GENTLEMAN JACK

The Real Anne Lister

ANNE CHOMA

WITH A FOREWORD BY

SALLY WAINWRIGHT

Edited by Stella Merz

BOOKS

3 5 7 9 10 8 6 4

BBC Books, an imprint of Ebury Publishing
20 Vauxhall Bridge Road,
London SW1V 2SA

BBC Books is part of the Penguin Random House group of companies whose
addresses can be found at global.penguinrandomhouse.com

Penguin
Random House
UK

This book is published to accompany the television series entitled
Gentleman Jack first broadcast on BBC One in 2019. *Gentleman Jack* is a
Lookout Point and BBC Studios production, co-produced with HBO.

Executive producers: Sally Wainwright, Faith Penhale, Laura Lankester and Ben Irving
Produced by: Phil Collinson
Directed by: Sally Wainwright

First published by BBC Books in 2019

www.penguin.co.uk

A CIP catalogue record for this book is available from the British Library

ISBN 9781785944048

Typeset in 10.5/17 pt ITC Galliard
by Integra Software Services Pvt. Ltd, Pondicherry

Printed and bound in Great Britain by Clays Ltd, Elcograf S.p.A.

All transcriptions are the author's own using primary source material from the Lister
archive via WYAS, Calderdale: (SH:7/ML/E/26/2), (SH:7/ML/E/26/3),
(SH:7/ML/E/1-24), (SH:7/ML/TR), (SH:7/ML/MISC), (SH:3/MS), (SH:7/
ML/5), (SH:2/M/1-6), (SH:2/CM), (SH:7/JN).

Penguin Random House is committed to a sustainable future
for our business, our readers and our planet. This book is
made from Forest Stewardship Council® certified paper.

MIX
Paper from
responsible sources
FSC® C018179

This book is dedicated to the LGBT community, and written in remembrance of Anne Lister and Ann Walker who had the courage and conviction to follow their hearts.

"Let us not lose ourselves in subtleties and sophistries. There is one straightforward path of right, and it is only in swerving from it to this side or that, we become entangled."

Anne Lister, 13th April 1834

CONTENTS

Foreword   vii

Introduction   xi

Chapter 1   1

Chapter 2   37

Chapter 3   67

Chapter 4   91

Chapter 5   111

Chapter 6   137

Chapter 7   161

Chapter 8   179

Chapter 9   217

Chapter 10   251

Chapter 11   279

Gentleman Jack   299

Acknowledgements   315

Index   317

FOREWORD

Anne Lister is unique and fascinating. She is known primarily as a diarist, and as a great lesbian lover who recorded her adventures with other women in a secret code, but there are a myriad other things to know about this extraordinary woman, who never fails to ignite the imagination.

Anne was unusually intelligent and remarkably physically fit. She had an enviable passion for life. What she didn't cram into her tragically short forty-nine years probably wasn't worth doing. And not only did she live a remarkable life, she recorded it in obsessive detail, every day, from her late teens to the last month before her death, from getting up, to going to bed. It is the diary of a perfectionist with an eye for detail; of a woman with a brilliant mind who was fascinated by the world and everything in it. In the coded parts it is often the stream of consciousness outpourings of a passionate human being who had more mental and physical energy than she knew what to do with.

Anne read as profusely as she wrote, keeping herself well informed in the latest thinking in a bewildering array of subjects. She was a true polymath; someone who could absorb complex information, process it quickly and use it effectively. She was a player, both in her professional life running her estate, and in her private life as a lover of women. Her mental and physical prowess and her love of life are inspiring, but there is another side to Anne Lister. She was an authoritarian landowner who believed firmly in a hierarchical social order. Her estate was modest in size (she was never well off), but it was rich in coal, and she owned mines in which people were employed to work cruelly long hours, enduring inhumane and humiliating conditions. As Suranne astutely observed when we started rehearsing *Gentleman Jack*, 'She's a bit Marmite, this one'. One of the many contradictions about Anne Lister is that she appears so far ahead of her time in having such an admirably healthy attitude towards her homosexuality, whilst being something of a dinosaur (even in her own time) in regarding those from the deprived classes as insensate commodities.

Anne Lister was a survivor in a world that could easily have had no place for her, a world that would have rendered her invisible if she'd had less about her. She was smart enough and confident enough to construct a self-identity that would allow her to live her life just as boldly, ambitiously and freely as she chose. She refused to be ignored or made invisible simply because she was born with a penchant for members of her own sex. As well as her robust physical health, it's clear (between the lines of the journal) that she enjoyed robust mental health too, and it was perhaps this psychological strength that allowed her, when it was convenient, to turn a blind eye to the hardship of others. Of course these contradictions and complexities are the things that make Anne Lister a gift to a dramatist. As Eliza Priestley points out in the first episode of

Gentleman Jack, whether we like Anne Lister or not, 'She's very entertaining'.

Thanks to Arthur McRea's generous legacy to the people of Halifax after John Lister's death in 1933, Shibden Hall has been part of my life ever since I can remember. As a child I came here all the time with my dad, Harry Wainwright, a keen amateur historian. He taught me how to row on the lake, and now and again we went up to the hall and the folk museum. I loved Shibden then, and I love it still. Something about it entered my soul. That it was once owned by the remarkable Anne Lister, odd as it seems to me now, is an entire coincidence. In the early seventies no-one mentioned Anne Lister. I can't remember how I became aware of her, but as a teenager I started to pick up on the fact that an extraordinary woman had once owned Shibden, but there was something about her that people didn't like to discuss. Times have changed and we now live in a world where we can celebrate a woman who – almost two hundred years ago – chose to marry another woman. We should also celebrate Anne's partner, Ann Walker, a shy woman who had the courage to make a conspicuous commitment to the woman she was so dazzled by.

I met Anne Choma fifteen years ago (through an initiative to try and transcribe the Anne Lister diaries) and we became friends. When *Gentleman Jack* was green lit by the BBC and HBO I invited her on board as my adviser and she has been a wonderful collaborator. I would like to take this opportunity to thank her, not just for her work, but for her support too. We've climbed our own little Vignemale together, and got down the other side, and there were a couple of times when I didn't think I'd make it, but she kept me going. The diaries are vast and complicated. To transcribe, absorb, and then dramatise the eighteen months we have covered in season one has been a mammoth task that perhaps only those familiar with the diaries will appreciate. One of the hardest tasks during that process was making choices about what *not* to include – choices which Anne Choma and I debated at length – choices that were invariably painful because the material is all so fascinating. This book therefore has the happy task of complementing the drama by providing further detail and context about this particularly dramatic period in Anne Lister's extraordinarily colourful life.

Sally Wainwright
The Café, Shibden Park
Sunday 7th October, 2018

INTRODUCTION

*'I have taken my fate into my own hands,
believe nothing till I tell it to you myself. I know
well enough what all the world will think, but all
the world may be wrong'*

It is a tantalising prospect to think that if Anne Lister had lived just a year or so beyond her forty-ninth birthday, we might have had a photographic image of her that would have shown us what she really looked like. There are a few portraits of her at her home, Shibden Hall in Halifax. There is one of her as a child with a broad, impish face. At first glance, it is not easy to say whether it is a boy or a girl. The hair falls tightly in short curls on either side of the cheeks, parted in the middle, but there is little else in terms of affectation. The clothes are plain and dull, the only concession to colour being the red scarf tied loosely around her neck. The pursed lips and haughty look in the eyes bear a strong resemblance to that of another portrait, of Anne as an adult, which, like the childhood image, shows the hair parted down the middle, with tightly packed side curls and eyebrows thickly drawn. The clothes are now more distinctive. The frilled collar of a white shirt shows itself fleetingly, peeping above a dark great coat, appearing to force the chin upwards in a lofty manner. The image is alluring, perceptively but stylistically drawn. Anne looks both handsome and feminine at the same time. Again, the steely, sideways glare draws you in. This is the unmistakable, iconic image that Anne Lister, mistress of Shibden Hall and the prolific writer of a five million-word diary, has become synonymous with.

Anne was very specific about how she wanted to look. She dressed according to her wishes and for her comfort. She rejected anything that might have been seen as pretty or feminine. She refused to be moulded into an image of nineteenth-century womanhood that was defined by bows, bonnets, frills and ringlets. Generally, she was very critical of the restrictive nature of women's attire, referring to it as an 'inconvenience' and 'incommodious.' She complained about the tyranny of large bonnets at public meetings 'over which nobody can see, and which too often prevents the unfortunate wearer herself from either seeing or hearing clearly' (27th February 1831).

In 1817, she decided to always wear black clothing, only occasionally making a concession to this rule when propriety demanded it. It was a choice that instantly set her apart from her contemporaries. Anne wore a worsted great coat, a plain, black dress, and a sturdy pair of black-gaiter, leather boots. When she walked through the narrow streets of Halifax she cut an unusual figure. She was 5 feet, 4½ inches tall and walked at a great pace with an imposing upright stance. She was flat-chested and she weighed a modest 8 stone, 4¼ pounds. Her voice was deep. It was said that physically she presented herself in a 'gentlemanly' manner. She was often called names and jeered at by people who she would refer to as 'vulgar' or common. The nickname 'Gentleman Jack' was attributed to Anne decades after death, passed down through Halifax folklore. To date no evidence has emerged from her journals to suggest that Anne herself was ever aware of it.

Being mis-gendered was a common occurrence for her, however. 'I, in my pelisse attract much attention,' she said, having once been mistaken for a man three times in one day when travelling through Strasbourg (Travel journal, 22nd June 1827). She was reminded once that a post-boy on the coach from Rochdale to Halifax said that she looked like a 'man in petticoats' (28th June 1833).

Courting unwanted attention, for being herself, was something she had grown used to. She writes in her childhood diary on 27th November 1806, aged fifteen, of the time she 'went to Mr Stopford's 1st concert in a habit shirt and was much stared at and well quizzed as an original – care despised on my part'. On another occasion, the Halifax vicar's wife, Mrs Musgrave, commented on Anne's 'thick pickles – tallowed boots', forcing Anne to defend herself, saying that she 'had no petticoats so short to take up, as they, ladies had', because she was 'too independent' (25th January 1833). Years later, at Shibden Hall, Anne remarked how 'evidently astonished' the visiting brother of her architect Mr Harper had been at the sight of her in her unconventional 'costume' (22nd March 1836).

Privately, the hurt cut deep – 'It is those who have known me least who have done me the most injustice,' she said (2nd August 1833). Whilst many people in local society viewed her with suspicion and were not so forgiving of her manner and ways, some of them were kinder. She wrote of people in Halifax having become accustomed to her manner and 'oddities'. A Halifax acquaintance jokingly said, in front of Anne, how the world could not do with two Anne Listers, and that one moving in such an 'eccentric orbit' was quite enough (11th February 1835).

Anne was born in Halifax in 1791 into a modest, landowning Yorkshire family. She was an eccentric child, full of energy and mischief. She was so unusual that her mother Rebecca and her father Jeremy struggled to know how to look after her. When she was supposed to be tucked up safely in her bed asleep at night she would escape from her maid through her bedroom window into the nearest town to see 'bad' things. However, her academic ability was never in doubt. She was clever, described by a teacher at her first school in Ripon as a 'singular' child. She excelled in mathematics and in reading the classics, counting Virgil, Homer and Tacitus among some of her favourite writers of antiquity. She was precocious enough aged eleven to call herself a 'young genius', as though anticipating that she was destined for something far greater than a life of predictability and conventionality (3rd February 1803).

In 1805, when she was fourteen years old, the decision was made to send her away to Manor House boarding school in York, with the hope that the institutional discipline might be able to do something to harness her out-of-control energy. The plan did not work, as there was another side to Anne that singled her out as being different, and which impacted on her stay and her behaviour at the school. Physically and emotionally she was attracted to other girls. At the Manor House school she embarked upon her first sexual relationship with another girl, called Eliza Raine. Soon she was asked to leave the establishment, not only for her deepening (and distracting) bond with Eliza, but also for her disruptive behaviour towards the other girls.

Over the next few years, Anne began to spend more and more time with her Aunt Anne and Uncle James at Shibden Hall, a pretty, rural estate on the outskirts of Halifax. She flourished under their love and care. She began a rigorous period of learning and her days became structured and meaningful. She took regular strenuous exercise, making sure that she timed her daily walks. Soon she began to involve herself in the management of the estate, becoming knowledgeable about farming. She read everything she could to improve her knowledge. She became as hands-on as possible by physically working on the land with the workmen. In 1815, aged twenty-four, she moved in permanently, settling into Shibden's south-facing Blue Room.

Fortune favoured her. In 1826, when Uncle James died, Anne inherited Shibden. Having displayed an entrepreneurial flair for estate management, all of the land and the income derived from it was eventually to become hers. Though full ownership would not materialise until 1836, on the death of her aunt and father, both of whom had been given a life interest to live at the hall and receive income from the estate, it was a milestone decision that was to change the course of her life.

Anne's inheritance was not an unexpected piece of news, though. The ambition to become heiress had been part of a long and carefully orchestrated plan. In 1822, when her father told her that if he outlived his brother (Anne's Uncle James), he would build another archway under the road to the house, Anne swiftly executed her first plan of action to protect and rubber-stamp her future inheritance. She took the opportunity to expose her father's costly, ill-thought-out re-modelling ambitions by explaining the folly of the idea to her uncle, who she immediately asked to 'sign the Will' [in her favour], so as to 'make all safe' [for her] (8th July 1822).

As Aunt Anne and her father Jeremy still drew income from the estate, it meant that Anne's access to money was restricted. For many years following the death of her uncle, she remained reliant upon her friends and on her father to keep financially afloat. Frustratingly, she had to defer to him for money whenever she wanted to make improvements to the house. Anne had to count the pennies and pounds, balance her books, and re-hem her old clothes. She recognised, though, that in a society which had very limited roles for women – usually as a wife, a mother, a governess, or an old maid – it was her fortuitous inheritance that enabled her to avoid what she called the narrow world of domestic life.

Anne's only surviving sibling was her younger sister Marian. Unable to compete with Anne's business prowess or her intellect, Marian was very much in her big sister's shadow. She was jealous of Anne's inheritance and remained so for many years. Through the early deaths of her three youngest brothers in childhood, and of her eldest brother Sam when he was serving in the army, Anne had escaped the restrictive inheritance laws that favoured the male line. Had Sam lived he would have been the natural heir to Shibden, and under those circumstances Anne might have become reliant upon him for lodgings and money.

Yet throughout her life, inheritance or no inheritance, Anne had looked to gain financial independence by realising a long-held ambition to earn a living through writing. She had talked of translating some of the classics and of writing about her travels, but she never became a published author in her own lifetime.

Capable, clever and with a natural gift for land and estate management, Anne had been the natural choice to take on the huge task of running Shibden. Not only had she impressed Uncle James with her skill in dealing with the renewal of leases and misbehaving tenants, he also knew that she would never marry and therefore the estate would not be broken up. In their conversations together, Anne had left him under no illusion that her emotional and sexual feelings for other women precluded the possibility of her ever entering into a marriage with a man, in which she stood to lose all that was hers. It was another four decades, on the passing of the Married Women's

Property Act in 1870 (thirty years after Anne's death), before women would be able to keep hold of and inherit property following marriage. So, remarkable as it may seem to us now, it was Anne Lister's lesbian sexuality (then with no name or legal recognition), which played a crucial role in helping her to keep control of her wealth at a time when it was thought that it was impossible for a woman to do so. That Uncle James, in 1826, seemed to understand and recognise this is even more extraordinary.

In becoming a landowner, Anne took on a powerful new identity, and it gave her greater visibility within the male-dominated Halifax business community – particularly with local men like Mr Christopher Rawson, the eldest son of the Rawson family, who Anne had known since her youth. Christopher Rawson was the leading banker of the town, as well as the magistrate and a landowner and profit-hungry coal magnate. In later years, when entering into complex coal negotiations, she would exasperate both him and his younger brother Jeremiah with her commercial business acumen.

The role of landowner suited what she described as her 'natural Tory' politics. Anne was a traditional thinker in that she believed that decision-making powers in society should remain vested firmly in the landowners. Representing the old order, she championed the traditional demarcation of the relationship between landlord and tenant. She lamented the passing of the Reform Bill in 1832 which gave greater democratic powers to men who did not own property. She poured scorn both on the working-class radicals who fought for those greater freedoms, and on her neighbours who supported their cause. Once, on hearing of the possibility that radical agitators could be selected as magistrates to the West Riding of Yorkshire, she replied caustically, 'what impudent absurdity' (29th February 1836). While some of her male tenants following the introduction of the Bill were given the opportunity to vote in elections, Anne of course wasn't. But, as there was no secret ballot she was still able to use her landowning powers to the full by exerting her influence and by threatening eviction if they did not vote the way she wanted – Tory Blue.

Anne developed an early love-hate relationship with her new inheritance. Shibden was a quaint, romantically situated house going as far back as the early fifteenth century. Generations of Lister vicars, apothecaries, clothiers, farmers, lawyers and teachers had at one time called it home. She was proud of its long history, although out of snobbishness she distanced herself from the side of her family who in the past had been involved in the cloth industry, or 'trade' as she would have called it. Despite her good fortune, she often complained bitterly about living at the hall, describing it as being full of 'deformities and nuisances' (6th June 1833).

Nestled on the lea of a hill, in a wooded valley, Shibden could be a damp, cold and draughty place to live. Great coats, blankets, thick dimity dressing gowns, window frames stuffed with old pieces of newspaper – all were used at one time or other in an effort to keep out the bitter west winds. However, Anne remained steadfastly loyal to Shibden. In later years she embarked upon a plan to nurture the creaky floors and the dingy, low-ceilinged rooms. Her vision was to transform the house into something far grander – and more befitting a woman like her who had designs on extensive (expensive) foreign travel, and on moving within the higher echelons of Georgian society.

Anne was socially and financially ambitious. She was keen to make connections with people of a higher class than herself. She saw her own Halifax family as 'drooping', both in fortune and status. It was an image she wanted to change, the first plan of which was to try bringing the estate back into profitability by maximising its industrial potential. Under her management, the tenanted farms were farmed more efficiently, leases were managed correctly and rents were collected on time and in full. She would think later about exploiting the estate's prized coal reserves by reopening the dormant Listerwick pit and by sinking a new one.

Anne Lister is most famous of course because of the journals she kept, which she wrote in tantalising and candid detail about her lesbian sexuality. Apart from a few loose diary pages written as a child, and two later smaller exercise books, they amount in total to twenty-four major volumes – 7,600 pages, spanning from 1816 until her death in 1840. She tailored the physical style of each diary to her own needs. When placing an order for a new one with bookseller Mr Whitley in Halifax she was specific: 'One quarto blank book, half bound, then covered with common calf as usual, not to have less than 370 pages' (27th August 1831). Now recognised as a document of global significance by UNESCO for being one of the longest social commentaries ever written, in 2011 the diaries were selected as one of only twenty unique items worthy of being added to the UK Memory Bank of the World Register.

These adult diaries, which Anne started in 1816 aged twenty-five, became a vessel and repository for her thoughts and feelings. Each diary was a pseudo friend and confidante. Anne's consistent self analysis reflects the cultural zeitgeist of the early nineteenth century – the search for an authentic identity explored through feeling, sensibility and a post-Enlightenment sense of individuality. She described the journals as being a private memorial to herself, and her writing style was influenced by reading the literature of some of the leading philosophers of the seventeenth and eighteenth century, including John Locke, Jean Jacques Rousseau and Emmanuel Kant. She made use of the privileged opportunities that came her way to develop the knowledge and skillset to write truthfully and with conviction. She wanted to write and tell her own story, but crucially only for herself. She hated the thought of being mis-represented by what she called 'second hand' comments:

> *Remember, our most familiar friend must judge of us in some sort by our own words, and we ourselves should watch these narrowly when we know that they are not in unison with, or do injustice to, our own feelings.*

7th January 1833

Anne employed two styles of writing in her diary – the first 'plain hand' and in the other what she called 'crypt hand', the latter comprising a secret code she made up from random Greek letters, numbers, symbols. In using the cryptic code to secrete information, hinting as it does as a means of self-censorship, Anne essentially presented a self that was separate and distinct from the one which flowed freely in her plain hand, a self which remains locked within a complex structure of esoteric symbols, numbers and letters. Anne said her plain hand would contain nothing of consequence. Descriptions of sex, money, bodily functions, scathing comments about people in both high society and in Halifax – in fact anything that she felt needed to be hidden – was written in code. The safe outlet provided by her crypt hand gave her an extra means of support in times of emotional need. 'What a comfort my journal is,' she said, 'How I can write in crypt all as it really is and throw it off my mind and console myself. Thank God for it' (29th April 1832).

When she was writing, Anne worked in a disciplined and structured way. She said that the 'greatest desideratum' [the thing most needed] was steadiness (17th March 1834). There was never a point in her life when there was any loss in form, no hiatus in production – just consistent, detailed, daily accounts of what she did, what she saw and what she felt.

The journals provide an opportunity for the reader to time-travel back to a lost world, full of fascinating and illuminating details of everyday life that would otherwise be lost to history. We witness Aunt Anne's stubbornly ulcerated leg being treated with 'lunar caustic', Indian 'orange-pea' capsules and 'fillet of diaculon plaster' (21st May 1836), and Anne ordering a prescription of the aphrodisiac 'cantharides' for a lover suffering a temporary loss of libido and sexual 'irregularity' (30th May 1836). We get to know that, in Halifax in 1836, the cow doctor was called Jabus Fawthorpe, the umbrella lady in York was called Mrs Bean, and that one of the Halifax doctors who used to visit Shibden was called Dr Mason Stanhope Kenny. We understand that the description Anne gave for her disorderly staffed house (for want of good, reliable servants) was 'hugger-mugger', and that on 7th June 1836, Anne invented a new euphemism to describe bringing a lover to orgasm: 'bring[ing] monsieur again'.

Anne Lister also kept fourteen volumes of separate travel journals. She was an adrenalin-fuelled thrill seeker. She scaled Swiss mountains, descended into French silver mines, clambered through Scottish caves and wandered into extinct foreign volcanoes. She slept in barns with Swiss peasants as well as dining at the table of the king and queen of Denmark. In 1838, she was recorded, along with her guide, as being the first person ever to conquer Mount Vignemale in the Spanish Alps. Notes about people and places were written, with precision, usually from the back of a bumpy travelling carriage. Personal detail was often comical, like the time in France in 1834 when she hid three newly purchased handkerchiefs from customs officers by pinning them to her knickers so that she didn't have to pay duty on them.

Anne's powers of observation meant that she went beyond the predictable description of rolling hills or a pretty church spire. She charmed her way into people's houses to find out how they lived. She would extract interesting anecdotes about famous people like Lord Bryon – a poet she revered and loved. Once, having stumbled on a place where Byron had stayed, she persuaded the 'nut-brown respectable farmer's wife' to let her see the very room where he had slept. Byron, said the woman, had paid her well. Anne, out of curiosity, wanted to know how much he had paid – 'a napoleon' the woman replied glowingly, he had 'une telle manière' ('such a manner'), she said. Upstairs, the obliging woman showed Anne another apartment, rented by an old couple for '9 or 10 napoleons a year'. On entering the room, Anne wrote how the old lady in excitement, aged eighty, 'skipped and danced and shewed us all her perfect set of teeth'. Before leaving, Anne was offered wine and cake, the generosity of the 'good people' being duly noted in her diary (23rd August 1827).

Travelling abroad meant that Anne was able to indulge herself, secretly, in some of her more unusual academic interests, particularly in the subject of human anatomy. Between 1829 and 1831 she managed to carve a secret niche for herself within a sphere of science where women were indeed absent, and in which they were also deemed incapable of understanding. Much of the interest in this section of the journals lies specifically in Anne's attempts to rationalise, through language, the complexities and anxieties of her own nature. The pages seem to become repositories of medical facts and descriptions of dissected body parts, where through death and lifeless bodies she tries to discover more about her own living being.

In Paris in 1831 she hired an attic room on the Left Bank and had body parts supplied to her so that she could dissect them. She dissected an arm, a head and a number of foetuses. She kept a full-sized human skeleton in her room to aid her knowledge. She attended as many public autopsies as she could. Her behaviour defied convention, and she ignored any feelings of doubt that she may have had about women in petticoats obtaining a greater 'command of the knife'. Of her first lesson in dissecting a corpse she wrote how:

> *Monsieur Julliart came at 1½ and staid till 4. Helping to clean all up. Had a male foetus – very small – might weigh about three pounds. Opened the abdomen. Studied the intestines and he showed me how the testicles slipped through into the bourse of scrotum. But somehow he is not very profound, and if I had as much command of the knife I think I should soon know as much or more than he does.*

18th February 1831

Anne studied under and became friends with two of the leading scientists of the day – Georges Cuvier and Etienne Geoffroy St-Hilaire. She took part in the cutting edge debates about evolution and the role of religion in science. Everything was driven by her unquenchable thirst for knowledge. Her life was dominated by her voracious appetite for reading and learning.

Anne's reliance on her books for mental well-being and personal happiness was clear – 'What is there like gaining knowledge?' she once said. 'All else here below is indeed but vanity and vexation of spirit – I am happy among my books – I am not happy without them' (2nd May 1829). Words on a page empowered, enlightened and educated. She said that it was our 'intercourse with the world that blunted our feelings, which made us suspicious, and mistrustful' and that living as she did among her books her 'heart was left unchanged' and her 'feelings rather sharpened' (2nd August 1829).

Of course, Anne Lister's written testimony dispelling the myth of the nineteenth-century non-sexual woman is what makes her journals truly unique. Tacit acknowledgement of relationships between women was then confined in populist thought to the 'romantic friendship' – a relationship defined by its beauty, innocence and asexuality. Anne herself commented to a friend that 'there was all the difference in the world between love and friendship' – specifically in terms of love encapsulating and fulfilling both the emotional *and* the sexual needs of the women involved (11th January 1824). Her diaries record in explicit detail that women were forming long-term relationships and that sex was a regular component of them. She lived in a world that had very different approaches to male and female homosexuality, with the former still being punishable by death, and the latter being left largely ignored. Anne Lister, while still exercising great discretion, was able to conduct her relationships without the threat of prison or at worst, death. Within her own social circles she carved out a niche where she could feel comfortable, accepted and safe.

When the journals were decoded in the late nineteenth century by John Lister, the last surviving member of the family to inherit and live in the house, the shock of discovering the nature of Anne's sexuality almost resulted in the diaries being lost forever. His friend Arthur Burrell, a retired schoolmaster who had helped him to crack the crypt hand, urged him to burn them. Speaking of Anne's relationships with women, Arthur Burrell said, 'Hardly any one of them escaped her.' John Lister, a learned man, recognised the historical value of his ancestor's documented life and so refused his friend's request. Instead, he decided to place the diaries back behind one of the oak panels in an upstairs bedroom. They remained there, untouched, with their secrets locked away, for another forty years.

Anne Lister was at ease with her lesbianism. It was rooted in healthy self-esteem. She said that it was her 'natural' inclination to love women. Her liberal interpretation of religious scripture also meant that her Anglican faith was never at odds with the desires of her body. She was at peace with her relationship to God and the church. She said to friends that she 'should never marry' and that she 'could not like men' (15th August 1816). She wanted to love women as a woman – and not as a woman dressed as a man. 'Thinking, as I had done last night,' she once said, 'of getting some country girl, Welsh perhaps, knowing that I was not a man, but yet to live with me apparently as wife' (6th January 1831). Her belief in traditional marriage in a Christian church at the altar before God was sacrosanct. And while she knew that she could not *legally* marry in church and exchange rings, she believed that she should still be able to stand before God, in front of a clergyman, take the sacrament with her intended wife, and thus solemnise their union.

Anne devised her own terminology to describe her butch lesbianism, seeing herself as the 'connecting link', and neither a man nor woman in society (16th August 1823). With pride she called herself an 'oddity'. In keeping with her keen interest in science, she explored her sexuality by examining herself internally to see if there was anything unusual about her body, only to discover the typical biology of a woman. She also read articles on subjects that spoke of an alternate identity, evident when in 1829 she lists in her literary index an article called 'intra-abdominal hermaphroditism'.

Anne was sexually uninhibited and curious. On 17th February 1831, after 'studying female organs of generation' in Virey's *History of Anatomy of Women*, she recalls 'finding out distinctly for the first time in my life the clitoris'. She had some years earlier described it as being 'just like an internal penis' (13th January 1825). Following this discovery, she spent the next few months getting better acquainted with it, periodically locking herself in her water-closet 'trying to enlarge' it through 'titillation' (24th April 1831). She often experimented with herself, once inserting her finger into her anus just 'to see what pleasure sodomy could give', ultimately declaring just 'for a moment or two' that she 'fancied it was going to be the thing' [sexually satisfying] (30th November 1824). With her partners she was the dominant one, the initiator. Oral sex, finger penetration (never the use of toys, which to her represented artifice) and 'queer' closeness, or vagina-on-vagina touching, were all part of her sexual repertoire.

Anne's writing about her sexual life offers a different truth to the one that has become dominant among some modern commentators, where strategically selected and sensationalist soundbites extracted from her diary have been used to cast her into the predictable predatory lesbian stereotype. Anne had eleven women-to-women sexual relationships in her lifetime (of varying intensity and genital intimacy), but many of her thoughts and sexual desires were fantasy, designed to be seen only by herself, concealed in her journal by her crypt hand. She stayed friends with almost all of her former lovers, a number of them forming petty jealousies among themselves when vying for *her* attention. Attempting to view her as a predatory stereotype diminishes her legacy and ignores the complexity of an identity that was formed at a time when there was no script for her to follow, no language to articulate what her place in the world might be.

Anne's social circle consisted of a diverse group of women. All of her friends were well bred, educated and, in the main, financially privileged. They paid visits to each other, often staying with each other for weeks at a time. They would talk, gossip, socialise, ruminate, argue, fall out, make up, progress and grow their relationships, be it platonic or sexual. Within this group, a healthy and fluid attitude towards sexuality allowed Anne's sexual relationships to flourish – with women like Isabella Norcliffe (known as 'Tib') from Langton Hall in North Yorkshire; Mariana Lawton (née Belcombe), the daughter of a doctor from York; the widow and single mother Maria Barlow from the island of Jersey, and the aristocratic

Sibella Maclean from Coll in the Scottish Highlands. Fleeting affairs, though still intense, included Harriet Milne, Anne Belcombe and a Mary Vallance who Anne met at a house party in 1818.

Her ideal woman was pretty, rich and aristocratic. More than often, her successes were a combination of these ideals, falling short of the full package, forcing a compromise. Isabella Norcliffe, who Anne met in 1809 when she was eighteen, was a butch, hunting-and-shooting, snuff-taking, larger-than-life extrovert character. Anne described her as 'shockingly brazen'. In the autumn months she would often keep Anne in a regular supply of partridges from the Langton estate. Polar opposite to Anne in terms of temperament, the relationship was not to last. Tib's liking for the wine bottle, for partying and for staying in bed till late in the afternoon was anathema to Anne. It meant that the relationship was only ever going to last until someone else materialised – someone prettier and more feminine. Throughout her life Anne continued to make many long and happy visits to the Norcliffes at Langton, forming a special bond with elderly Mrs Norcliffe, who, like Tib, was to remain a life-long and treasured friend.

Mariana Belcombe was the most passionate of all of Anne's relationships. They met in 1813 when Anne was twenty-three years old and Mariana was twenty-four. She was sister to Eliza, Louisa, Anne, Harriet and Dr Stephen. This was the woman who Anne Lister had loved and had wanted to marry. And she was the woman who, in 1816, broke Anne's heart when she married the wealthy Cheshire landowner Charles Lawton of Lawton Hall (the 'blackguard', as Anne called him). Many years later, Anne referred to the marriage as 'the day of doom that sealed so many fates' (2nd March in 1832).

In 1824, Anne went to Paris and began a relationship with a woman called Maria Barlow, a widow and mother to a teenage daughter called Jane. Maria was intrigued and instantly attracted to Anne, and at the hotel Place Vendôme where they were both staying flirtation soon began. Maria was besotted, passionate and sexually forward, but when she learned that Anne's real affections were still tied up with Mariana back home their relationship crumbled and she was left devastated. Anne felt guilty knowing that what Maria craved could never be given, but she decided to remain friends with her. They continued to meet and travel with each other and experienced many adventures together.

Even after her marriage, Mariana Lawton continued to play a pivotal role in Anne's life. Visits between the two of them did become less frequent, but the recriminations and vestiges of old love remained a dominant theme in much of their correspondence. Anne realised the futility of their situation, but she stayed positive, believing that someone else would appear who she could spend her life with – 'I always look on the bright side,' she said. 'My conviction is daily strengthened that all things work together for the good.' By 1830, her feelings had changed irrevocably towards Mariana. She had started to cultivate new and more exciting relationships, crucially with women of higher rank. Mariana had only the prospect of an unsatisfactory, financially unstable future to look forward to with her husband. She had it all to play for to try and win back her friend's affections.

In November 1830, Anne received the news that former lover Sibbella Maclean had died. Sibbella, a sophisticated, elegant woman of the minor aristocracy, and the daughter of a Scottish landowner, was a woman of breeding who Anne had found irresistible. Their relationship became sexual in 1824, but had failed to develop long-term because of Sibbella's prolonged bouts of ill-health. Before Sibbella's death, Anne had become acquainted with members of her family – most notably with elderly Lady Stuart, Charles Stuart her son, his wife Lady Stuart de Rothesay and their two children Louisa and Charlotte. Vere Hobart, a young woman in her twenties and Sibbella's niece, had been introduced to Anne the year prior to Sibbella's passing, when it had been suggested that Anne accompany her to Paris.

Anne was instantly attracted to the Hobart and Stuart family, not only because of what they could offer her in terms of improved social status, but also because they had important foreign connections that might be of use to her when travelling. Within this social circle, Anne was also introduced to a Lady Caroline Duff-Gordon, a widower, mother and great socialite. Lady Caroline, two years older than Anne and the daughter of former politician Sir George Cornewall, offered Anne the exciting possibility of becoming her next new travelling companion.

Anne's relationship with Sibbella Maclean had sown a lasting seed of hope for her that a life of opportunity lay beyond people that she now described as 'medium' or second-rate. As she approached her fortieth birthday, Anne became more serious about finding a woman of rank to settle down with – someone perhaps like Sibbella's niece, Vere Hobart. Between 1829 and 1832, she set about trying to realise this ambition in earnest – first on a stay in Paris with both Vere and the Stuart de Rothesays, and then afterwards on a lengthier stay in Hastings just with Vere. During this period, Anne got to learn much about how to conduct herself in society, but she often felt gauche and ill-equipped to deal with the demands made of her at social events. Lack of money remained an issue, as her inheritance at Shibden had still not been fully realised. With no carriage of her own and with nothing decent to wear to events she had little to impress her friends with – apart from her engaging company.

In 1832, when our story begins, we see Anne returning to Shibden from Hastings after having spent many months away from her family. Uncharacteristically she is disillusioned about what the future holds for her, and is at one of the lowest ebbs in her life. While processing past events with Vere in Hastings, she describes herself as having narrowly escaped the same fate as Icarus, the mythical character of Greek legend, who dies having flown too close to the sun. Typically, she soon rallies herself into a more positive frame of mind.

Anne returns to a household at Shibden consisting of: Aunt Anne, aged sixty-six and suffering with debilitating rheumatism; father Jeremy, aged seventy-nine and a weakening man suffering from deafness, and sister Marian, aged thirty-four, who, in Anne's absence, had been busy playing mistress to Shibden servants Elizabeth Cordingley, Rachel Hemingway and John Booth. Anne quickly re-asserts her dominant position within the Shibden household and throws herself back into the management of the estate, determined to improve the look of the hall and the land around it.

Then, following a chance visit to Shibden by a neighbouring woman called Ann Walker, Anne's story takes a new and unexpected turn, opening up another chapter in her event-filled life. Using her own words, we follow the twists and turns of a complex and unlikely love affair, where we witness Anne being pushed to the brink of emotional ruin as she tries to understand and care for this troubled woman who, she said, 'had everything to be wished for but the power of enjoying it' (19th December 1832).

Anne Lister said that she owed a good deal to her journal. She rejoiced in the power of language to help her at times of personal uncertainty and through heartbreak. She stood proud in a hostile world that could be cruel and unforgiving in its treatment of her. The future never really looked bleak for the woman known locally as 'Gentleman Jack' of Halifax, and who had to face many challenges in her life – *Non si male nunc et olim sic erit*, she wrote poignantly, quoting from her beloved Horace, or, 'If it is ill now, it will not also be so hereafter.'

CHAPTER 1

HIGH SOCIETY AMBITION AND HEARTBREAK IN HASTINGS

'Tis well my heart should run no risk.
She found it warm and open as a summer's day.
She'll leave it closed in wintry mists,
and as cold as they'

On 5th November 1831, Anne Lister began settling into a new apartment overlooking the sea at 15 Pelham Crescent in Hastings. Assisted by her 'noodle' of a servant, Cameron, she started by unpacking some of her extensive library of books, among them Mary Shelley's *Frankenstein*, de la Beches's *Geology*, Dr Scudamore's *Observations on Pulmonary Consumption* and Edward Gibbon's *The Decline and Fall of the Roman Empire*.

It was a rainy, blustery day, and Anne was pleased to discover a comforting piece of Yorkshire Parkin in her packing box. Choosing to ignore the fact that, judging by its label, the cake was intended for her manservant George Playforth, she shared it with Miss Vere Hobart, who along with her servant, Norbury, was busy unpacking her things in the bedroom across the landing. Anne's aristocratic travelling companion was delighted by the sticky Yorkshire delicacy, describing it as 'next to vanilla cake in goodness'.

Vere's approval pleased Anne, who remarked in her diary that Miss Hobart 'spoke as if with some regard for consideration for Shibden'. With the bills for the groceries, servants and the carriage being sorted amicably, Anne commented drily how Vere liked her enough to let her *'pay for, and give her as much as I like'*.

It was providence – or 'dame destiny', as Anne sometimes liked to call it – that brought her and Vere to Hastings together in the winter of 1831. Anne's original plan to travel to Spain with another friend, Lady Caroline Duff Gordon, had failed at the last minute, leaving her unsure of her next move. She didn't like the idea of returning to Shibden, where she found living harmoniously with her younger sister Marian – the 'cock of the dunghill' – a challenge.

However, while it was a disappointment not to be going abroad with 'quick, clever and agreeable' Lady Gordon, who had already proven herself a 'woman of the world' and ideal travel companion on a tour of the Pyrenees with Anne in 1829, Anne herself recognised that the aborted travel plan was financially serendipitous. Still to receive her full inheritance of Shibden Hall, Anne had to watch how much she was spending. On top of that, the threat of cholera made the prospect of travelling to Europe, with anyone, less attractive. Anne noted on 20th September 1831 that 'people were in great alarm' over the disease. They included Lady Stuart de Rothesay, a relative of Vere Hobart, who had by now been settled upon as Anne's travelling companion. Concerned that travel would exacerbate Vere's persistent and debilitating cough, Lady Stuart de Rothesay warned Anne that 'to go abroad was madness ... even to Milan'.

Anne agreed. She was fearful of cholera too. By now, the epidemic had reached the village of Wibsey, only three miles from Shibden and, while nothing could compare to the 'health breathing gales' of the West Yorkshire dales, she conceded that Hastings and the healthy, bracing winds of the south coast could suit her and Vere both.

Anne Lister had been introduced to the Hobarts and Stuart de Rothesays in 1829 by Vere's late aunt, Sibella Maclean. They were important society people; Vere's cousin, Charles Stuart, the husband of Lady Stuart de Rothesay, was ambassador at the British Embassy in Paris, and Vere was the daughter of the Honourable George Hobart, Earl of Buckinghamshire. They had stylish residences dotted around London (in St James's Park, Richmond and Marylebone), as well as the palatial Highcliffe Castle in Dorset. Theirs was a world far removed from draughty Shibden and Anne's own family. But Anne was a skilled social networker. Always ambitious to forge links with the upper echelons of society, she charmed herself into their circle with her charismatic personality – and perhaps a slightly romanticised vision of her ancestral seat.

When Lady Stuart identified Anne as a 'highly respectable person' to accompany her great-niece to Hastings, Anne was more than satisfied with the arrangement. 'Well,' she wrote in her diary, 'I shall have more society with Vere at Hastings, and I had better be with her there than wander about the continent thro' cholera alone. I do the kindness and it suits me well' (21st September 1831).

Doing 'the kindness' was something Anne was already practised in, having acted as a chaperone to Vere during the Stuarts' stay in Paris two years previously. As well as a milestone in Anne's conquest of her new aristocratic friends, it proved significant in her love life: it was during this trip of 1829–1830 that Anne determined to win Vere's heart.

However, Anne's first impressions of Vere were not entirely favourable. On 8th July 1829, when the two women paid a visit to the Conservatoire des Arts to look at the horology exhibition, Vere had to be persuaded to go in. At twenty-seven years of age, she lacked Anne's natural confidence. She did not like the look of the gathering crowd outside, made up mostly of men. Anne, who had no such qualms about propriety, thought to herself that Vere was a 'goose'. In another diary entry, she branded her a 'noodle'. Later, when comparing her with Mariana Lawton, the on-off lover for whom she still harboured complicated feelings, Anne decided, unkindly, that Vere was simply 'a good humoured fat girl' (30th July 1829).

But as the two women got better acquainted, and Vere became more comfortable in her company, Anne changed her mind. She became 'decidedly attentive' towards Vere, 'playing the agreeable' at every opportunity. She began, slowly, to make Vere aware of the nature of her liking for her, recording in her journal every detail of the flirtation that was developing between them. She wrote that she was allowed to unhook Vere's gown on going to bed (but was not permitted to untie her petticoats), and that Vere played love ballads for her on the piano. When she told Vere that 'she was pretty, had the prettiest mouth I ever saw', she noted that Vere took the compliment very well. Having initially thought that her 'chance would not be great with Miss Hobart', Anne soon reassessed – 'tis now clear she likes me' (Travel journal, 13th–14th October 1829).

Vere would go on to describe Anne as 'the most extraordinary person' she had ever met. It is clear that she was increasingly cognisant of Anne's sexuality. When Anne asked why, unlike their mutual friend, Lady Gordon, she was not allowed into Vere's bedroom, Vere's reply was revealing: Lady Gordon would 'not remember what she saw, and you [Anne] would never forget it'. On a separate occasion, Vere told Anne that when Anne happened to touch her, it led to a 'ticklish' feeling she could not quite fathom (Travel journal, 17th October 1829). Buoyed by this encouragement, Anne stepped up her efforts to forge a romantic connection with Vere.

Anne told Vere that she was going to construct a special cryptic alphabet, a secret language in which they could write to each other. Sharing her crypt hand with potential lovers was a technique Anne had used before, and her imagination started to run away with her. 'What will she write to me?' she wondered.

Vere wavered, worried about the attention such a pointedly private correspondence might bring to her friendship with Anne. Noting her concern, Anne reported, 'People might think if she used it she was writing something improper – it would not look well to use it.' Anne nevertheless succeeded in talking Vere 'off her scruples' and into using the secret code (16th October 1829).

Anne enjoyed making gifts to Vere. As well as a beautiful hand-embroidered handkerchief with a 'pretty, coloured gothic border' and expensive bottle of eau-de-cologne, there was a bottle of 'golden ink':

Gave her the little bottle of golden ink. She kissed me for it of her own accord. I laughed and said the skies would fall. We all sat in her bedroom, writing journal and accounts. She showed me a line or two of nonsense and asked me to write 'festina lente', which I did.

Travel journal, 19th October 1829

Vere's request for 'more haste, less speed' was a significant acknowledgment of Anne's attentions. What Vere wanted was for Anne to slow down, to moderate her occasionally overbearing manner towards her. Anne might have anticipated this, having noted in her journal some months before:

I cannot quite make Miss H out – whether she does not like me much, whether I have overdone it with attention – or whether she likes me and does not want to show it – and rather flirts with me. Is the latter possible?

31st July 1829

Throughout her stay in Paris, Anne was eager to make a good impression on Lady Stuart de Rothesay and elderly Lady Stuart. She made sure to act with what she felt was the utmost propriety, careful not to raise eyebrows with her eccentricity. It was an approach which yielded mixed results, not least because Anne found it hard to resist acting in a decidedly gentlemanly fashion.

'We get very cozy and good friends,' wrote Anne, after a late night in Lady Stuart de Rothesay's company. 'Talked about women's characters. She very liberal. We quite agreed on this point. She talked to me exactly as she would to a married man, and surely feels quite at ease with me' (30th July 1829).

Anne was becoming more relaxed around her new 'high-ton' (i.e. 'posh') friends, as she called them. Just three days earlier, conversation between the two women had been more guarded. Anne, not wishing to demonstrate an intellectual prowess above that of someone of superior rank, had given Lady Stuart de Rothesay the last word on the subject of Creationism:

> *Got onto the first chapter of Genesis. The light created before the sun. She talked some moments of which I, too civil to take any advantage, in spite of her saying the sun was created afterwards. She thought it not necessary to believe it not existing before the creation of our world. There were many suns and systems.*

(27th July 1830)

Having already forged connections with leading French scientists, Anne was in a position to treat her friends to some unusual cultural experiences in Paris. Now, at the invitation of the scientist Etienne Geoffroy Saint-Hilaire, she took Vere and the Stuart de Rothesays to see the inside of a skeleton of a female whale. Lady Stuart de Rothesay, her two young daughters, Charlotte and Louisa, as well as Vere and elderly Lady Stuart, gamely followed Anne up the 'carpeted ladders' to take their seat inside the skeleton, 'in which' wrote Anne, '30 persons can sit' among 'tables and books and newspapers'. When Monsieur Saint-Hilaire had to leave the party temporarily, she took over the lecture with panache. 'All listened with attention,' she said, 'and the thing went off well.'

Vere, it seems, agreed. Anne reported their conversation in her diary: '*Said she*, "I do not know whether you will think it a compliment but the children [Louisa and Charlotte] *said to me*, 'We wished Miss Lister would begin again for we understood her much better than Monsieur Hilaire'."' Anne gave herself a pat on the back: 'That will do well enough' (10th July 1829).

Those children who had been so captivated by Anne Lister would go on to lead extraordinary adult lives themselves. Charlotte Stuart became Viscountess Canning when she married the son of the former Prime Minister George Canning. By 1842, two years after Anne's death, Charlotte Canning was Lady of the Bedchamber to Queen Victoria. She achieved success in her own right as an artist of Indian landscapes.

Charlotte's younger sister Louisa Stuart, who became Marchioness of Waterford, also trained as an artist, under the tutelage of Dante Gabriel Rossetti. Her image was said to have inspired some of the Pre-Raphaelite painters. Augustus Hare's 1893 biography, *The Story of Two Noble Lives*, gives great insight into the characters of the two women, and gives a flavour of the elevated social circles in which Anne Lister had found herself moving by the 1830s.

Vere was quick to offer Anne unsolicited pointers about how to behave in high society. Anne recorded more than one occasion in Paris when Vere indicated that she felt Anne's inquisitive mind was getting the better of her in the company of people of rank. Vere only wanted Anne to make a good impression. It was not the 'done thing' to have asked Lord Cosmo Gordon to name his 'favourite hero of antiquity'. 'You will puzzle him,' she said. Similarly, when Anne had asked Sir Charles Bagot, a member of the Privy Council who served as British Ambassador to Russia and to the Netherlands, why he 'disliked Petersburgh people' Vere was quick to tell her that such people 'cannot always answer such leading questions' (18th October 1829).

Initially defensive – 'If people express a decided opinion, they subject themselves to a decided question as to why and wherefore' – Anne, who was given to periods of introspection and self-analysis, went on to absorb Vere's remarks about her behaviour. She was aware that she was used to being in a position of control. At Shibden, she took charge of running her own estate and managing the people who lived and worked on it. There, she behaved in a manner befitting her rank, as landowner and employer of men. She was looked up to. It was becoming clear to her that she would need to learn a new set of behaviours if she was to succeed and be accepted in this social circle:

But, thought I, there is a good hint – never ask a too decided or abrupt question. She little thinks how much I have had to learn – when to talk and when not. I was too new among such society to quite know how to manage for the best. I was anxious not to appear too familiar. My manner wants to be more easy and liante [sociable] *without being too much so, but I do not fancy people see thro' the real person. Better think me stupid and reserved and cold than the contrary ...*

I must dress well, and having everything nice, and reading all the works of the day, and studying at the same time – nothing but this to bear me thro'. I must see to about having a carriage. I can then be useful to people and this will do something.

Travel journal, 18th October 1829

Anne was painfully aware of the gulf that existed between her and her monied friends. Vere was somehow under the impression that Anne had an income of £5,000 a year, a piece of misinformation which Anne chose not to correct. 'Oh, if they saw my father and Shibden and knew all,' she wrote in her travel journal on 15th October 1829, horrified at the prospect of them discovering her real circumstances.

In other ways, though, Anne felt that she did belong in the company of the Stuarts, Hobarts and Stuart de Rothesays, writing that 'I know not how it is that I am at heart so pleased with the really high ones of the land. Their stateliness and dignity suits me.' She told herself that 'medium people' (meaning her family and, as time progressed, her provincial ex-lover Mariana Lawton), did not suit her any more. She put out of her mind the unattractive way in which the 'high ones' had poked fun at her manservant George Playforth and 'all laughed at his stare', with Lady Gordon telling Anne that she 'could not have him in London – his vulgarity is too evident'.

Though nothing overtly romantic developed between Anne and Vere during their time in Paris, the experience was eye-opening, particularly for Vere. She arrived in Hastings with a good understanding of what her 'extraordinary' friend Anne Lister was about. The expensive gifts, the secret code and the gentlemanly displays of attention had made the intended impact. Vere told Anne directly that their conversations 'seemed to her more like that of a lover than a friend, so affectionate' (2nd August 1829).

What Anne did not know as she prepared to travel to Hastings in the autumn of 1831 was that Vere had an agenda for agreeing to stay in the country, besides dodging the cholera in Europe. She was keeping a secret from Anne about her own love life.

Donald Cameron of Lochiel would have been a formidable love rival for anyone. Having distinguished himself in the Napoleonic Wars, and more recently for his heroic conduct as a lieutenant in the Grenadier Guards, he was soon to become the 23rd Chief of the revered Cameron clan in the Scottish Highlands. This man 'was not to be sneezed at' (20th September 1831). What's more, he had the backing of the de Rothesays. Unbeknown to Anne, plans to marry him to Vere had been underway for some time.

And it appeared that Vere herself had high hopes for the match. It fell to Lady Stuart de Rothesay to break the news to Anne that Vere had a 'particular reason' for not wanting to go abroad that winter: 'not liking to be out of the way of a Captain Cameron (Donald) who had lately paid her decided attention.'

Publicly, Anne Lister responded with sangfroid. 'Ah,' she said to Lady Stuart de Rothesay, 'I will not say a word of this, but I am glad you have told, I now see my way clearly.' In private, she thought Vere had been disingenuous in not telling her about the prospect of the match:

> Oh, thought I to myself ... She might have been more candid and ought to have been. I have had my amusement in flirting and shall get off early. I may take the society this winter at Hastings, and then Lady Gordon will suit me much better.

20th September 1831

It's clear that Anne was hurt, but she was not entirely surprised. Indeed, she remembered an instance in London in which Vere had spoken of a secret that, when pressed, she had refused to reveal.

The news of Vere and Donald's match did not deter Anne from setting up rooms in Hastings with Vere. Though she admitted, initially, that any affection between them (by which Anne meant not only sex, but long-term commitment) seemed 'out of the question', the truth of the matter was that she did feel that she could compete with Captain Cameron. She had much to offer Vere. Vere, in turn, represented Anne's ideal woman. She was engaging, clever and sophisticated, with connections to the social circles in which Anne aspired to move. Anne wasn't about to let her slip away without a fight.

In 1831, Anne was as determined as she had ever been to find a female life partner. She didn't feel it was in her nature to live alone – the nature which also dictated that settling for a man was never going to be part of the plan. She was prepared to risk heartache and pain in pursuit of a happiness that she believed was as much her right as it was Captain Cameron's. She was also acutely aware that time was not on her side. Anne was approaching forty one, and no matter how much she told herself that she was 'comfortably enough indifferent' about the outcome with Vere, she was not. It was now or never. She would later write in her journal that 'the woman that deliberates is lost' (7th February 1832). Anne was willing to gamble her own heart to win Vere as a companion for life.

<hr />

'Her high opinion of me is evident'

One of the first things Anne did after arriving in Hastings was write to her beloved aunt at Shibden Hall. She was keen to tell her how well she and Vere were settling in, and how cosily they were getting on together:

> We are sheltered here by an enormous, perpendicular, sand rock cliff, close behind us, and circling round a little on

each side, so as to keep all winds but due South. We are even close upon the sea than at St Leonards. Yet they say, [we] shall not be so incommoded with the spray in winter. In fact, after all, Hastings is well and picturesquely situated, is a nice little town, and might be a comfortable residence were it possible to get a well built, air-tight house, and dry the atmosphere a little … The box contained all I expected – Miss Hobart liked the Parkin – [we] walk for a couple of hours before breakfast – breakfast at 11 or 11¼ – dine at 6½ or 7 … then music – tea at 9, and go to bed about 11½. Our 2 bedrooms over our drawing room and dining room … 4 flights of stairs from the kitchen. We have soup, one dish of meat, 3 dishes of vegetables, and a pudding or tart every day, and are, so far, from 1st to last of us, very harmonious and agreeable. Must begin, and stick to my writing soon.

9th November 1831

It is a typically detailed account. Even away from home, one of Anne's preoccupations was the structure and order of her days. She was keen to maximise her time in Hastings, and made regular visits into town on her own. She took the opportunity to expand her burgeoning library, spending a massive 19 guineas on 'Boydell's Shakespeare in 9 volumes' at a local book auction, in what she called a bout of 'temporary insanity'. She instantly regretted the expense, and started thinking of ways that she might be able to recoup some of the money. She wondered about writing a book of her own, about a recent visit to the Pyrenees:

Thinking to write my tour there, and afterwards if that answers, a sort of sensible, popular travels. The buying of Boydell's Shakespeare has roused me to think of making money ... I must try ... May go again to make my words more perfect?

16th January 1832

The as yet unwritten 'Wanderings of Viator, Pyrenees 1830' would, she fancied, be dedicated to Lady Stuart de Rothesay.

On Sundays, the vicars of Hastings bore the brunt of Anne's critique. One unfortunate preacher was deemed 'affected' and 'slightly impedimented' as he delivered a sermon from the Epistle of St John. Anne visited medical men and apothecaries, making sure to record in detail the special trip to order 'sulphur electuary' for Vere's persistent piles. Back at Pelham Crescent, her greatest indulgence was reading. Books were reviewed on a regular basis. Edward Bulwer-Lytton's true-crime novel *Eugene Aram* was 'Powerfully written, at least the last volume'. Mary Shelley's *Frankenstein* was a 'strangely odd, genius-like cleverly written thing'.

Meanwhile, there were some domestic issues to deal with. Anne's servant Cameron was proving incompetent. Vere was the first to notice:

Miss Hobart not satisfied with the grocer's bill, and with good reason – Cameron for any good she does in these matters is not worth her meat – she is indeed an uncommonly great noodle, and my heart fails me at the thought of taking such a person by way of being trusted to abroad.

10th January 1832

This didn't prevent Anne and Vere from enjoying each other's company. They spent their days reading, walking on the sea front, shopping and attending church together. In a letter to Lady Harriet de Hageman, Vere's half-sister in Copenhagen, Anne described 'a degree of quiet, comfortable wholesomeness' that 'can't fail to do us good' (21st November 1831).

As the days passed, there was a return of the flirtation that had characterised Anne and Vere's relationship in Paris. Though there was a hint of childishness on Vere's part that made her intentions hard to decipher – pushing for attention and sulking when it wasn't adequately delivered – it was behaviour that gave Anne hope. She saw the potential for more serious affection.

In the evenings, Vere played the piano and gave Anne German lessons. Anne presented Vere with an amorous poem – 'When in my hand thy pulse is prest I feel it alter mine, and draw another from my breast in unison with thine.' Vere was not aware that Anne had originally written the verse in 1824, for a woman she met in Paris.

The following day, Anne upped the ante by reading to Vere from William Collins's 'The Passions. An Ode'. Vere's response was difficult for Anne to interpret; she swung between laughing at and seeming to appreciate the 'beautiful' passage.

Vere recognised that Anne was a brilliantly clever woman, and increasingly enjoyed her company. When Anne asked if she should read some of Gibbon's *Decline and Fall* aloud, Vere told her that she 'liked her talking better than reading', because it was 'better than Gibbon'. Anne relished the compliment and reported in her diary that 'her high opinion of me is evident' (11th February 1832).

Vere also trusted Anne's medical opinion. She took advantage of Anne's interest in bodily functions and disease to ask for her thoughts on the 'suspicious greenish dark indurated phlegm such as she spits up occasionally'. Anne readily 'took the opportunity of observing'. Trust and intimacy between the two women was growing.

Anne knew that her love of science was unusual and intriguing. In fact, she told Vere more about her experiences under the tutelage of the renowned natural philosopher Georges Cuvier than she had ever disclosed to other friends or lovers:

> *3 hours talk anatomical ... told her of my having Juliart and of my dissection. She really seeming interested about it, and not sorry to find I had never named it even to M* [Mariana Lawton], *she said as if thoughtlessly, 'What pleasure you will have some time in dissecting me.' I merely said, 'Oh, no, even if I felt it a duty to have her opened, I should not, could not, be there to see. No one dissected those they had loved or had even much known.' But I took no further notice. I think the idea of being with me eventually is somehow getting more familiar to her mind. She really*

begins to flirt a little with me and looked very pretty when
playing this evening. Well strange things happen – she may
like me after all.

14th November 1831

The discussion resumed over breakfast the next day. It was an uncommon seduction technique, but Anne's use of her scientific knowledge to deepen Vere's interest in her is telling. There were no shared conventions of lesbian love available to her to call upon. She had to rely on her intellect and wit to court women. And with Vere it seemed to be working. Anne had taken a risk in telling Vere about her transgressive studies (although she assured Vere that she had 'never assisted in dissecting adult corpses'); Vere's suggestion that Anne should enjoy 'dissecting' her too demonstrated that she was interested in playing along.

Though later Anne privately indulged some of her less optimistic thoughts about what Vere might really be thinking of her – 'The fact is,' she wrote on 26th December, 'she thinks me odd – more as she once let slip – like man than woman' – she was, in general, confident that the relationship with Vere was on a good track as 1831 drew to a close. As midnight struck on 31st December, Anne kissed Vere gently on the lips. Vere looked at her but didn't say anything. 'Will she, can she, suit me?' was the question on Anne's mind as the new year chimed in.

'She is not worth a heart or friendship like mine ... she said she always told me I cared too much for her ...'

Unfortunately, the year got off to a poor start. Anne found Vere increasingly critical of her, and the atmosphere at Pelham Crescent quickly became cold and tense. It appeared that Vere struggled particularly with Anne's lack of femininity:

> *She certainly treats me oddly, and so she thinks of me too. For yesterday morning on my saying something that the occasion brought forwards about petticoats, 'Indeed,' said she, 'I think from your difficulty in getting accustomed to them, you must have spent a great part of your life without them.'*

2nd January 1832

Looking back, there had been warning signs. Before they had arrived in Hastings, Vere had indicated that she sometimes felt stifled by Anne's manner and could not 'bear' her looks (3rd November 1831). As they settled into co-habitation, she found Anne 'tiresome' and imposed allotted times in which she could visit her rooms. It was a blow for Anne's self-esteem. Vere was 'le jeu ne vaut pas la chandelle' – not worth a candle – she wrote frustratedly in her journal (26th November 1831).

As 1832 progressed, the situation between the two women deteriorated further. Anne recorded the details of a disastrous trip to Eastbourne, during which she and Vere argued to the point that Vere slammed out of their carriage and refused to get back in. Incidents like this caused an uncharacteristic downturn in Anne's spirits. She suffered a dip in her usual energy. She was so reluctant to say or do anything to upset Vere that she completely withdrew her attentions. There were no more goodnight kisses.

Any residual hopes Anne had of a relationship with Vere were dashed by the appearance of Captain Donald Cameron on 9th January 1832. Anne's first impression of her rival suitor was that he was an 'amiable, agreeable enough person'. The tall, red-haired Highlander had clearly come to establish his interest in Vere's hand. His short visit to 15 Pelham Crescent was enough to convince Anne that a marriage between them, if not yet officially decided, was a *fait accompli*.

Anne's rather bullish diary entry betrays the insecurity she felt, knowing that her chances of winning Vere's heart were slipping away:

> *I think she will have him but what do I care? I shall have*
> *all the good I can out of her acquaintance, and not having*
> *more will not break my heart. Lady Gordon may suit me*
> *better. Somehow poor Mariana at all events seldom occurs to*
> *me, as destined for my future companion.*
>
> 9th January 1832

By 17th January, Anne was ready to pour out her feelings in a long, heartfelt journal entry. She was entirely candid about the ways in which Vere's behaviour were hurting her:

Thinking of Miss H – annoyed and hurt ... My whole life with her is one effort to be what I am not naturally. I feel it more this morning than I did last night. It began with – she came out from dinner to get her bag – and I followed to light her [light the way with a candle], *and unluckily, was going to kiss her forehead which she refused, saying it was indecent, not a usual time. I laughed but submitted. I had not seen her of so long. The seeing now put me in spirits. I then, at table (George was not by), joked about having taken three glasses of wine and would have more. Then, said she, 'I shall have a headache and go to bed.' All this passed off, but when I repeated afterwards how little I had seen of her during the day (only the half hour at her breakfast and eleven minutes on coming home), she said, 'Oh, I had seen as much of her as usual,' and my allowed time was an hour counting from the time she had done breakfast, and from seven to twelve in the evening. It is the thinking over this that so annoys me. For she said she could not lock the drawing room door (insinuating or meaning the room was as much mine as hers) ... When she was cross on Friday morning, and as I told her without the smallest reason, she would not allow this, saying she did not know I did not mean to stay. For I often went in for a minute, and staid twenty, when she was busy. Thus there is now no doubting that I am in fact excluded from all but my own bedroom, save as above ... No great love therefore, of my company. Besides, I now begin to feel that I must look a little like I know not what to all her friends, who never see, and now never will see me, downstairs in a morning.*

But, why write so much about her, why waste so much time and paper? I hope it may instruct me afterwards, and cure me of all folly about her, by forcing me to remember what sort of time I have really passed with her. How chequered with mortification and pain. I have in fact never been so solitary. We can hardly be said to have one feeling in common, and here I am alone in heart and sighing under mortifications. That shame can never let me breathe, but which is all my consolation that none can dream of ... Do I, or do I not know what I wish? Lord have mercy upon me, thou orderst all things wisely, and thy will be done. No more of her at least at present ... If I had indeed five thousand a year, how all things would be smoothed over, and easier than now, when I ought not to spend seven hundred. I must employ my mind, get all my accounts done and then think seriously of authorship. Why not try myself to make a few hundred? Would do some good, and at least that of diverting my attention. Thought of Miss H, with all these mortified feelings as I walked ... She began to joke at dinner, about not having come down to her for my half hour. I merely replied I had come in after my walk and had been very busy, but not being inclined for joking or much conversation, no more was said, and my gravity was unmoved during the evening ... Surely no more nonsense, no more playfulness and ease. She will like it better. Let her. I shall get accustomed to it, and find it easier or less irksome

by and by ... Let all this fire my ambition to write, and cut
some figure, and in the race, leave Miss H a little behind.
How surprised she would be, and how silently delighted, I.

17th January 1832

Vere seemed oblivious to the pain Anne was feeling. To Anne she appeared callous. 'She said I was too different,' she wrote on 8th February. 'Wished I was a little more blended [ordinary]'. Vere told Anne that she 'wanted what she [Vere] could not give'. It was 'a great pity' that she 'expected so much'. It was becoming painfully clear to Anne that Vere did not want her particular brand of love.

'It is not pleasant to hear one cannot be loved, and that others not more worthy must be preferred,' wrote Anne some weeks later on 18th March 1832. 'Let Pett be my watchword,' she told herself, recalling the day of yet another memorable argument at Pett Levels. Anne's instinct for self-preservation was kicking in. She resolved to be more guarded around Vere, who responded to Anne's complete withdrawal of affection with tantrums and tears.

Finally, on 6th February, the two women attempted to resolve the emotional impasse. Anne told Vere that she was 'cured' of the 'unaccountable phrensy [sic]' of emotion that Vere had found so unattractive. Vere explained her shock at Anne's latterly cold behaviour; she had not expected 'such a violent change'. This open exchange enabled a truce. Their normal backgammon schedule was resumed, and Anne continued with her reading of Gibbon. However, the change in Anne's manner from loving to distant was felt deeply by Vere. She appeared to be missing the tenderness that Anne had once offered. When Anne noticed Vere looking at her on the sofa, she remarked, 'Well, how will it all end. She certainly likes me, and seems almost as if she could not bear to lose me … well after all, I am in for it now. How strangely things turn!' (7th February 1832).

Between their 'tiffs', which Anne described as 'like lovers' quarrels', there were still affectionate moments:

After dinner she sat down on the sofa. I asked her to put her feet up – 'Yes – if you will put them up'. I stood by her and after looking for a moment as if I intended the thing, took this kiss to which she made no resistance, and I pressed her lips thrice – once with mine rather open or finding hers so. She merely joked and said she afterwards could not possibly close her lips again after this. It was all fun, and I took notice but sat a proper distance and quietly at her feet. We then had music. On going to her room, I said I should only stay two minutes, but she kept me, and her eyes filled with tears.

10th February 1832

A week later, Vere's encouragement was beginning to confuse Anne:

I gently leaned down my head. She placed it to lie on her knees. I perceived without looking that she was a little moved and attendrie [touched]. *All the little she said was kind, and gentle. I felt the tears in my eyes, and after some moments or perhaps minutes, silence made an excuse to stir the fire, with my back turned. I just said I think I will go upstairs, and left her – will she end in liking me better than she thinks, or in fact, and in coolness wishes?*

16th February 1832

It appears that Vere was genuinely conflicted. When Anne kissed her forehead, there was a hint of what Anne interpreted as sexual feeling: 'She said she did not like it, it tickled her down to her knees and all down her back'. 'So we are all right,' wrote Anne. 'She certainly likes me, and really I myself cannot guess how it will end' (20th February 1832).

Either way, the emotional uncertainty of her relationship with Vere was getting to Anne. 'Is society worth this to me?' she asked herself, in a searching crypt-hand diary entry on 20th February 1832.

Anne was always careful about disclosing details of her private life to people she did not fully trust. Though she had revealed very little about her former relationships to her, Vere was aware on some level that Mariana was a person of significance to Anne. For her part, Mariana would have hated to know that Anne was spending a six-month sojourn in Hastings with an aristocratic mystery woman. She still held out hope for a relationship with Anne after her husband's death. For Anne, it was not so simple. Though Mariana had been the love of her life, their shared past was full of 'bitter remembrances'. Mariana's marriage to Charles in 1816 had broken Anne's heart. It was part of the reason she was so loath, now, to play second fiddle to Donald Cameron.

❧

'Liberty is still mine. She shall lose me almost without perceiving it'

A 'newsy' letter from Aunt Anne, including details of the theft of three dozen bottles of wine from the Shibden cellar, provided a welcome distraction from the claustrophobic atmosphere at Pelham Crescent. Aunt Anne also had news of Anne's younger sister, Marian:

> *I can't help smiling at Marian saying she goes nowhere, when at the same time she is going everywhere, dining, lunching, or calling – she has not the happy knack of getting rid of acquaintances if she tires of them, but whether she does or not, she retains them, as she says, 'she likes to know everybody'*
>
> 23rd March 1832

Anne's sister was able to annoy her, even at a distance of nearly three hundred miles. 'Well! I can't change her in anything,' wrote Anne to herself, 'however much it might be for the better – she has always liked to be cock of the dunghill. I have no taste for scratching at her; and the less we are in each other's way the better.'

By this time, Vere had started to think about leaving Hastings. But she was aware that her future was not yet certain. It appeared that she was keeping Anne within her sights as a potential 'companion' in the event that Captain Cameron did not make an offer of marriage. When Anne mentioned travelling with Lady Gordon, Vere became jealous. Despite everything, Vere did not want to lose Anne's affections to another woman, especially their mutual friend Lady Gordon.

By mid-April, Anne was making preparations to leave Hastings herself. On the thirteenth, she wrote to her aunt with instructions about the books she was sending ahead of her, including, of course, the Boydell's Shakespeare:

> Thought the Shakespeare, had better be put on top of the mahogany drawers in the blue room ... the first volume ... to be put in the top end drawer next the window of the deal chest in the blue room ... should be off from here on the 23rd, stay the 24th at Tunbridge Wells, and dine in London on the 25th – ask Cordingley to get me 2 pair of small, men's-sized black worsted stockings at Mounsey's – to be washed and sent in the parcel.

Two days later, Anne received the news that she had feared. Captain Donald Cameron had proposed marriage, and Vere had accepted. 'We talked it over,' Anne wrote simply. 'She will not say no. So, 'tis done' (15th April 1832). It was not a surprise, but the fact that her aristocratic ideal woman was destined to find happiness with a man drove a dagger through Anne's heart.

In an act of either masochism or catharsis, Anne wrote a detailed journal entry about the day leading up to Donald Cameron's proposal. She began with the afternoon walk she had taken with Vere. As they had approached the High Street, she recounted, Vere had spotted an odd-looking man in the distance. 'How very long that man's arms are from his side,' Vere had pointed out, 'I don't like that.' Anne too had noted how strange it was that 'one saw the light between the upper arm and side'.

On closer inspection it emerged that the long-armed man in question was, in fact, Captain Cameron of Lochiel. As they walked with him past the nursery garden and along George Street, Anne noted that Vere's misgivings about her suitor's physical attributes had evaporated. Indeed, she seemed 'very satisfied' with him, going so far as to ask him to dine with them that evening. 'I shall be very glad to see you,' Vere told him. 'Will you really?' Captain Cameron replied, in what Anne described as 'a low voice'.

Surely fearing what was to come, Anne left Vere and Captain Cameron to dine alone. When the news of their engagement subsequently came, it had a devastating impact on Anne. 'Flow on my useless, miserable, foolish tears,' she wrote. 'She little guesses the misery of this tearful moment.' Vere had made no attempt to soften the blow or hide her excitement from her.

The following morning, still in 'an agony of grief and tears,' Anne stayed hidden in her room:

Cried and sobbed miserably ... I was ashamed of my swollen eyes, but doing very well till about near 9 ½ when Miss H knocked to ask if I was up ... I faintly answered yes, but the sound of her voice set me wrong, the tears started and I was bad again as ever.

16th April 1832

All day Anne lay in her great coat, with a handkerchief over her face. She refused all food apart from a 'spoonful or two of the soup' and 'a bun with brandy and water'. Vere, catching sight of her tear-stained, swollen face, seemed to understand the reason for Anne's grief. 'Ah,' she said, 'you are thinking of me.' She expressed surprise, rather than sympathy, that Anne 'should take on so'. She 'did not know what she should do' to make things better for her. For Anne, the pain of rejection seemed intolerable:

Miss H tapped at my door ... asked if I was up, let her in. 'Oh,' said she, 'you do not look ill, I see what it is, what an odd figure you are' (in my great coat). She asked if it was her fault ... she is not worth a heart or friendship like mine ... she said she always told me I cared too much for her ... what I feel now will pass away and then she has no qualities to engage me. Let me make what I can of her as an acquaintance, and that perhaps will not be much ... my pride might be wounded, but no I shall not care for all that. She may think what she pleases.

Tis 4½ as I write this last word – my head aches shockingly yet I feel better than I did – cannot sleep – it seems to me she is flippant ... she is selfish, as witness her

whole conduct in not letting me slip till she was sure of
another … proud her prudery was, more pride than modesty
… vain, for she said the first thing there were many people
it would be so nice to tell (of her engagement), and where
is her real modesty for now that he has offered … perhaps
my feelings are more those of mortification at failure than
anything else. Well my journal does not flatter her much –
proud, vain, not good tempered, selfish, flippant, proud and
vain, heart-doubtful, certainly none towards me.

16th April 1832

Vere was a young woman about to embark on a bright married future. Anne was two weeks past her forty-first birthday, without a life-partner and lacking the funds to restore her crumbling ancestral home. But she would not stay cast down for long. With a typical rousing of spirit, her thoughts turned to foreign travel. At the end of the blisteringly raw, painful day, she 'looked at the road map of France to go to Geneva by Calais, Arras, Laon, Chalons, Chaumont and Dijon', wondering where her next adventure might take her.

From Hastings, Anne travelled to London. But with more time alone to reflect, the failure of her society plans played heavily on her mind:

Fine day, but I too fine to take a good walk out. What
splendid slavery. Fine rooms, dressed in my silk redingote,
all for company and nobody to see. Musing of … Mariana
again, giving up finery and fine people … I have had a

32

little trial of great people. I have had my whim, which has
cost me pretty dearly. Now there shall be an end of it? Well,
I wait but to see Lady Gordon.

29th April 1832

Visiting Lady Gordon in Cheltenham was a bold move, and
one by which Anne laid herself open to more hurt and humil-
iation. Lady Gordon was surprised to see her, declaring Anne
'the queerest creature in the world' for turning up so suddenly
and without warning. She made it quite clear to Anne that
travelling together would mean separate bedrooms: 'different establishments and independent of each other' – in other
words, it would require access to the kind of money Anne just
didn't have. Her mortification was complete:

I felt myself, in reality, gauche, and besides, in a false
position. I have difficulty enough in the usage of high society
and feeling unknown, but I have ten times more on account
of money ... my high society plans fail ... I shall now get
out my scrape as well as I can ... Well, I have gained
experience. Lord have mercy on me. I will eventually hide
my head somewhere or other ... The mortification of feeling
my gaucherie is wholesome.

29th April 1832

Anne continued to muse on what she thought of as her fail-
ures. The importance of her diary to the maintenance of her
mental equilibrium is especially clear in passages like this one:

May never see Miss Hobart or Lady Gordon again ...
muse of having my aunt back ... Lady Gordon's proposal
to be independent of each other opened my eyes. She would
not be bothered by having me to society for Florence ... I
may bury myself somewhere in comfortable seclusion and
study and then have fortune enough for happiness ...
What a change in all my plans and thoughts ... What a
comfort my journal is. How I can write in crypt all as it
really is and throw it off my mind and console myself –
thank God for it.

29th April 1832

By 4th May, Anne was staying with Mariana at Lawton Hall in Cheshire. The brief visit did not do much to lift her mood. 'I had little need to speak,' she wrote. 'She enjoyed her own volubility, and I sat, tired to death, but too civil to shew it. Well, I am reconciled to be off.'

The two women found their way to bed together, but for Anne, the sex was mediocre, only 'tolerable'. It was spoiled, in part, by Anne's fear that she would catch a sexually transmitted infection from Mariana (who contracted it from her husband) as she had done some years before in 1821. Now, Anne described how she 'felt hot after it, it frightens me though I have washed twice ... she is not, I fear, to be touched with impunity'. A few days later the situation had not improved: 'Mariana still thinks me altered and fine, and feels restrained, I am sure, and this has destroyed our chance of our being together – she would live and die where she is' (7th May 1832).

These desperate detours could only put off the inevitable for so long. Halifax and home beckoned. On 7th May 1832, at twenty-five minutes past eight in the evening, Anne arrived back at Shibden Hall. She was physically as well as emotionally weary, having chosen to alight from her carriage and walk the final few miles from the turnpike.

The following morning, she had breakfast with her aunt. Aunt Anne was taken aback by her niece's unusual despondency. When Anne asserted that she might as well up sticks and move to America, her advice was immediate and touching: 'There is all England for you to be in.'

CHAPTER 2

SHIBDEN HALL, TRESPASSERS, GEORGE PLAYFORTH'S DEATH, MISS WALKER OF LIGHTCLIFFE AND COAL TALK WITH JEREMIAH RAWSON

'Nothing is wanted but a little energy and determination to set your mind to rights'

Hidden behind one of the oak panels in a downstairs room at Shibden Hall is a rough, white-washed wall. To its right is a finely hewn inglenook fireplace, its opening forming a handsome, curved arch, which is almost tall enough to walk through standing upright. It is a relic of the old Shibden, which was built in 1420 as a modest yeoman's property, and a reminder to visitors today of how different the hall would have looked before Anne made it over with dark oak panelling as part of her grand renovation in the late 1830s. It offers a glimpse at the Shibden Anne inherited, an opportunity to imagine the house in its original condition. It was this Shibden that Anne returned to. It was shabby and scruffy, and she felt ashamed of it.

Anne's relationship with her ancestral home was complicated. Its cluttered rooms, eccentric layout and draughty windows were a physical reminder of the gulf that existed between her grand aspirations and reality. She felt stifled by it: there was some truth in Mariana Lawton's assertion, in a letter referencing her friend's desire for frequent adventure away from home, that Anne would succumb to the 'Blue Devils' [become depressed], if she stayed there for too long. Anne responded:

> *I cannot imagine why you are so bent upon thinking and believing that I shall never live here long together. You have never seen my interest in the place decrease, even though both you and I have lived to see the hope that cheered me on in early days blighted for ever. You ask 'what makes you so devoted to a foreign clime' because as I have said I wish not to make myself a home in England except at Shibden. However lovely the green Alp near Grenoble, it could not seem to me a restful place.*
>
> 30th November 1832

Here is an insight into the complexity of Anne's feelings about Shibden. Despite her dissatisfaction with its condition, and though she would have to defer to her father for permission at every stage of her efforts to improve it, the idea of being parted from it permanently was unbearable.

The Lister lineage meant everything to Anne. Her identity and self-esteem were dependent on Shibden because it was a visible manifestation of the connection between her family and an ancient landed class. For hundreds of years, her research told her, there had been Listers at Shibden Hall, and it was a continuity that Anne would endeavour to maintain at all costs. Her snobbish streak prevented her from publicising the family's historic involvement in the cloth trade, which she judged common.

Later, following Anne's full inheritance of the hall in 1836, she would go as far as establishing a Lister family motto. 'Justus Propositi Tenax' – 'just and true of purpose', inspired by her admiration of the poet Horace. It can still be seen today in finely carved panelling on the oak stairs leading off the central housebody of the hall. The initials A and L are carved on either side, as a permanent reminder of Anne's role in the reinvention of the Lister seat.

Adjusting to life back at Shibden after the disaster of Hastings and Vere proved challenging for Anne. On 17th May 1832, she spent almost ten hours secreted away in her room, ostensibly sorting out her books. Having ignored her aunt, father and sister all day, she found her family intolerable over dinner: 'sat with them all … all vulgar. My aunt the best, but with all her goodness to me sadly tiresome as a companion. The rest – insufferable to the point of vulgarity. Marian's emphasis in speaking terrible.'

As for Halifax, it was 'vulgar' too. The pull of domestic and foreign travel had meant that Anne had been away from her home town for long periods of her adult life. On returning, she found its society parochial and insular. Though much of Halifax had grown accustomed to the eccentric figure Anne cut around the town, she herself could never shake the feeling that she didn't quite fit in.

On 30th June 1832, only a month after returning home from Hastings, Anne found herself tempted by the idea of leaving again. She was drawn to an advertisement in the local newspaper 'of a cottage and 12 acres of land to sell near

Missenden, 3 miles from Wendover, 6 from Aylesbury and 8 from High Wycombe – under the Chiltern Hills in a pretty glen'. Ironically, the area happened to be home to a side of Vere Hobart's family. 'Have been musing about this,' Anne wrote in her diary, 'It is a nice neighbourhood'.

The Halifax of Anne's day was home to appalling poverty as well as a burgeoning industrial middle class. The urban poor and the privileged of the countryside lived side by side. Anne had only had to step out of her front door, walk up the hill to Conery Wood and down the Old Bank past the parish church of St John to find herself among the filth of Woolshops, one of the town's worst slums. Sanitary provision was non-existent; slops and effluent ran down narrow, cobbled streets, spreading disease among the stone cottages and densely populated cellars and over-dwellings. Any person who dared venture down the back streets of Woolshops would have experienced an abominable stench. Mortality rates, needless to say, were horrifyingly high.

Anne Lister seldom strayed into the dark, dirty alleys of the Halifax slums, but she was not ignorant to the contemporary arguments surrounding the experience of the poor working class in her town. It was a period in which the use of child labour in local mills and factories was beginning to be challenged. Anne denied gaining anything herself by the forced labour of the local worsted cloth mills (some of which belonged to her business rivals the Rawsons). She wrote to a friend:

Our respectables say there is much misrepresentation about the factory children. I, myself, no judge. Would rather err

*in ignorance on the side of humanity than, from want of
experience, sacrifice the innocent. No politician, or should hope,
Mrs Norcliffe, would not find I had got any wrong-sided warp.*

28th April 1833

While the Listers' patronage of various local charities indicates
that they were not indifferent to the suffering of the poor, like
many of the landed gentry who had assets to protect, the family
were keen to keep the town and its people at a safe distance.
One of Anne's long-term preoccupations was the network of
public footpaths that ran through the Shibden estate. With the
help of her solicitor, Mr Parker, she was able to have many of
the paths stopped up or redirected. She recorded every success
in her diary. 'Ordered a plan to be taken of the new footpath
I have made of James Smith's Brow, and of the Daisy Bank
footpath and Lower Brea wood, Bridle Road, that I wish to
stop,' she wrote on 28th November 1832. A day later, 'Took
Washington's plan of the footpath and Bridle Road in Lower
Brea wood that I wished to stop – explained all.'

Anne's biggest victory was to close a public path near
to the hall which she had long seen as a magnet for thieves.
According to her journal, she had frequently hung out of the
upper windows of Shibden with a shotgun threatening to blast
the head off anyone who contemplated stealing her chickens.
The fact that she was known to be a competent markswoman
was handy in frightening people away. She kept a loaded gun
at the ready for all eventualities, though in reality her targets
were most often the rats that populated the Shibden kitchen.

Trespass was a persistent threat on the Shibden estate, and the undesirables who encroached upon Anne's land came from all quarters of society, not just the poor. Shortly before she left for Hastings in September 1831, Anne took the landowner and businessman Christopher Rawson to task over the errant behaviour of one of his gamekeepers. Out walking with Mr Sunderland, a local doctor, Anne was infuriated to find a dead bird at the top of one of her fields. 'If one of the fellow's dogs had been near enough,' she had told her walking companion, 'I would have begged the loan of his (Mr Sunderland's) double-barrelled gun and shot the dog myself.'

But her real venom was reserved for Mr Rawson. She wrote a letter to him as soon as she got in:

Dear Sir. A man of the name of Mark Wilcock, calling himself your gamekeeper, after being discharged 3 times in the course of today from shooting on the grounds belonging to Shibden Hall, persisted in returning, and shot 2 partridges to my knowledge, one of them under my own eye, and that of several other persons. I can hardly believe such a man to be your keeper, but, if he is, I think it right to inform you of his conduct, and that I have given instruction to Messrs Parker & Adam to summons him before the magistrates on Saturday, if the matter can be so settled, and if not, to bring an action against him. I am, dear sir, very truly yours, A. Lister, Shibden Hall.

1st September 1831

At 7.45 the next morning Anne received a limp reply. Mr Rawson clearly hoped to put the matter to bed quickly:

Dear Madam. I was very sorry to hear Mark Wilcock had been trespassing over the grounds at Shibden Hall, as he ought to have known better, and I think must have been in a little liquor. But, will take care he does not offend again in the same way. Yours truly, C. Rawson. Hope Hall.

2nd September 1831

The response did not pass muster, and Anne was having none of it:

Dear Sir. I am much obliged to you for your note of this morning. Nothing can be more satisfactory as to the future conduct of Mark Wilcock, who, I am happy to find, is your game keeper, as in this case, you will doubtless be able to settle the matter for me. I am sorry this annoying business has occurred, and still more so to feel obliged to say the man was not in liquor when I discharged him, and that such was the man in which he set me at defiance in the presence of the two men who had before discharged him by my authority. I am really called upon to beg you will be so good as insist on his coming here, and giving me a proper written apology in the presence of the two men in question, and of such other persons as I may choose to have present. Had you said ½

a word about the game, I should have had the greatest
pleasure in giving you run of the estate. I am dear sir,
very truly yours, A. Lister.

2nd September 1831

Mark Wilcock did come to apologise. A week later, Anne visited Rawson's Bank in Halifax. Under the auspice of making 'good friends' again with Mr Rawson, she could not resist a little gloating:

Saw Mr Rawson – very good friends. Very sorry I had not
seen his mother – going away tomorrow after church. He
thought I should be quieter in France than they would here
– no trade – people turning off the workpeople – there be
a sad winter. Said I had near gone to spend winter with
a friend in Spain, but the journey so long and sure to be
robbed near Madrid and Seville, that we had given it up.
Said I had let off his gamekeeper as easy as for example's
sake I could – better for us all to keep people in some sort of
order.

Christopher Rawson was a prominent figure in Halifax, and his influence was felt widely among its people. In fact, it is highly likely that if Anne had brought an action against Mark Wilcock for trespass, Mr Rawson would have been the Justice of the Peace called upon to preside over his own employee's trial. Anne's solicitor Mr Parker knew this; it is probably the reason that Anne chose not to take the matter further.

Rawson had clout. To a landowner, banker and magistrate of his standing, the Mark Wilcock episode was probably nothing more than a minor annoyance. For Anne, it was more important. She needed to demonstrate that she was not a person to be messed with. It was an approach that was to stand her in good stead in the coming years, as she locked horns with Christopher Rawson in complex coal negotiations.

Today, as you walk through Halifax town centre, the Rawson influence remains visible. Christopher Rawson's home, Hope Hall, stands as a monument to Georgian grandeur, with fine fluted pillars and handsome porticos still intact. Rawson's Bank, on Rawson Street, retains the architectural impact of its former days, despite its current use as cafes and offices.

The unlawful use of her footpaths was not the only estate matter occupying Anne on her return to Shibden. Partially to prevent herself from dwelling on how things had ended with Vere, she threw herself into dealing with the eviction of an elderly tenant, Benjamin Bottomley. From Hastings, Anne had already brushed off Marian's concern that Bottomley was too old to be ordered off the land, writing to her aunt that:

I really hoped he was wise enough to be persuaded that at his age (nearer ninety, I presume, than eighty) it was time to give up farming, as much for his own sake as that of anybody else. Marian herself told me of his being obliged to go to bed after returning with his milk cans from Halifax, and considering the strong symptoms of decrepitude, and

*how unaided he is for anybody in whom one can place
any confidence, I had supposed Marian herself must, on
reflection, be of the opinion that if he has no money, he is
unfit for the farm, and if he has money, the farm is unfit
for him.*

9th December 1831

Anne had a hard nose for profit. Her uncompromising treatment of Bottomley exposes the harsh reality of the power
imbalance between the nineteenth-century landlord and
tenant. Anne's father, she decided, had given away too many
concessions during his years of managing the estate. She would
not follow suit.

Anne was firm, and sometimes merciless, but she always
believed herself to be fair. Each decision she made was backed
up with careful reasoning. She valued openness in her communication with her tenants, offering praise for good farming as
well as admonishment where she felt it was needed.

Rent collection day, hosted at the Lister's Stag's Head
Inn about a mile from Shibden Hall, was a significant site of
interaction between Anne and her tenants. Accompanying her
father and land steward to the twice-yearly event, Anne would
have cut an unusual figure in an inn full of burly working men.
But once the business of collecting the rents had started, there
was no mistaking that Anne was the one in charge. The publican knew it, her father knew it and so did the tenants.

'Saw poor George in his oaken coffin, very neatly shrouded with greens and laurels round his head – this struck me more than all I had seen of him before – poor fellow! It was for the last time'

In June 1832, not long after Anne's return to Shibden, the Listers experienced a tragedy: the sudden death of their coachman, George Playforth.

George had been in the Listers' employ for many years. Though he was a loyal servant, his relationship with Anne was dogged by what she called his 'forever stupidity'. She had accepted that he could never 'speak or look beyond the grade of a stable boy' (19th April 1829). Early on, she had taken exception to his filthy nails. Anne did not like dirty hands on anyone; it was one of the first things on which she judged those who made her acquaintance. Her most recent contretemps with George had occurred a few months earlier, on 11th February, when he had got drunk and scared a gentleman's child in the street in Hastings.

In the past Anne had often complained of his incompetence as a footman and his over-use of the whip on her horses, for whose welfare she was always concerned. Yet when he had come over the reins of Anne's beloved horse Percy, injuring himself quite badly, she had been quick to get him medical treatment:

Percy came down. George flew over his head and sprained his knee – the horse wanting shoeing. Sent George off with

him to Blamires and desired [him] *to go to the leech woman
and have six leeches set on his knee while the horse was shod.*

24th March 1824

Clearly, some affection had built up over the years between mistress and servant.

In June 1832, Anne and George had travelled to Langton Hall, the country home of Anne's audacious, snuff-taking, hard-drinking friend (and ex-lover) Isabella Norcliffe. The accident in which George ultimately lost his life was outlandish and improbable. It is described by Anne in characteristically gory detail:

*The half hour bell had just rung at 3½ when a man was seen
returning up to the house … come for a ladder – the keeper had
shot a man in a tree – all in alarm – soon learnt it was George
– shot in the head – was dying – prepared for the worst. He was
soon brought up and laid on a bed in the dressing room down
stairs … By 4¾ Mr* [Dr] *Cobb and his son arrived – no wound
of any consequence but for one gram of shot that had entered
the socket of the left* [eye] *– small shot – at the distance of about
30 yards – in the top high tree near a carrion crow's nest – the
keeper shooting the old birds – this one shot must have pierced
the socket, from the stupor and insensibility, and the catching
convulsive clothes-pricking motions of the hand and arms – this
always takes place in cases of apoplexy and any pressure on the
brain from extravasated blood or otherwise.*

1st June 1832

Climbing the tree in an attempt to scare the carrion crows out of their nest for the Langton gamekeeper to shoot, George had been shot himself. Anne was determined to get the best treatment for him, asking the doctor, Charles Cobb, 'to stay here all night if he thought there was the least occasion' to aid George's recovery. Later, curiosity prompted her to examine George's hat: '16 or 18 shot had entered it – of the 5 or 6 that had entered his head, none of any consequence but that that had entered the eye'.

George died three days later:

Found the pulse fluttering, perspiration on the skin … at 5.50 the rattling (like the gentle boiling of water) came on. At 6.5/11 – the poor fellow expired without a sigh – he seemed to suffer no pain … Mr Charles Cobb came about or soon after 7 – the head to be opened.

3rd June 1832

Anne was upset, but not squeamish. Having dissected a human head during her time in Paris, she was comfortable with the sight of blood, and fascinated by the workings of the brain. She stayed to watch George's autopsy, having insisted to Dr Cobb that, as George's employer, she should be present over 'two of the men' from the estate. She suggested that Burnett, Langton Hall female servant, should attend too. Dr Cobb agreed to her demands, and the detailed post-mortem instigated by her, recorded on 4th June, reads almost as if Anne were holding the scalpel, or *bistouri*, herself:

Mr Cobb had sawn and prized off the upper hemisphere of the cranium, and laid open the brain in ¼ hour. The whole surface including a little bit over the right eye covered with coagulated blood, and the ventricles full of liquid blood. Mr Cobb thought 6oz at least coagulated, and liquid in the ventricles. Could not find the shot. It had made a large opening through the orbit and must be hid deep in the brain – impossible to have saved life in such a case – of this I was quite satisfied. The cap of the skull was then replaced and the skin so neatly sewn over it, that all looked as if nothing had been disturbed.

4th June 1832

Anne recorded in her diary how, that day, George's 72-year-old father walked nearly sixteen miles across the Yorkshire Wolds to see his son's body. Broad-shouldered in times of crisis, she treated him with great sensitivity:

Said everything I could most comforting (no hint at the examination) … mentioned that ¾ years wages would be due on the 19th – gave him £5 for the present, and his watch and all that poor George had here … did not pay him more now not knowing whether George might have left any debts behind him … would have £10 more to receive – would send him an account.

4th June 1832

Finally, Anne gave the Langton servant, Burnett, a note containing the message for George's coffin plate: 'George

Playforth died on the 1st June 1832 aged 31.' It was a rare mistake for someone so obsessed by detail and accuracy. George had died on the 3rd June. It seems as though Anne had taken the date of his death to be the day he was shot and lost consciousness, and not the day he drew his last breath.

Back at Shibden, Anne turned her energies towards the renovation of her hall and estate. For some time she had envisioned building a *chaumière* – a kind of rustic thatched hut that she had admired during her travels in France – on her land. She liked the idea of a cosy space into which she could retreat when she wanted a break from working outside. It might be nice to take a nap, or read the newspaper. She started to make definite plans and consult with workmen over where the hut might go.

She also began to think seriously about how she could improve the monetary value of her land. By the 1830s, coal mining had become a hugely important and profitable industry in Halifax, and Anne had hopes that the dormant family pit, Listerwick, could be brought back into operation. Knowing she would need expert advice before plotting her next move, she determined to approach her coal steward tenant, James Holt, from Highroyds in Northowram.

Though Anne appeared to be settling back into estate life at Shibden, she frequently reminded those around her that she would only be staying for as long as it took to plan her next foreign adventure.

Anne had proven that she could manage lengthy periods abroad in conjunction with the profitable running of Shibden's 400 acres. With her elderly father now little more than a sleeping partner, she was able to deal with estate matters in a way that suited her, running things remotely from whichever part of the world she was in. She left orders with her staff via a relentless trail of letters. She even roped in her aunt to make sure the workmen were planting the right hedges and sowing the right seeds.

During a trip to York in 1831, she wrote to Aunt Anne to check up on how her tenant, Jonathan Mallinson, was getting on with the job of renovating Shibden's back room. Anne's physical absence did not mean that her presence should not be felt:

> *I hope Mallinson would quite understand about his job in the back room. There is to be a brick wall of a brick length in breadth built across the room from the pillar. A new window of two lights nineteen inches wide each, to open sash-wise, and a door to communicate with your room, and the back room, or that part of it taken in is to be lowered as much as it can be conveniently – six or eight inches at least, and is to have a boarded floor ...*
>
> *Let them begin this part of the job earlyish in the morning, and all may be pulled down and made up again at night.*
>
> 26th June 1831

It wasn't uncommon for Anne to take advantage of the flexibility of her tenants and their skills. Mallinson was also the publican of her inn, the Stag's Head. On this occasion, however, he appeared to have overstretched himself. Anne wrote to her aunt again on 7th July: 'Do pray tell Mallinson he must begin the job as soon as he can, and stick to it, that is not leave it on any pretense whatever, till it is done.'

Until now, the Shibden estate had been run using methods of coal mining, stone-quarrying and agriculture that went back centuries. Anne knew that to fully capitalise on her land and its wider tenanted farms in a rapidly changing landscape bursting with industrial competition, she would need to embrace the new methods of her mill-building, pit-sinking rivals. She also knew that to keep up, she would have to seek the advice of professional men who were better versed than she was in the latest business trends.

When her long-standing land steward, James Briggs, died a few months after her return from Hastings, Anne took the opportunity to rethink exactly how her estate would be managed. Dutifully, she had attempted to visit Mr Briggs before he passed away:

Note from Mrs Briggs with my rent book to say Mr Briggs easier but no better otherwise – would like to see me if I chose and Mrs Briggs thought seeing him would not disturb him ... down the old bank to Mr Briggs – in much pain – in bed – not well enough to see me.

30th June 1832

Even before Briggs became ill, Anne had her eye on his potential successor. Samuel Washington of Fenny Royd also managed the nearby Walker estate at Lightcliffe. Following a few glasses of wine and a conversation about the possibility of building '£15-a-year houses in the Sheep Croft for £200 each', Anne wrote that she had given Washington 'good hope of being my steward, should anything happen to Briggs' (26th July 1832).

The day of her visit to ailing Mr Briggs, who finally died some months later on 17th September, was packed with other errands. Anne's trips into Halifax always were; they are a testament to both her mental stamina and her physical fitness. She walked everywhere. She broke up the endless meetings with surveyors, solicitors and tenants by calling on friends and catching herself up on political news which, in the summer of 1832, was dominated by the impending Reform Bill. 'Stocks had been haranguing his party for 2 hours today in the assembly room – a radical firebrand sort of speech against present institutions,' she reported on 29th June 1832.

On her return home from the visit to Briggs, she managed to 'fit in' a translation of *Theocritus*, then order surgical implements for future anatomical studies from Rogers in Sheffield:

Six French bistouries with tortoiseshell folding handles at 3/6 each, and 2 scalpels with ditto at 2/, and 2 best lancets at 2/6, and one Russian leather case containing the four best razors at 21/, two ditto containing 2 best razors at 11/, and a … pruning knife. Will you be so good as to let me know if you have made knife and fork and spoon and corkscrew all shutting up in one handle, and at what prices?
29th June 1832

The pace at which Anne's brilliant mind worked had its drawbacks. She often felt frustrated by what she judged to be the glacial tempo of the majority of her day-to-day interactions. It was important to her that the professional men she employed had a level of intelligence that could match her own.

Samuel Washington, her soon-to-be land steward, fitted the bill perfectly. Living with his wife, Hannah, and young family less than a mile from Shibden Hall, he was both sharply intelligent and of sound moral fibre, a characteristic that Anne looked for in all her employees. He was a skilled draughtsman, able to produce the accurate and precise estate maps that would be vital to her ambitious remodelling plans. Over the coming years, his services would become indispensable to Anne.

❦

'Your letter is just like yourself – sensible, agreeable, and to the purpose'

Lady Gordon's description of Anne Lister fitted her friend perfectly. One of the many reasons people sought Anne's company was because her brisk sense of purpose was matched by a deep-rooted optimism. Periods of melancholy, though they occurred, were never lengthy. Anne was a believer in the power of positive thinking, long before it became fashionable. She trusted that all would work out for the best in the end and everyone, she felt, had the power to be their own 'fortune teller and ... fortune maker'. 'Providence leaves us free,' she wrote, ''tis we enthral ourselves' (7th January 1832).

Anne could also be intimidatingly measured and cool. Arguments in Hastings frequently ended when Vere Hobart stormed out of the room in tears, frustrated by the calm dignity that Anne was able to maintain in the most fraught moments.

Though, of course, as events in Hastings had proven, Anne was not always as in control as she liked to appear. The raw emotion of her tear-stained diary pages gives an insight into what she referred to as her bouts of 'womanish weakness'. But what Anne was able to do was critically appraise her mistakes – and she used this ability to help herself move on efficiently, be it from a broken heart or an erroneous business decision. She was skilled at disarming those who confronted her in either situation, too.

Writing her journal gave Anne the opportunity to distil and analyse the subtle detail of her own life. Between her straightforward, if heavily abbreviated, English (plain hand) and passages of secret code (crypt hand) she had the freedom to catalogue every detail of her public and private life. Anne's diaries were more than an *aide-mémoire*; she used their wealth of data to improve herself.

There was much material for Anne to reflect on after her return from Hastings. She needed time at home to process the 'tyranny of disappointment' she had felt over Vere, and recover from the embarrassment of her visits to Lady Gordon and Mariana Lawton.

Though Anne would never allow her pursuit of love to be thwarted by fear of refusal or social constraints, the failure of

Hastings was a watershed moment in her life. Vere's rejection of her represented to Anne a rejection by high society, and it brought about a significant change in her thinking regarding what she wanted for her future.

Anne's return to Shibden, though to a degree a decision that was forced upon her, offered the new possibility of finding a love interest closer to home. The reinvention of her ancestral seat was part of a bid to establish financial and emotional stability on her own terms and 'within her compass' (29th April 1832).

There would, of course, be challenges to making a match on home turf. It was an audacious plan that required next-level confidence. In Hastings, Anne's failure to win Vere had taken place behind the door of 15 Pelham Crescent. She had been hundreds of miles from the eyes of Halifax society. At closer range, she knew she would be subject to scrutiny and gossip. If things went wrong it would be not only excruciating but excruciatingly public. Even though Anne had never tried to mask her 'oddity', she fully understood that diplomacy and discretion were crucial if she were to live as she wanted to.

Mariana Lawton had been a consistent figure in Anne's romantic life for nearly twenty years. Now, as the two women approached middle age, they acknowledged the changes to their relationship the years had wrought. Anne put it succinctly when she wrote that 'nobody felt at forty as at fifteen'. But though things between them had grown less ardent, Mariana maintained her role as chief advice-giver to Anne in 1832. She told Anne that her 'unsettled life' was having a bad effect on her temperament and resulting in her 'odd and particular' treatment of others. 'I am as I am,' Anne responded stoutly. 'How can I change myself all at once?' (3rd May 1832).

Mariana also believed that Anne would never settle permanently at Shibden. Anne's response reveals the degree to which her decision rested upon finding love: 'A great deal will, and must, depend on that someone known or unknown that I still hope for as the comfort on my evening hour.'

In fact, by the time Mariana was dispensing advice, Anne already had her eye on the wealthy heiress of a neighbouring estate.

Anne Lister and Ann Walker had met several times before 1832. References to the Walkers of Lightcliffe – a grand estate near Shibden – are scattered through Anne's diaries of the 1820s. Her early descriptions of the family, and particularly Ann, are not auspicious. There is certainly nothing to hint at the hugely significant role Miss Walker would go on to play in Anne's life. 'A stupid, vulgar girl indeed', was how Anne described her on 18th June 1822. Later, along with her sister, Elizabeth, she was 'deadly stupid' (19th August 1822).

Nor did the other Listers seem particularly enamoured of the Walkers. Despite their geographical proximity, the families were not on regular calling terms. It may have been that the 'old money' Listers of ancient (if shabby) Shibden believed themselves to be socially above the 'new money' Walkers, whose enormous wealth and sparkling new houses derived from recent trade. Anne recollected encountering Miss Walker, her elder sister and their mother in the aftermath of a carriage accident that had occurred on Shibden land in 1820. The Walkers were offered a cup of tea and a lantern to light their way home, but not friendship.

In 1832, the reacquaintance between Anne and Ann began very respectably. On 6th July 1832, eight weeks after Anne's return from Hastings, Miss Walker accompanied her relatives, Mr and Mrs Atkinson, on a chance social call at Shibden. 'Received them and was very civil,' wrote Anne of the unremarkable afternoon. Reading the day's diary entry more closely, there is to be found a tiny hint of flirtation in a joke she makes with Miss Walker 'about travelling' together.

A week later, Anne returned the social call. At Lightcliffe she found Ann in the company of members of her wider family, Anne's own friends, Mr and Mrs Priestley, as well as the Atkinsons.

Anne was given a tour of the three properties on the enormous Lightcliffe estate. Lidgate, where Ann lived, was cosier and more contained than the ostentatiously grand Cliff Hill, home to Ann's aunt (who was also named Ann), and the Walkers' flashiest property, Crow Nest. Anne did not seem overawed, limiting her comments on the visit to a few journal lines. She preferred to write of her efforts to avoid the heavy shower that came on as she walked home 'along the fields and by Lower Brea' and record that for the rest of the afternoon she read the first volume of Voltaire's letters, in French.

Born in 1803, Ann Walker was twelve years younger than Anne Lister. She does not seem to have had a happy childhood. Her father, William Priestley told Anne in 1822, was a 'madman', who had been 'spoilt all his life' and who 'blackguarded [ill-treated] his wife and daughters' (9th July 1822). Whether this was the source of the low self-esteem and anxiety which dogged Ann Walker throughout her adult life, we cannot know. It was Mrs Priestley who expanded on the nature of Miss Walker's mental illness to Anne some years later:

> *Miss Walker's illness likely to be insanity – her mind warped on religion. She thinks she cannot live – has led a wicked life, etc. Had something of this sort of thing occasioned by illness at seventeen, but slighter. The illness seems to in fact be a gradual tendency to mental derangement.*
>
> 28th August 1828

In fact only a few months after this conversation Mrs Priestley entered into the subject again with Anne about Miss Walker's mental health, saying that if nothing was done to help the girl that she feared she would 'end in idiocy' (6th November 1828).

By the 1830s, with her sister Elizabeth married to Captain George Mackay Sutherland and living in Scotland, Ann Walker had little to occupy her at Lidgate. She looked forward to occasional visits from relative Catherine Rawson and friend Miss Parkhill, and lessons from her drawing master, Mr Brown. Otherwise, she filled her time as best she could with sewing, knitting and small philanthropic works. The typical pastimes of a woman of her class were just enough to keep her feeling that her life had some value.

Though they had very different personalities, there were similarities between Anne Lister and Ann Walker's circumstances. Like Anne, Miss Walker was close to her aunt, Ann's mother and father having died years previously. Like Anne, she had come into an inheritance that wouldn't have been hers but for the unexpected death of a brother.

The vast estate that Ann and Elizabeth Walker inherited in 1830 came with great responsibility. Their acreage dwarfed Shibden's. Ann Walker had a private income far beyond anything that Anne Lister could ever dream of. On 2nd February 1833, Anne worked out that her own income was somewhere between £830 and £840 per annum. She made light of her financial straits in her diary: 'I will make it do, and perhaps I shall be happier than if I had none' (2nd February 1833). By contrast, Ann Walker had more than double that amount at her disposal.

The wider Walker family contrived to keep a close eye on Ann Walker. Some of them had ideas for where she, and her enormous wealth, might end up. Her brother-in-law's mother, Mrs Sutherland, hoped to marry her to Sir Alexander Mackenzie, a relative who had recently fallen on hard times. Having been ejected from the army for insubordination, his baronetcy was redundant. He had his mother to keep. It is fair to assume that Mrs Sutherland had a financial motive in wondering if he might be a catch for Ann.

Through the marriage of her cousin Mary Priestley, Ann Walker had become linked to the Rawson family, of which Anne's soon-to-be business rival, Christopher Rawson, was a member. The extended Walker, Rawson, Edwards and Priestley network dominated Halifax society, with combined political and commercial influence. Ann Walker may have been shy, but the reality was that as an unmarried woman of private means at the heart of such a family, she held considerable power. Anne Lister knew this.

In fact, it was on 13th July 1832, the day of Anne's visit to Lightcliffe, that she received a note from another Rawson family member, Jeremiah: 'Mr Jeremiah Rawson called and left his card for me this morning. I conclude he wanted to speak about a few coals at the top of the hill, that Hinscliffe wants.'

Anne was now firmly in business mode. She wasted no time in working out exactly what the coal on her land might be worth. Following a consultation with her coal steward, James Holt, and based on a series of precise calculations, she found the answer: £226.17.6 per acre. She would be ready for Jeremiah Rawson's next visit on 19th July.

Anne had a good head for figures. Over many years she had become practised in balancing her own books. It stood her in good stead; her mathematical skills were required on a daily basis in her life as an estate owner, from buying and selling property and everyday goods to bidding for the stone of a tumble-down building at a local auction. Now, if the need arose, she was able to quickly measure the amount of stone required for walling, or evaluate the going rate for 'hurrying' and 'getting' a corve of coal.

On Thursday 19th July 1832, as planned, Jeremiah Rawson came to Shibden Hall to talk business. With her calculations sorted, Anne was able to spend a leisurely morning awaiting his arrival. Breakfast was at nine, followed by the appraisal of some new surgical instruments – 'razors, bistouries, etc.' – that had arrived from Rogers Cutlers in Sheffield. She checked over her stone and coal plans before mending stockings till just after eleven.

The Rawson brothers had known Anne since their shared youth in Halifax. She was friendly with their mother. Why had Christopher Rawson sent his brother to see Anne, rather than visiting her himself? Possibly he knew she would be formidable to negotiate with, so perhaps he thought that Jeremiah would pull off the deal better than him.

As Jeremiah was ushered into the hall, just after 11.30am, there were few pleasantries. He cut to the chase, telling Anne she must set a price for her coal. 'I have made up my mind,' said Anne, 'not to take less than my uncle sold it for – £230 for what came out of Trough of Bolland pit, and £205 for what was pulled at Willy Hill pit.' The visit lasted no more than twenty five minutes. The price, wrote Anne, 'frightened him'.

CHAPTER 3

MORE OF MISS WALKER, VERE'S MARRIAGE, BELOVED AUNT ANNE, ANNE'S HEALTH AND SHIBDEN'S ERRANT TENANTS

'Here I am at, at forty-one, with a heart to seek.
What will be the end of it?'

Anne Lister's account of her third visit to Lidgate signals a surprising shift in her feelings about Ann Walker. Outwardly, the social call she paid on 10th August 1832 was unremarkable; the polite tea-drinking and exchange of amusing local gossip between two respectable ladies might have been taken from one of Jane Austen's Regency drawing rooms. But as Ann chatted on with a description of the 'queer questions' and 'odd remarks' of her medical man Dr Kenny – who she believed, despite his being married, would like to become 'intimate with her' – an insight into Anne Lister's inner thoughts make the story quite different. Miss Walker's 'civil and agreeable' behaviour meant more to Anne than her neighbour knew. For Anne, there was romantic promise in the fact of their getting on so 'very well together'. The possibility of courting Miss Walker had entered her mind 'several times before of late'. 'Thought I,' she wrote in her diary that evening, 'shall I try and make up to her?'

A week later, Anne called on Miss Walker again. On her way, she paid a visit to New House on the Lightcliffe estate, home to Ann's cousin, William Priestley, and his wife, Eliza.

Anne had known the Priestleys for many years. She was friendly
with Mrs Priestley in particular, who thought her interesting
and kind, and was endeared to her eccentricity. They talked,
'confidential as usual', about Anne's sister, Marian. When
Anne excused herself from the company, which now included
two other members of Miss Walker's extended family, Mrs
Priestley seemed disappointed that she was leaving 'so soon'.
Anne told her friend that she was 'as busy as ever', and headed
briskly to Lidgate, where she spent the next three hours with
Ann Walker.

This would be the longest amount of time the two women
had ever spent together. Ann Walker spoke candidly about her
relatives, giving Anne a rather cutting take on William Priestley who, along with Mr Edwards, had been appointed trustee
of the Walker estate. Neither, she felt, 'behaved like a gentleman'. Anne was alarmed to learn from Miss Walker that the
Priestleys 'knew all' of the Listers' financial concerns.

While they were talking, Anne managed to break an ivory
book knife that had been gifted to Miss Walker by her cousin,
Catherine Rawson. Initially ashamed of her clumsiness, Anne
turned the situation quickly to her charming advantage. It
would, she suggested 'be a good excuse for my giving her
one someday from Paris, which she hoped she would value as
much as the one destroyed'. Miss Walker replied, encourag-
ingly, that she would value any gift of Anne's even more than
the thing she had broken.

At a friendly parting, Ann Walker gave Anne the Saturday
edition of the *Penny Magazine* to take away with her. Though

no follow-up date was arranged, Anne's intentions were being formed with increasing clarity. The crypt-hand entry she made in her journal that night is revealing: 'She has money and this might make up for rank. We get on very well so far and the thought, as I returned, amused and interested me' (17th August 1832).

Until now, the combination of wealth and ancient pedigree had been a prerequisite in Anne's vision for a life partner. She had been attracted to the idea of sharing her life with a woman of a distinguished lineage. But after the disappointment of Vere and her rejection by society, Anne's mindset had shifted. A woman without rank, but with Ann Walker's kind of money, might do very well. The Lister lineage could be enough for them both.

Clearly, Anne's intentions towards Ann Walker were strategically inclined. She was working within a frame set by her heterosexual peers: for the middle and upper-classes in the nineteenth century a 'good match' was a marriage that made financial sense, with love a secondary consideration. This was the context in which Mariana had been married to Charles Lawton, twenty years her senior, in 1816. A grand estate like Lawton Hall in Cheshire would always be more important to Mariana's family than a romantic connection. Despite her own heartbreak at Mariana's betrayal, Anne Lister had understood that. She had nothing to offer Mariana in terms of immediate wealth. Nor did her passionate love and intense loyalty mean anything in Georgian society. A private lesbian relationship like theirs had no value.

Sixteen years later, Anne was able to think differently. With her impending inheritance, she had something to bring to a match with Ann Walker. The combination of their incomes would cement her own financial future. And they did get on 'very well together'. It was time to move the friendship on to something more serious. 'She little dreams what is in my head,' wrote Anne to her diary. All that remained was to bring Miss Walker up to speed with the plan.

⌦⌫⌦⌫⌦

'Have patience with Dame Destiny, and she will pay everybody'

On returning from her lengthy visit to Lidgate on 17th August, Anne spent five hours of the afternoon digging on the land with her men – 'Banking up the new part of the walk in Tilly Holm'. Returning to the hall almost twelve hours after she had left it, she was greeted with relief by her aunt, who had been uneasy 'at my being out and nobody knowing where I was'. Only a few days previously, servant Rachel Hemingway had injured herself climbing over a wall on the estate, trying to locate her mistress.

Anne often went out for long periods of time without telling anybody how long she was going to be away for. For someone as attached to her fob watch and obsessed with recording the precise timing of her comings and goings, ... it was an interesting habit to have.

The following day was quieter. Anne wrote a thank you to Burnett at Langton Hall, the servant with whom she had attended George Playforth's autopsy:

My very good Burnett. I send you a silk gown which I hope you will think pretty, but which I count upon you wearing for my sake. You may be quite sure I can't forget all your valuable attentions to poor George, or the many little kind services you have so often done myself. I shall be much obliged to you to let Joseph Booth, the boy at Scott's, have the parcel directed to him.

18th August 1832

Despite her incubating designs on Miss Walker, Anne was unable to put the thought of foreign travel out of her mind. She had been on the hunt for a new lady's maid and manservant for some time, and was determined that her new servants should be suited to travel. She had offered the role of manservant to a local man called James Greenwood of Conery Wood, but he had declined, confiding in Matty Pollard (Anne's only female tenant) that he would have been interested had Miss Lister been more 'settled'. It was the second time in recent months that someone had questioned Anne's restlessness. Mariana had told her back in April, after she had left Hastings, that she should 'be more happy settled than wandering about'.

A plain-speaking Yorkshireman, James Greenwood told Anne that he was not disposed to travel. Anne agreed, having her own doubts about his credentials as a potential companion abroad. There was the language barrier to start with. 'He should not like … to go where they could neither understand him nor he them,' she wrote. He 'was right and had judged very well'.

Anne had taken advantage of her time on the south coast to cast a wide net for potential servants. From Hastings, she had placed an advertisement in a London newspaper for:

> *Thoroughly trustworthy, clever, active, enterprising, cheerful, good humoured person, who is not given to making difficulties, and whose constant attention to her mistress's interests and comforts will best secure her own.*
>
> 3rd February 1832

Her criteria were exacting. Of seventy-nine replies, she had 'burnt all but twenty'.

Now, Marian dared to make a suggestion of her own. It was rare for her to offer advice to her sister, with whom her interaction in this period seemed limited largely to domestic arguments:

> *Marian stood an hour talking & arguing that she did not order the carpets to be shaken once a week when I was here in 1828, and I persisted that they, or a large carpet was shaken so often. Tis odd enough, we never agree and something always turns up for us to get wrong about. I had come in in good spirits and was rallying her a little and thus as usual, it ended. She cannot like my company much better than I like hers.*
>
> 13th August 1832

On this occasion, Marian came up with the goods. Anne found her suggestion of 'a soldier, or a Highlander for a servant' very sensible. 'I will think about it and try what I can do,' she wrote. 'Such a man would be orderly and a good traveller, and might suit me best' (22nd July 1832).

Of course, foreign travel might have to be put on hold if Anne was to achieve the desired outcome with Miss Walker. Now, she sought her aunt's advice about her potential new relationship.

Aunt Anne – the younger sister of Anne's father, Jeremy – was a hugely significant person in Anne's life. Even before the death of her mother in 1817, Anne had looked up to her aunt as a maternal figure. She was loving, loyal and a sympathetic listener with a keen understanding of Anne's emotional needs. When things were falling apart in Hastings with Vere, it was to her aunt that Anne turned:

My dear aunt. I never think of all you have done without far more affectionate gratitude than I have ever been able to express. And so as to the interpretation of all my thoughts, words and actions ... you are the only kind, reasonable person I have to count upon.

23rd March 1832

Anne was twenty-six when her mother died, but there is scant mention of Rebecca Lister (née Battle) in her diaries. What there is suggests that she suffered from alcoholism. When Anne does write about her 'poor mother', there is a protective tone.

In 1829, Anne confided to Lady Stuart that her mother was the subject of an unsettling recurring dream:

> *Before Lady S went to bed, talking of dreams. Told her my three, of my mother's last confinement, the snake and black eggs, and the black bull with a golden horn at Paris.*
>
> 10th September 1829

There is evidence, too, of a loving early relationship, in letters that have survived from the summer of 1803 between twelve-year-old Anne, who was staying with her aunt and uncle at Shibden Hall, and her mother. Anne is eager to impart news of her singing lessons with Mr Stopford, who was in charge of the music at Halifax parish church. She wants her mother to know that on Sunday she will be wearing a 'new bonnet, a new white Tippet, a pair of new Stays, and my new Frock made up'. Rebecca writes back to Aunt Anne proudly of Anne's 'charitable act' in playing the organ at a local event. She comments on Anne's ability to 'write large hand exceedingly well'. Tellingly, perhaps, Rebecca also describes young daughter as 'a little high flown' and 'giddy'.

Anne's precociousness and physical restlessness were to have an impact on her relationship with her parents as she grew older. In the sporadic remembrances of her childhood that appear in her adult diaries, Anne talks of being too much for her mother and father to handle, resulting in her spending increasing amounts of time with her aunt and uncle at Shibden Hall, before moving there permanently in 1815.

Over the years leading to 1832, Anne had grown reliant on her aunt as a confidante. In a society which struggled to place Anne, Aunt Anne offered her niece unconditional support and held liberal views that were in many ways ahead of her time. She was an emotionally astute woman who exhibited a tacit understanding of her niece's lesbian sexuality. She appeared to apportion equal importance to Anne's desire to settle down with a woman as she did to Marian's pursuit of happiness with a man. She understood that when Shibden Hall came into Anne's full ownership, she would want to inhabit it with a female life partner.

Aunt Anne would not have batted an eyelid at Anne and Mariana Lawton sharing a bedroom on 31st July 1832, whether she had been aware of her niece's sexuality or not. Before and after her marriage to Charles Lawton, Mariana was a frequent visitor to Shibden Hall and always stayed with Anne in the 'blue room'. In fact, it was not unusual in the culture of the time for female friends – who were assumed to be platonic – to sleep in the same bed. At compact Shibden Hall, where spare beds were non-existent, there would have been no other option. Those Shibden staff who were in the know were discreet enough to keep their thoughts to themselves. Elizabeth Cordingley had served for many years as Anne's lady's maid and had long-standing knowledge of her mistress's preference for women.

Curiously, Mariana's visit fell on the same day as Vere Hobart's wedding to Donald Cameron of Lochiel. Anne had received the details in a letter on 24th July. 'A thousand thanks for all your good wishes and kindnesses to me in times past, and a happy meeting to us all somewhere hereafter,' wrote Vere. Anne was less gushing: 'Well, and there is an end to me of V. Hobart.'

Though Anne decided not to attend the wedding, which was to take place at St Martin-in-the-Fields in London, propriety required her to send her good wishes to Lady Stuart de Rothesay and Vere's elderly great aunt, Lady Stuart. 'Congratulations,' she wrote, 'Never match seemed made with fairer prospects of happiness.'

Mariana arrived by stage coach that afternoon at the Stump Cross Inn on Godley Lane, and Anne walked across the fields to meet her. Given the nature of her recent visit to Lawton Hall, Anne's hopes for this visit were not high, and she was greeted by a woman who had clearly had 'a bad night' and who, she said, 'looked wretchedly'. Typically, Anne expanded on the medical details of Mariana's wretchedness in her journal: 'suffering from inflammation of the left ear produced by over syringing for deafness – too much wax taken away – the drum or tympanum laid too bare' (31st July 1832). She was sympathetic, but did not appear to receive much support in return:

> *Told Mariana Miss Hobart was married today to Mr Cameron younger of Lochiel, but she made no remark ... Very civil and kind and attentive to M in walking home she had seemed to take rather more interest about things than she did before. Got into bed as soon as I could. Not much conversation. She was in pain from her ear.*

Anne found Mariana's visit tiring, writing that, by the time her guest left the next day, she 'felt relieved to get rid of her'. For Mariana, the visit appeared to have stirred up old feelings. On 5th August, she wrote to Anne that she regretted having betrayed their relationship by marrying a man: 'The last of my sins is that of willingly disappointing you.' Though Anne had chosen not to tell Mariana about her interest in Ann Walker, perhaps Mariana had picked up a hint that Anne's affections were becoming vested in someone new.

Money, or the lack of it, was an ongoing issue for Anne in 1832. Though she hated being reliant on her father for the funds and permission she needed to improve her estate, he did at least appear to be obliging. On 2nd August she asked for, and was given, a loan of £200, 'promising to pay it any time on having a week's notice'. When she 'mentioned my wish to have a stove in the library passage – he said nothing against it'.

Alongside her courtship of Ann Walker, Anne found plenty of time and energy to cultivate Shibden's land. *Merat's Botany* and *Paxton and Harrison's* gardening magazine were particularly useful:

> *'Annual pruning – take out not less than 3 or more than 5 of the most vigorous branches beginning at the top – never injure the tap root of timber – sow where the plant is to remain … cypress wood the most durable known.'*

6th August 1832

Keeping trespassers off her newly cultivated land remained a preoccupation for Anne. She was determined that her more lenient father and sister shouldn't prevent her from dealing with the culprits in the official way she hoped to. Telling James Greenwood that she was 'going to speak to Mr Parker about trespassers and desired all might be taken to him', she specifically asked James not to 'say a word to my father or sister as I would have no one excused in future'. It was better that they didn't know, in case they tried to stop her.

The men on her estate colluded with Anne's demands when they were asked to. She liked to think of them as her eyes and ears, recognising that a flow of information from her workers could be of benefit to her. It helped that she wasn't afraid of mucking in with their physical outdoor work.

As the summer progressed, things began to take shape to her satisfaction. Anne's thatched *chaumière* was under construction. George and Robert Pickles were levelling and widening an elegant walk in the Lower Brook Ing Wood, partly at the suggestion of Mariana Lawton. Sister Marian took the opportunity to give her opinion that Anne would soon 'not have income to keep these things up' (12th August 1832).

On 13th August, Anne received Mr and Mrs Edwards of nearby Pye Nest. Following Miss Walker's words about his lack of gentlemanly conduct as trustee of her estate, Anne harboured a mistrust of Mr Edwards, but seems to have entertained him civilly on this occasion. He and his wife approached the hall from the steep, new Northowram Road, which lay to the east of the house and offered (as it does today) a stunning view of Shibden's grounds. They told Anne that they had been admiring the 'beauties' of the estate. Anne joked that in order to get the full impact of the place they needed to see all the other 'beauties' too, including the crumbling barn. She gave them the full tour, telling Marian after they had gone that her self-deprecating manner surely meant that they could not think she had any 'affectation about the place'.

Anne was keen to press on with the renovation, despite her limited funds and her sister's scepticism. Her next innovation was a 'long chair', a rustic red seat built by her father-and-son tenants Charles and James Howarth, and set at the bottom of Calf Croft, towards the lower end of the estate. She wrote to her friend, Isabella (Tib) Norcliffe, of the 'jobbing of all sorts in hand' that was keeping her busy. She could not give serious thought to any travel until at least after Christmas.

The 'all sorts' of Anne's letter to Tib might have included the sporadic misbehaviour of her tenants. The evening of 16th August was marred by the arrival of a drunk workman at the door: 'About 7 Pickles called at the door to speak to me – saw he was quite drunk – told him to come tomorrow and bade Rachel to shut the door in his face.'

George Pickles was not Anne's favourite employee. He wanted 'looking after ... trust the man as little as possible ... he will take advantage if he can', she wrote to herself. The next day Anne gave him some very clear instructions: 'To do his job and stick to it and not come drunk to speak to me.'

This directness was typical of Anne's approach to her workers. It was better that they knew from the off, she felt, that 'this sort of thing would not do with me' (17th August 1832). It was important to her that they submit as fully to her authority as mistress of the estate as they would to a master.

If Pickles gave Anne the most trouble of her tenants, John Booth gave her the least. 'Of all the workmen I like Booth the best,' she wrote on 30th August 1832. In December of that year, Anne would go so far as to seek out for his fourteen-year-old daughter, Charlotte, a placement as a dressmaker in Halifax – but not before checking her ability to read:

Heard her read tolerably and made her read the four lines one of Plutarch's lives (easy, again and again, 5 or 6 times till she could tell me what it was about). Set her to write her name and put a few words together. But she could not well do this on account of spelling. Knows nothing of accounts but seems a niceish little girl – well enough. Talked very gently and kindly to her and on her promising to do the very best she could at learning, said I would speak to her father about her going for half a year to a reading, writing and accounts school, and then perhaps she might learn dressmaking.

23rd December 1832

Martha Booth, aged fourteen, and John's other daughter, was also being considered for employment as part of Mariana Lawton's household. After an exchange of letters between her and Anne she wrote back to Anne saying that she thought an 'under housemaid's place must be the upmost height she is fit to aspire to' (6th January 1833).

The majority of Anne's tenants were industrious, hard-working people. In addition, many of them had ambitions for their children outside the farming, mining and quarrying industries that dominated the Shibden valley. Two of Anne Lister's notable tenants – Samuel Sowden of Sutcliffe Wood Farm, and John Mallinson of the Stag's Head Inn – had sons who went to Cambridge University. Sutcliffe Sowden, who became vicar of St James Church in Hebden Bridge, officiated at the marriage of Charlotte Brontë and Arthur Bell Nicholls on 29th June 1854 in Haworth.

Between visits to Lidgate and dealing with inebriated workmen, Anne found time to read. On Sunday 19th August 1832, she recorded eight hours spent on scientific, classical and travel volumes. Anne read with purpose as well as for pleasure, wishing to draw improving connections between books, their authors, and her own lived experience.

The neatly catalogued literary indexes Anne kept are testament to the staggering range of literature she consumed. Books were her obsession. She thought frequently about her home library when she was absent from it, writing to remind Cordingley to open the windows to air the books on the shelves. The construction of a passage next to her bedroom, now underway, would give her even more space for, and easier access to, her archive.

The purpose-built gothic library tower adjoining the west wing of Shibden Hall was not to come until years later. For this, Anne would need not only vision, which she had in abundance, but significant finance, which she did not.

<hr />

'She thought ladies had never any business with politics. I said entirely, but there were exceptions'

The months of Anne's life following her return from Hastings were all about reinvention. The renovation of Shibden Hall represented much more than a practical desire to smarten up an old building: it was a symbol of Anne's personal healing. Her immersion in the land was cathartic and it excited her, because to Anne change meant progress.

The estate was particularly important to Anne at this moment in her life because it was a realm over which she had dominion. The deterioration of her relationship with Vere had been a painful reminder that she could not always be in control of her romantic life. Shibden, on the other hand, was her domain. The gradual transformation of the landscape around her was a daily reminder to Anne that she was creating a legacy, writing her own narrative.

Time was healing her emotional wounds, too. Vere Cameron, as she now was, would become a lifelong friend of Anne's. And though their courtship was at a tentative stage, Anne's visits to Miss Walker filled her with optimism. They heralded, she rightly hoped, the beginning of a new chapter.

Mariana Lawton's role in Anne's life remained consistent. She continued to provide epistolary dispatches of her unhappy marriage to Charles: 'All would be well if Mr L would be a little more consistent, a little more sociable, a little more forbearing, a little more pleased to see others happy, and a little better tempered' (20th August 1832).

Anne suspected this was never going to happen. Over the years, Charles Lawton had proven himself a gambler and philanderer, and had fathered a child with a servant. The marriage seemed so hopeless that Mariana's complaints simply annoyed Anne. 'Well,' she wrote on 20th August 1832, 'I trust I have done with her. I rarely think of her without irritation.'

As August progressed, Anne remained deeply involved in the day-to-day management of the estate. She was a hard taskmaster:

> *Pickles and his men and William Greenwood and Robert Pickles the sick boy there ... Found them cutting through the old pit hill bottom of Calf Croft all wrong – made them do it again ... loitered about while the men dined at 12 ¼ – all at their work again under the hour.*
>
> 21st August 1832

Her assessment of her workmen's competence was even bleaker the following day: 'Found I could not safely leave them – they would have cut through the roots.'

On the plus side, she had finally decided on the location of her *chaumière* – 'Near Lily bank or rather at the entrance of Lower Brook Ing wood'. She envisaged that nine small oaks would be needed to build the moss hut, which would be complete with thatched roof, and dressed prettily with '3 or 4 little hollies opposite'. She hoped that it would be finished by the end of September. Its secluded location and cosy interior were designed with intent: the *chaumière* was an intimate site that was to become crucial in Anne's seduction of Ann Walker.

Though the routine she detailed in her diary suggests a person with boundless energy, Anne had in fact been suffering from exhaustion. The most personally distressing of her symptoms was that found she could not stay awake to read or write. Dismissing the idea that her physically challenging, sixteen-hour days were the root of the problem, she sought help for another long-standing medical issue, constipation. Writing to the York-based practice of Dr Stephen (Steph) Belcombe – whom she trusted more than the 'local quacks' that were found around Shibden – she asked for advice on her 'intestinal obstinacy'.

Dr Belcombe was Mariana Lawton's brother. He and Anne had been friends for many years and she was not prepared to spare him any detail that she thought could aid an effectual diagnosis:

> Long letter to Dr B – re 'I have never since had any sufficient or proper alvine evacuations ... found that I had parted with, to all appearance, a large garden worm, but rather thinner or flatter and paler – I eat and sleep well and am out all the day ... have a sensation of fullness in my head and ringing in my ears ... If you can make anything of all this do pray tell me what I had best do.
>
> 26th August 1832

Anne was clearly frustrated. Her bowels were a lifelong preoccupation and analysis of their imperfect function appears frequently in her journal. The many books she had read on the subject had not helped much. After a period of eating only vegetables, she had recently returned to an omnivorous diet. Now, Steph prescribed senna for her 'intestinal torpor'.

The quest for a cure continued for years to come. In 1835, Anne was testing various approaches. She wrote about castor oil and 'bathing the bottom of the back with salt and water or vinegar and water' and 'digestive pills of aloc and myrrh before dinner (it would produce one solid stool)'. Her continuing obsession with her bowels suggests that an effective cure remained elusive.

Anne did not seem to mind that Dr Belcombe did not address the other ailments she had described in her letter: backache, a compression against the lower vertebrae and an unquenchable thirst. He remained her trusted practitioner. And soon she would be consulting him about another patient, whose symptoms it would prove far more difficult to diagnose and treat.

Anne's month ended in a typically busy fashion. On 30th August a local coal merchant, James Hinscliffe, called at Shibden to offer her £150 per acre for her coal-rich land. He was in direct competition with the Rawsons. Though Christopher and Jeremiah had maintained a silence since Jeremiah's meeting with Anne, she remained cool and non-committal with Hinscliffe:

I was not anxious about selling – the coals would pay for keeping. I might one of these days get them myself ... after

> *a great deal of talk irrelevant of the business in hand (these*
> *people will always have their talk) on politics, it ended with*
> *H seemed inclined to give my price.*

If Hinscliffe guessed that Anne was in negotiation with the Rawsons, she neither confirmed nor denied it. She maintained, enigmatically, that she was engaged in several conversations over her valuable commodity, but had committed herself to nobody. Anne may have been dismissive of Hinscliffe on this occasion, but as a pawn in her negotiation with the Rawsons he was to become pivotal in her quest to establish herself as a leading coal player in Halifax over the coming months and years.

Outside the bounds of the Shibden estate, there were political stirrings. Charles Howarth kept Anne up to date with the instances of radical agitation that were becoming increasingly frequent in Halifax. Men, he told her, had joined up to unions in unprecedented numbers as the march towards reform had accelerated.

Anne was critical of the unstoppable force of industrial and political change. A landowner with deeply held conservative views, she disagreed with the idea of extending the franchise to unpropertied men of an inferior class. Part of it was pure snobbishness. 'So much for the spirit of reform,' was her response to the news that a friend's carriage had been set upon by thugs (5th November 1831).

On 31st August 1832, she gave Jonathan Mallinson strict orders not to allow local masons' and delvers' meetings to take place at the Stag's Head. Her inn would not be the home of left-wing agitation; if Mallinson did not comply she would revoke his licence.

Anne described herself as someone with little interest in politics, but she certainly knew how to use the power she held as a landowner. Before the introduction of the secret ballot in 1872, it was commonplace for landowners to tell their tenants how to vote. Anne's influence was felt among the frequent elections of the turbulent 1830s. Her opinion on the role of women in politics, demonstrated in a letter to her friend Harriet de Hageman, is brilliantly, and conveniently, specific:

> *She thought ladies had never any business with politics. I*
> *said entirely, but there were exceptions, for example ladies,*
> *unmarried who had landed property had influence arising*
> *out of that property and might perhaps use it moderately.*
>
> 6th June 1830

Lady de Hageman was Vere Hobart's half-sister. Anne's letter, sent from Paris in 1830, was written at the time Anne had been out to impress the aristocratic Hobart and Stuart de Rothesay families. In this instance, she wondered if she had overstepped the mark with her opinions, which she conceded may have been 'too energetic' for the 'milk and watery' Lady de Hageman: 'I always forget to be restrained till it is too late,' she wrote in her diary. 'I am too much a man at heart.'

THE DEMANDS OF PROPRIETY, PROGRESSION WITH MISS WALKER, 'LADY' VERE CAMERON, A NEW FRENCH LADY'S MAID, MONEY AND COAL

'I am more and more astonished when I think how marvellously things work together in my favour ... I am thankful enough for all the blessings I enjoy'

In the first days of September 1832, Ann Walker was preparing for a holiday in the Lake District. The trip, which she would make with her relative, Catherine Rawson, would take her away from Halifax for over three weeks. By now, Anne Lister felt confident enough to ask Miss Walker if she would be thinking of her while she was away. Though Ann's response to this rather romantic question was encouraging – 'yes, she would not forget' – Anne Lister remained circumspect. The scrape with Vere and the historic disappointment of Mariana tempered her excitement about this new relationship. 'Who knows how it may end,' she wrote, 'I shall be wary this time' (31st August 1832).

The two women arranged to spend an afternoon together in Halifax before Miss Walker's departure. Their first public outing would be meticulously planned. Theirs was a courtship destined to take place within the bounds of propriety; nothing could have appeared more respectable than the 'sundry shopping' and social calls of two landed women.

Anne spent the evening beforehand planning her outfit. She personalised a new pelisse, 'sewing [on a] watch pocket' and 'putting strings to petticoat and getting all ready to put on tomorrow'. It was a measure of the seriousness with which she viewed this first show of togetherness in Halifax society. Anne wanted to make a good impression, not only on Ann Walker, but on the wider family who she hoped would, one day, become her in-laws.

Ann Walker arrived at Shibden Hall on the morning of 3rd September. She was early, and made conversation with Aunt Anne until Anne was ready to leave. At 11.50am, the two women set off for Halifax in Miss Walker's carriage, which had been selected as the smarter vehicle. An ambitious itinerary of social calls had been planned: after a visit to the recent widow of local banker Rawdon Briggs, came a trip to Willowfield to see Mrs Dyson, who was dutifully thanked for her recent call at Shibden, but warned by Anne not to expect regular visits in return. Stopping next at Throps, the garden merchant, for shrubs and flowers, the women called finally at the home of the Saltmarshes. Disappointingly, the Saltmarshes were not in, but Anne and Ann left calling cards, expressing 'particular inquiries after Mrs Saltmarshe'.

In the name of civility, Anne encouraged Miss Walker to extend their visit to Mrs Edwards, in spite of a 'huffy letter' Ann had recently received from her relative. Anne noted with pleasure in her diary Miss Walker's willingness to follow her advice: '[she] seems inclined to consult me and tell me all'.

By 5.30pm, the carriage was back at Shibden Hall. Miss Walker departed for Lidgate, and, within ten minutes, Anne was out of her smart pelisse, back in her work clothes, and in the fresh air. A few days later, Ann Walker left for her holiday. She was not to return to Yorkshire until 25th September.

Anne Lister was confident she would not be forgotten during their separation. By effectively acting as Ann's chaperone, she had taken a valuable opportunity to step visibly into Miss Walker's life and society. For Ann Walker, who until very recently had had to be content with observing her charismatic neighbour from a distance, the trip was excitingly intimate. For both women, the public show of unity marked a new phase in the relationship. Anne was living by her motto: 'the woman that deliberates is lost.'

Two days after Ann Walker left for the Lake District, Anne 'incurred a cross' while thinking about her. It marked the first time she had used the phrase about her. Always recorded in crypt hand at the top of the day's diary entry, this was Anne's preferred way to describe an orgasm she had achieved by masturbation. It was frequently used in conjunction with the name of her current or would-be lover, and sometimes followed with the specification that she had been thinking of that woman 'merely as a mistress'.

Without an accessible language of female sexual pleasure to draw on, Anne had devised an idiosyncratic lexicon by which to record her sexual activity. 'Grubbling' meant using her hands to bring another woman to orgasm. A 'kiss' was another word for orgasm, and 'going to Italy' referred to making love or having full sex.

Anne was a confident and experienced lover of women. The sexual preference she records in her diary is characterised by a desire to give her partners pleasure before taking her own. She displayed a deep interest in their arousal and preferred to touch than to be touched. Though her partners would also initiate lovemaking, Anne felt comfortable when taking the dominant role during sex.

Anne enjoyed the company of women, indeed, her social life was overwhelmingly female. In some ways, the forced secrecy of her lesbianism worked to her advantage and without it she would not, as she recognised, have been so free to pursue platonic or intimate friendships with women.

However, in a society in which she was not able to openly express her desires, finding a sexual partner was challenging, and could be dangerous. Advances had to be made carefully and incrementally; with so much that couldn't be said it was difficult to gauge how each woman would respond to her courtship. Her diaries reveal only two women as having a similar sexual identity to her own. These two 'regular oddities', which from the detailed description contained in Anne's journals we might read today as butch lesbians, were Isabella Norcliffe and Miss Pickford. Like Anne, they had expressed a disinclination ever to marry a member of the opposite sex.

Anne could safely assume that same-sex love would be an alien concept to Miss Walker. She had no reason to speculate on her previous sexual experiences. But it is likely that Ann Walker, though she had lived a sheltered existence at Lidgate, would have heard rumours of Anne Lister's liking for women. The cloak of incomprehension that existed around female same-sex desire did not render Anne Lister's 'oddity' completely invisible.

If Ann Walker had heard rumours, it did not impede her desire to pursue the friendship. She arranged to take breakfast with Anne as soon as she returned from Wastwater on 25th September.

But Anne Lister was aware of the speculation that could follow her close friendships with women, and was eager to protect Ann Walker's reputation as well as her own. Over the coming months, as their liaison deepened, she would try hard to deflect the attention of others. This would be an onerous task, given the keen spread of local gossip, and with Ann Walker's many relatives keeping a close eye on her every move, and fortune.

<hr />

'A little of politics – the people not a bit more contented for the Reform Bill – now want to be rid of the national debt'

On 9th September 1832, Anne heard that Vere Cameron had received a title. Lady Stuart had written to tell her that 'his majesty had granted Vere and her sisters to take the rank of Earl's daughters' and that consequently, Vere was now a Lady too. Swiftly writing to congratulate the new Lady Cameron, Anne's tone was affectionate. 'All is now right – everything seems to go well with you. My dearest Vere, I am quite happy for your sake, and know not that I have one wish concerning you unsatisfied.'

If sincere, the letter reflects that a change of heart had occurred in the time since Hastings. Continuing, Anne was able to thank Vere for 'her discretion' and applaud her for staying faithful to 'her own very self'. She went so far as to look inwards, at the 'less proper grain of my own nature', to help explain what had gone wrong at Pelham Crescent. Whether Anne's recovery from the disappointment of Vere's rejection was as complete as she wanted to project, her desire to maintain a friendship with Lady Cameron was heartfelt.

Besides, she saw no reason to lose contact with Vere's high-society connections. In a correspondence with Vere's half-sister Lady Harriet de Hageman – whom she was keen to visit at home in Copenhagen – Anne celebrated the happiness of the newly married couple:

> *Thought Mr Cameron's place on the banks of Lochiel one of the most beautiful situations in the Highlands – Vere will be the Laird's wife, My Lady of Lochiel, head of the Camerons, and quite a personage in Scotland – the people think of him with something like adoration – many a bonfire on many a hill will greet Vere's arrival, and I do believe she will be happy.*
>
> 9th September 1832

Despite Anne's frequent assertions that she had no interest in it, the subject of political reform was one which arose in her letters to both Vere and her half-sister. To Vere, she confided her fears of 'a bad prospect for the winter ... A fearful number of people have turned out for increase of wages ... they vow vengeance against the machinery'. To Lady Harriet, she wrote 'A little of politics – the people not a bit more contented for the Reform Bill – now want to be rid of the national debt'.

Anne's anti-radical and anti-reform views were shared by her high-ranking friends. James Wortley, related to Vere via her great aunt Lady Stuart, would soon be standing as Tory MP for Halifax. He would become a familiar name in the pages of Anne's diary in 1835 as she vociferously supported his bid for election.

The 9th September was a busy day in Anne's correspondence. Writing to Dr Belcombe, she admitted that she had forgotten to take the remedy prescribed for her 'intestinal torpor', but joked that it would have to wait 'till my out-of-door jobs are done, and I have leisure enough to make myself ill enough by thinking about it'.

There was word that day from Steph's sister, too. Mariana Lawton, currently staying in Brighton, wrote to Anne with the news that she may have found her a new lady's maid:

Met with a person ... Eugenie Pierre, at 23, lived with Lady Herbert ... wage 23 guineas ... does not associate with common servants but always civil and attentive to them ... not smart but always neat and clean, and very tidy and methodical ... Brighton very full and gay, but Charles does not like it.

9th September 1832

After a protracted search, here, finally, was a servant who might fulfil Anne's criteria. Mariana knew that a faculty for foreign languages was a prerequisite in a servant who would complement her friend's wanderlust, and here she had gone one further by producing a French native.

By this time, Anne's dream travel plans had expanded beyond Europe – France, Italy, Spain, Switzerland and Denmark – to include further-flung destinations like Algiers and Niagara Falls. She had recently told Mariana that she felt it against her nature to be tied to one place, and instead was fated 'to wander on the face of the earth, the where and how, never to be fixed till the last moment' (20th January 1832). The question that began to cross her mind was whether Miss Walker might suit her as a travelling companion.

For the moment, though, Anne had more pressing domestic concerns. She was worried about Aunt Anne, who had been suffering from painful spasms in her joints, and began thinking about fitting up Shibden's downstairs north parlour as a more accessible bedroom for her. Though she didn't share Marian and Rachel Hemingway's gloomy view that the 67-year-old would 'hardly get over next spring', her aunt was elderly by the standards of the day. Extended periods of travel were out of the question, at least until she could be assured of Aunt Anne's recovery.

Anne took advantage of Miss Walker's absence in the Lake District to deal with the time-consuming vexations her tenants presented. On the morning of 10th September, Mr Dodgson came to dish the dirt on Mr Kirton of Lower Place. Kirton, Dodgson reported, had been selling off valuable clover from his land to

Mr Carr. Stopping only to deal with a dead cow at the bottom of Hall Croft ('had got a grave dug 5ft deep and had almost dragged (by 2 horses) the carcass into it') which she then insisted on having dissected to establish the cause of its death, Anne set off to see her solicitor and tell him 'what Kirton was about'.

Standing over him as he wrote, she demanded Mr Adam issue a summons, threatening that 'If he [Kirton] did not immediately make a compensation for the clover he had sold off, and if he sold anything else contrary to the covenants of his lease, I should commence an action against him.'

The following day, Kirton came to make amends. He claimed that he 'Did not mean to defraud me – had sold four little loads of clover, but would bring back as much manure – wanted the privilege of selling on this condition'.

Anne did not grant this request, and told Kirton that he must stick to the tenancy agreement he had made with her. Pleased that his intervention had allowed her to act so swiftly, she took Dodgson further into her confidence, asking him to 'keep a good look out, and tell me if anything more was sold off' (11th September 1832).

The week presented other challenges. John Oates insisted on keeping his gate open, allowing George Pickles to access it as a free, public cart road, to Anne's annoyance. Having set Oates right on the matter, Anne was happy to move on to the subject of blowpipes – a contemporary tool used to ignite a flame:

John thought that for 2 or 3 pounds he could make me a
portable one (reservoir of air like that for air gun and filled

in the same way), all to go in a box of 6 inch square – one reservoir full would keep up a strong and regular blast for ¼ hour.

12th September 1832

Anne liked Oates' idea and wondered if his invention might come in handy for the stove that was being fitted in her new library passage. Her *chaumière* was almost complete too. What with this, and the 'long chair' at the bottom of Calf Croft, the place was, finally, starting to look a bit more elegant.

***

'French femmes de chambre seldom famed for discretion, or the adventurous spirit of travelling, or understanding or being interested in the common run of English character, much less one like mine – but Eugenie might be superior to all the rest'

Anne was optimistic about the prospect of Eugenie Pierre as a lady's maid, but characteristically thorough in her considerations. She replied to Mariana that, while it certainly sounded as if Eugenie 'might have sense, might suit me', she would feel more confident if 'M had seen her, or Lady Stuart had seen her, or I had seen her'. In spite of, or perhaps because of, her Francophile leanings, some of Anne's reservations were related to Eugenie's nationality: 'She would either leave me in 6 months, or, as most tolerably well-bred French women could do, talk me into what she pleased.' Anne had flirted with a number of French women over the years. At least Eugenie was from Normandy, 'the most English part of France'.

Anne was keen to ensure that Eugenie possessed the other qualities she saw as essential in a maid. 'Her age, family and native place in her favour, but her health must be good. She must like travelling, travel outside, and have upon her mind to make no difficulties.' She would need to receive more details before deciding either way. Perhaps, she replied, Mariana would know 'better what to do' than she.

The 'dirty business' of coal remained on Anne's mind. The pits she saw springing up across the Shibden Valley – the vestiges of which can be felt today in place names like Pit Hill, Spiggs and Lands Head – were a constant reminder of her land's untapped potential. In a dynamic industry that was growing exponentially (and that was yet to wake up to the plight of its workers) Anne's preoccupation, like that of her industrialist peers, was profit.

Anne knew that before she could make any serious money, she had to decide exactly how to exploit her coal beds. Frustratingly, weeks after his visit to the hall, she was still to hear from Jeremiah Rawson about the £226.17.6 per acre she had set for their potential lease.

Mr Holdsworth, a local man from whom Anne had recently purchased a quantity of stone, arrived at Shibden on 22nd September with some interesting information. The Rawson brothers, said Holdsworth, who leased his own quarry from Christopher and Jeremiah, were already mining coal dangerously close to Shibden land. Christopher, he went on, 'had bought Mr Hall's coal for £1,000 ... had bought it very cheap at a thousand, and Mr R never said a word but gave the price at once ... they were getting all they could on the top of the hill ... they must be getting very near my [Anne's] land now'.

Anne digested the implications of this information. She had been warned that trespass and theft were commonplace among competitors in the cut-throat mining industry. She would not put anything past Christopher and Jeremiah Rawson.

While this was going on, Anne's rolling programme of estate improvements needed urgent funding. The precarious state of her finances is clear from a letter she drafted on 23rd September, in which she wondered if her friend, Mrs Norcliffe, could be a candidate 'to help me out with a hundred pounds for the last month or two of the year if I wanted it'.

Anne was close to Mrs Norcliffe as well as her daughter, Isabella (Tib). She was frequently and enthusiastically welcomed as a visitor to the Norcliffes' North Yorkshire home, Langton Hall. It is likely that Mrs Norcliffe would have obliged Anne's request willingly, had she not, in the end, 'determined not to send the letter'. Mrs Norcliffe was elderly, and Anne had begun to have doubts about how the whole thing would look. The money would have to be found somewhere else.

Optimistically, Anne pressed on with her improvements. The next project – one she had been considering for some time – was to build a road through a thick, wooded area at the back of Shibden Hall called the Trough of Bolland. It would provide access to the hall from the newly constructed

Godley Road – an important public access route which now connected Halifax to places like Leeds, Hebden Bridge and Manchester. Major excavation would be required for Anne's road, but George Pickles had given Anne hope that the work could be done for a good price:

> *He said he could make it for 100/ less than Washington ... 30/ a rood, 14ft wide, and put a foot of boulder on it ... Mr W said he durst engage to make it for £300 ... Told Pickles if he could manage to do it at 30/ a rood thought I should not hesitate much about having it done.*
>
> 22nd September 1832

A few days later, Anne was struck with another bolt of design inspiration, this time for major renovation inside the house. She told her father she had 'a new idea and the best on the subject that had occurred to me yet': to 'move the hall stairs altogether and turn them up the little buttery and to come out in that part of my father's room that is over it, and so be lighted from the north or west as one chose'.

In reality, Anne would not have the resources to carry out this work (the benefit of which can be seen in Shibden Hall today) until several years later. In 1832, though he may have recognised the over-ambitious nature of her plans, Jeremy voiced no objection. At eighty, he was resigned to his energetic daughter's determination to bring about change.

'Miss W and I very cosy and confidential ... she said she knew not when she had spent so pleasant a day and I believe her'

The day after Miss Walker returned from the Lake District, Anne joined her for breakfast at Lidgate. She strode the few miles across the fields briskly, pausing just long enough to order Joseph Pickles 'To pursue and kill game and rabbits for and during this present season of hunting and shooting, and to proceed against all persons found trespassing on the estate in my name and on my behalf' (26th September 1832).

Once there, she stayed talking with Ann for an hour and a half. 'Very civil, our conversation quite confidential', she wrote in satisfaction to her journal afterwards. She was touched to find that Miss Walker had brought back a 'presse papier' (paper weight) from the marble works at Kendal as a gift for her. 'We really get on very well – yet she said she could not go to Italy.' In this instance, Anne's 'going to Italy' was meant literally, rather than as a sexual reference. But, demonstrating as it did Miss Walker's indisposition to the idea of foreign travel, the answer remained a cause for concern. Anne put the matter on ice for now.

Just ten minutes after she arrived back at Shibden that morning, Anne found Miss Walker's servant, James Mackenzie, at her door. He had come, he said, to collect some books which Anne had forgotten to bring to Lidgate for Miss Walker. Anne scribbled back a note, offering 'a thousand apologies' for her oversight, and sent Mackenzie away with them at once.

The fact that Anne and Ann had plans to meet for breakfast the next morning gives a twist to an otherwise unremarkable anecdote. It seems unlikely that the return of the volumes might not simply have waited until then. It is tempting to speculate that it was a desire of Ann Walker's to establish further communication with Anne Lister before their next meeting that prompted her to send her servant to Shibden, more than any impatience to read her books.

Either way, the visit from James Mackenzie gave Anne Lister an opportunity to further her cause. The language of her return note operated within the romantic conventions of the day. She told Anne that she had 'played truant' by staying longer than she had intended at Lidgate. The visit had given her 'so much to think of afterwards, that is long after I have actually left you'. It was the Georgian equivalent of texting your date afterwards, to tell them you've had a good time.

Breakfast at Lidgate the next morning was served just after 7.30am. Anne Lister was used to early mornings and had already been up and about for some time. Her breakfasts at Shibden, usually just bread and milk, were frequently taken after hours of physical work on the land, or a trip into Halifax. At Lidgate, she was greeted with a more formal spread. After eating, she and Ann Walker 'adjourned' to another room.

Anne's supreme confidence in company served her well when two of Miss Walker's relatives paid an unexpected social call. Mrs Stansfield Rawson and her daughter Delia Rawson, of Gledholt, might reasonably have expected Anne to retreat politely to Shibden on their arrival at Lidgate. Indeed, Anne noted that they 'looked odd on finding me here' in the first place. However, having waited in the wings for the three weeks of Miss Walker's visit to Wastwater, Anne was not about to let her visit be cut short. She stepped self-assuredly into the role of joint hostess. While the Rawsons appreciated the opportunity to become 'better acquainted' with her, they recognised well that she had determined to outstay them. They were no match for her stamina, and eventually returned to Huddersfield. Ann Walker told Anne that she was 'glad' of it.

Anne's visit continued into the afternoon. After lunch, she suggested to Miss Walker that they might stroll the three or so miles back to Shibden for a tour of her elegant new walk and recently finished moss hut. 'Walked slowly by the new road and Lower Brea, and sauntered to nearly Hall Wood gate in my walk,' she wrote later, 'then on returning rested in the hut and must have sat there a couple of hours' (27th September 1832).

Miss Walker was the first person to be invited inside Anne's *chaumière*. Located a good distance below Shibden Hall, close to the babble of the Red Beck brook, it was both privately and romantically situated, offering the perfect space for the advancement of their fledgeling courtship. This was no coincidence; Anne's *chaumière* was the realisation of a long-held dream of creating a space in which she could discreetly entertain women. As a much younger woman, she had fantasised about frolicking in sheds with her conquests. She had already decided that she 'would pay due court' to Miss Walker in the moss hut.

Miss Walker was duly enchanted. 'She sat in the moss house, hardly liking to move. Of course I made myself agreeable, and I think she likes me even more than she herself is aware,' wrote Anne.

Anne took advantage of this mood to enter into the subject of travelling together. In previous conversations, Miss Walker had wondered if Anne's tentative propositions of foreign travel had been 'all a joke'. Now, Anne hoped that Miss Walker 'would understand that I was more serious than she supposed'. Her endeavours appeared to be successful, and the conversation took a decidedly romantic turn. 'We laughed at the idea of the talk our going abroad would [make],' wrote Anne in that evening's long crypt-hand diary entry. 'She said it would be as good as a marriage. "Yes," said [I]. "Quite as good or better".'

It was more than Anne Lister had dared hope. The timid Miss Walker had uttered the word marriage, and Anne's mind was working at a hundred miles an hour. 'She falls into my views admirably,' she wrote, 'I believe I shall succeed with her, and if I do, I will really try to make her happy.'

After the disaster of Vere and protracted disillusionment of Mariana, Anne felt herself 'set at liberty' to love again. The tide, it seemed, was beginning to turn in her favour. Life could be curious:

> How strange the fate of things, if after all, my companion for life should be Miss Walker. She was nine and twenty a little while ago. How little my aunt or anyone suspects what I am about.
>
> 27th September 1832

The future looked to be full of surprises. Anne thanked merciful heaven 'for bringing me home'.

at 6¾ tho. at 7 in spi. of heavyish r— & a thay driv. full ag.ᵗ
causeway 5 or 6 t.ᵉˢ &c. hard. get in at our own gate — j.ᵗ y.ᵉ tartan
on me kept me tol.ᵇ dry — chang. my clothes — din. at 7³⁵ — for 3 or
immed.ᵗ aft.ʷᵈˢ w.ᵗ my at. & fath. — told y.ᵐ gradvent. &news opp. d
been at Lidgate yest. & to day — X·5·do —726·∿ Ⓢ58·3·7·5·? ∗8w.·42·—+p
4·f·32:·7·√·56·6n·∿·Ⓝ·∦·82·=· Ɔ·;·f·4·∿·2·c·56·∿·2·d·∿·p·3·⅞·—4·∿·Ⓝ·+·3·p·Ⓢ·2·∿·=·∩·4·∿·3·6·+·½·
= at \0·ᵒ⁻ — damp rainy morn.ᵍ tile 7½ —aft.ᵈ fine day till bil
r— & though. rainy for y.ᵉ most opp day & w.ᵈ, & rainy night — =·2·∿·b·+·
·7·56·=·4·X·82·∩·4·∿·5·6·∿·=·∿·24·=·∩·∩·3·=·4·∿·3·0·4·∿·3·p· —

busk.ᵗ of grape
8·⁰⁻ w.ᵗ √ fath. — ⅜ h.ʳ — un. y.ᵉ who. of gut. — at \0½ no. fr. huss.¹ (
3 pp. of ½ sheet in envelope
my at. &no. to me, to consult me ab.ᵗ her tent. Collins who h.ᵈ y.ᵉ Lidgate far
Wilks thou.ᵗ s.ᵗ his cows away w.ᵗout say.ᵍ a word or w.ᵗ knowl. au. y
& her cook told h.ᵐ y.ᵗ morn.ᵍ she h.ᵈ no milk — ask.ᵈ wh.ᵗ to do — y.ᵉ hu
we w.ᵈ y.ᵗ on y.ᵉ main's count. to pk. to h.ᵉʳ she sh.ᵈ be ver. civ.ᵗ, say she w.ᵈ va
dept. she w.ᵈ th.ᵏ ab.ᵗ it — being cautious to avoid giv.ᵍ an. hint of all. th
it. do — & to let h.ᵐ & h.ᵉʳ see.ᵈ be as lit. al. as poss. to cale.ᵗ fr. w.ᵗ man.
of do.ᵍ — prob.ᵗ y.ᵉ man want.ᵈ to annoy doing so.th.ᵍ on otter he c.ᵈ turn to
rant. b.ᵗ her perf.ᵗ self comm.ᵈ & temp.ᵉ w.ᵈ foil all chances of y.ᵗ sort —
& s.ᵈ n.ᵗ serve h.ᵐ in a case like y.ˢ — n.ᵗ to mind y.ᵗ — Collins h.ᵈ prop
hold with of her — my 1.ˢᵗ impulse w.ᵗ to go to her y.ᵗ aft. b.ᵗ it
& on 2.ᵈ th.ᵗˢ n.ᵗ prud.ᵗ & best, determ.ᵈ n.ᵗ to go till 8 a.m. on the
3·∩·4·∿·=· Ⓢ·58·&·2·∿·p·d·3·0·4·0·4·∿·—·2·∿·4·3· 8·Ⓢ·3·∿·83·4·2·p·∿·30·d·2·=·∿·4·∿·Ⓝ·√·2·∿·4·∩·5·6·d·o·=·5·=·¹·
32·=·6·p·3·∿·2·0·p·3·?·4·∿·—·756·—·7·0·32·p·∿·p·4·3·∿· 6·∿·0·3·p·∿·√·3·p·3·4·p·∿·6·—·=·∿·2·∿·3·=·4·∩·5·6·do·
30·∿·5·∿·2·∩·3·6·+·—·7·+·3·∩· (6·∿·√·3·+·d·3·2·∿·=·5·b·√·3·4·∿·4·∿·—·756·p·20·Ɔ·4·33·=·j·—·=·2·∿·d·32·=·∩·
4·y·∪·24·p·3·W·Ɔ·6·=·3· √·3·∿·75·—·3·=·√·3·=·6·c·4·33·∿·∿·75·:·4·∿·= 3·∩·04·∩·∿· 84·√·—·71·4·∩·∿·p·
=·∿·3·p· c·3·+·2·3·Ɔ·3·—·3·756·p·=· Ɔ·3·p·7·=·4·∿·3·p·3·dy·2·2·8·2·d·3·p· — H.ᵗ Booth y.ᵉ mason
& y.ᵉ carpenter & settled w.ᵗ y.ᵐ p.ᵈ in full, for Geo. Naylor's stable au
y.ᵉ work done in y.ᵉ lib.ᵗ pass. & flue makt. in y.ᵉ hall chim.ʸ & stove sett.ᵈ
& in & our new light, op.ᵉᵗ in — y.ᵉ blue r— — un. & s.ᵗ at 11½ by ½.ᵃ
— 2 — no. 4 pp. of ½ sht. in envelope men.ᵗ writ. y.ᵉ latter sh.ᵈ been
cloak w.ᵗ n.ᵗ brush.ᵈ by man w.ᵈ w.ᵈ to wait ½ h.ᵉ — 4·c·3·∿·2·2·8·4·∿· 7
·6·p·+·p·4·=·3·=·—·3· (6·∿·=·6·p·+·p·4·=·34·=·∩·5·∿·√·3·∩·√·75·p·√·3·6·∦·3·p·—·5·=·∿·∪·; d·∿·∿·8·Ⓢ·4·+·3·∿·
Ɔ·3·756·∿·54·—·2·∩·∿·3·8·Ⓢ·2·∿·4·—·32·∩· ∪·5·f·=·6·p·3·d·756·2·d·p·32·0·7·∩·58·—·3·∿·!·83·:·∿·5·7·3·∿·
o·—·4·=·3·756·—·2·784·∩·∿·5·—·2·∩·3· √·3·∿·∪·5·:·58·=·—·7·2·∿·Ɔ·4·33· 2·c·5·6·∿·
3·84·∿· 42·—·∿·√·2·∩·756·Ɔ·3·p·7·—·6·∿·∪·5·p·√·3·∿·p·2·+·3·=·8·Ⓢ·∿·∿· 84·√·756·p· b·=·6·2·d·∩·!·0·460·
·0·4·p·3·3·∿·30·∿·5·—·72·6·∿· 42·—·0·5·6·c·d·y·∪·d·2·∿·3·p·3·∿·5·6·c·d·y·5·2·d·4·∿·30· &·3·d·5·2·∩·82·=·5·∿·√·3·
∿·5·—·3·2·=·∿·4·∿·Ⓝ· 3·W·3·4·∿·2·—·∿·∩·2·d·4·=·X·+·7·p·3·∿·;·= 4·∩·5·8·=·∿·8·Ⓢ·3·∿·4·Ⓢ·2·Ɔ·3·c·;·∿·
·5·7·—·∿·p·24·X·Ⓢ·p·4·3·2·∿·3·∿·&·∿·o· 8·Ⓢ·4·∿·7·2·=·∿· 82·=·?·5·=·∿·p·∿·2·4·∿·=·∿·—·3· √·2·∿·482·=·d·

CHAPTER 5

EARLY WARNING SIGNS AND SEXUAL CONFIDENCE

'I think we should be happy together –
I should gently lead her into my own ways
and soon be really attached to her – to the
exclusion of all care for anyone else'

Mariana Lawton could little have predicted that shy Miss Walker would be the woman to finally dethrone her in Anne's affections, though it would be months before she would discover the nature of Anne and Ann's deepening relationship. Anne's attraction to Miss Walker was, in part, a reaction against how manipulated she had felt during her on-off relationship with Mariana. Of the nearly twenty years the two women had been involved with each other, Anne would later write, 'The history of her acquaintance may be summed in, she accepted, refused, accepted, married, offended, refused, repented' (16th March 1834).

In Ann Walker, Anne found a refreshing lack of worldliness. Unlike Mariana, or Vere, Ann Walker was uncritical. She looked up to Anne, and took her affection at face value. She was not bothered by the unusual way Anne dressed, or how she curled her hair, or the 'mannish' way in which she walked. Mariana had frequently expressed her embarrassment at being seen with Anne in public; Ann Walker never would.

In turn, Anne Lister believed that it was within her power to fulfil Ann Walker emotionally. She was keen to take on responsibility for her happiness, 'that she shall have no reason to repent'. Though she recognised that her match with Miss Walker did not represent a meeting of intellect, confidence or even physical energy, she perceived that their partnership could be a loving one. Her relationship with Mariana had been fraught, her pursuit of Vere had been messy. In Ann Walker, Anne Lister saw someone with whom she might share a life of uncomplicated and mutual affection.

By the end of September 1832, Miss Walker had accepted Anne's invitation to travel abroad with her. For Anne Lister, there was some pleasure in the idea that their plan must be kept private. Secrets, she knew, could be seductive:

> *Our liaison is now established – it is to be named to nobody*
> *but her sister and aunt and my aunt, and that not till*
> *a week or ten days before our being off. We shall go on*
> *swimmingly, and our courtship will progress naturally – she*
> *already likes me – perhaps she scarce knows how. We shall*
> *both be in love seriously enough before our journey.*
>
> 28th September 1832

At the prospect of the travel plan, Anne redoubled her efforts to ingratiate herself with the wider Walker family. On 29th September she turned her charm on the Priestleys. Dropping in at New House en route to Lidgate, she was 'friendly, open and consulting' to William, and flattered Eliza with the news that people in Halifax had been talking about what a 'fascinating person' she was.

Having accomplished one objective, Anne walked the half a mile to Ann Walker's house. From the diary entry she made that night, it appears to have been an extraordinary day:

We now get on beautifully ... In moralizing a little on how much we had both to be thankful for, how happy we should be, etc. She said, 'yes, she had often looked at all her things and said what was the use of having them with nobody to enjoy them with her?'

She said it all now seemed like a dream to her. I told her I had made up my mind in May, the moment I was at liberty to do so, so that it had been well enough digested by me, however sudden it might seem to her, and that I gave my happiness into her keeping in perfect security. Said I had built the hut on purpose for her.

29th September 1832

In fact, Anne had not built the hut for Miss Walker, but it was a timely piece of flattery. The level of feeling between the two women was moving, emphatically, beyond the bounds of common friendship.

However, while it marked a confident step forward for their intimacy, their conversation also signified choppy waters ahead. The lack of self-confidence, wavering commitment to travel and initial reaction against the idea of inhabiting Shibden Hall – all of which Ann Walker demonstrated – would, in the coming months, constitute significant obstacles to the future of her relationship with Anne Lister.

For now, Anne was content to dismiss them. She chose to interpret Miss Walker's admission that she 'had been think-ing last night whether she could make me happy and be a companion for me' as sensitivity, rather than low self-esteem. To Miss Walker's suggestion that they delay their plan to travel until after the visit of her friends Mr and Mrs Ainsworth – 'she wishes not to put them off, and all other things suiting, would rather not go till February' – Anne simply agreed. In fact, she said, the extra month would put her mind at rest and allow her to spend more time with her ailing aunt. About Miss Walker's reluctance to engage with the idea of eventually moving away from Lidgate Anne appeared relaxed. She privately conceded that it had been 'too early in our day to mention' her plan for Miss Walker to let out her property and move into Shibden. At this stage, she was happy to have planted the thought in Miss Walker's mind.

Anne's *nous verrons* approach to Miss Walker's insecuri-ties and procrastinations suggests that she saw and heard what suited her in the early stage of the courtship. She remained typically confident that, in time, she would 'gently mould Miss W to my wishes' (27th September 1832).

Whilst maintaining, thus far, a level of secrecy regarding her sexual orientation, Anne had opened up to Miss Walker about herself in other ways. Within her first visits to Lidgate, she had spoken in depth on the subjects closest to her, bearing her soul on the topics of education, travel, family and home.

But in the early autumn of 1832, there was still much for Anne Lister to discover about Miss Walker. She did not know whether or not Ann had ever had an intimate relationship, but assumed that Ann was sexually inexperienced, which reinforced her instinct that she must tread sensitively and carefully. 'I see I must be uncommonly and fastidiously delicate,' she would write on 1st October. As September drew to a close she was astonished at her own progress:

> We are in smooth waters now, and she tells me more and more of her affairs. She feels at ease and happier with me than perhaps she could easily explain, and probably we shall both be impatient by and by to be off. I myself am surprised at my so rapid success.

> 28th September 1832

Now, as Anne returned home late, having spent the entire afternoon and evening of 29th September with Miss Walker, Marian took the opportunity to air her irritation at what she considered Anne's selfishness:

> My aunt has been miserable about my being out so late, and Marian set on my entering the room, that I must do so no more, in that sort of to me dictatorial manner, that I as usual could not stand it, and it ending in Marian's crying and having a nervous fit.

> 29th September 1832

While this account paints Marian as an hysteric, the truth is that she and her aunt had every right to be concerned for

Anne's welfare. Crime was not confined to the urban slums of Halifax; pockets of lawlessness existed all over the Calder Valley, and the road that led from Lightcliffe to Shibden was particularly dark and secluded.

Knowing this, Aunt Anne and Marian had taken the step of dispatching Eliza Cordingley and Rachel Hemingway into the night to find their mistress. By the time she returned in their escort, the whole house was up and about.

But Marian's fury could not detract from the excitement Anne felt following the events of the day. She turned to her aunt with her hopes for the new relationship:

> *Telling her of my real sentiments about Miss Walker and my expectations, that the chances were ten to one in favour of our travelling and ultimately settling together. My aunt not to appear to know anything about it, even to Miss W* [Ann Walker's aunt], *till I had mentioned it to the latter.*
>
> 29th September 1832

Anne had been confident of her aunt's approval and indeed, the elder Anne Lister admitted that the idea of the match had already crossed her mind. She 'seemed very well pleased at my choice and prospects', wrote Anne, and 'thought my father would be pleased if he knew, and so would both my uncles'. Just as it would have if the match had been a heterosexual one, Ann Walker's well-publicised fortune played its part in the enthusiasm of Anne's family: 'I said she had three thousand a year or very near it.'

The genteel femininity that attracted Anne to Miss Walker as a prospective sexual partner was also a part of what made her acceptable to Anne's family. Ann Walker was highly respectable. She fitted neatly into her period's received ideal of womanhood, of the image of a 'proper lady' as depicted in contemporary conduct manuals. She exercised her wealth and influence in a manner befitting of her sex, by showing regard for the needs of the less fortunate. She was the right kind of woman, and would be made welcome at Shibden.

Meanwhile, Anne's thinking was less genteel. Her sexual fantasies about Miss Walker – from which she 'incurred a cross' in the early hours of 30th September – were increasingly frequent and meticulously logged.

At nine o'clock that morning, Dr Kenny called to see Aunt Anne, who was still suffering from painful spasms. He thought her 'state precarious', recorded Anne, whose medical interest prompted her to dog his every move, 'but ten days will show the effect of the combination of alternatives he has now given her'. Anne's lack of faith in Dr Kenny was compounded by Miss Walker's recent confidences about his unwanted attentions, as well as the fact that he had, a short time ago, been seen arm-in-arm with none other than Marian.

Anne remained preoccupied with Marian's reaction to her late return from Lightcliffe the previous night. She had slept on it, and decided that she still found Marian ridiculous. During the resulting row that afternoon, Marian threatened that 'she would go away'. Anne resolved to 'never mention Marian in any way to anyone' in the future.

After Dr Kenny had left, Anne turned her attention to her correspondence. She appealed to Mrs Norcliffe to help her find a replacement for George Playforth, who had died that June, before moving on to a general update:

> *Ask if Bell is really to marry Dr Travis's younger brother ... ask if Burnett got the parcel I sent her ages ago ... ask if Richard the groom at Langton, knows of a good groom who could act as footman and likely to be at liberty in January – almost determined to take an English groom, and a courier too.*
>
> *Nothing would delight me more than to go to Langton now, but can't, for business – my steward died ten days ago, and my aunt had been so far from well this last fortnight, that I should be uneasy to leave her ... all pleased with my friend's marriage with Lochiel ... mention that the younger children are now to take the rank as if their father had come to take the title.*

30th September 1832

Anne's second letter was to Eugenie Pierre's sister. To Miss Pierre, who was working as a teacher at Mrs Swinley's School in Brighton, she reiterated her exacting requirements for a lady's maid:

> *I want a clever lady's maid who is at the same time thoroughly respectable and steady, obliging in her manner, neat in her person and habits, who has good health, and is sufficiently fond of travelling to make the best of everything,*

and have no objection to go outside, or to go to wherever I may wish.

If your sister is such a person, and if, as Mrs Lawton seems persuaded, she has really profited by many advantages of birth and weather, I feel certain that she would, in a very short time, understand my habits and wishes, and find her place as comfortable as it would be in my power to make it.

Eugenie had, indirectly, been warned. Anne's maid would have to do more than cut her hair, prepare her food and mend her clothes; she would be expected to interpret every one of her mistress's complex wishes, and quickly.

<hr />

'She said she had thought of me every day at Wastwater, and could not help thinking now of the very great anxiety she somehow felt to get home again. She had always an idea that her thirtieth year would be an important one'

Anne's *chaumière* had proven a worthwhile investment. Within only a few weeks of its completion, she and Miss Walker were visiting the moss hut on an almost daily basis. It provided a romantic sanctuary among the otherwise utilitarian, and still scruffy, grounds. Cows, to Anne's chagrin, were liable to break through the neighbouring Calf Croft and reap destruction on the rest of the land. They had, she had written, 'cropt [sic] to

121

destruction' her 'fine young lime tree and a fine arbutus and several young oaks' on 7th September.

Outside the thatched hut, Anne had other preoccupations. She began to make plans in earnest for an access road from the Godley turnpike on the perimeter of the estate grounds. Pickles was costing it, so Anne recorded his calculations in her diary for subsequent perusal and cross-checking.

Tensions with her sister had been temporarily calmed by Marian's decision to go and stay in Market Weighton, a town sixty miles away. Before she departed by the 11am Highflier on 1st October, Anne had the good grace to wish her a pleasant journey. She hoped that Marian's holiday would clear the air and improve her mood.

Having done her sisterly duty, Anne left the hall to see Miss Walker. The women met at the half-way point between their homes, a junction called Hipperholme Lane Ends. As they walked back slowly to the *chaumière* together, Miss Walker commented that she had not been feeling well. It was the first time that Anne, who already knew a little of Miss Walker's history of mental ill-health from Mrs Priestley, was able to note how it affected her physically. Today, Ann's lack of energy was striking.

Once they had arrived, the two women remained inside the moss hut, locked in intense conversation, for six hours. Anne Lister had described their conduct in the previous days as like that of 'engaged lovers', and, with Miss Walker more responsive than ever to her courtly attentions, it was a dynamic that was set to continue.

Their *tête-à-tête* began with Anne's return to the subject of Shibden Hall. Her ancestral home, she 'advocated skilfully', countering Ann's attachment to her own property, would be the perfect place for them to settle as companions. The ancient lineage of the Lister land would give Miss Walker not only a certain 'éclat', but a level of independence that she would never know under the watch of her tribe of relatives at Cliff Hill. Besides, Shibden could be run at a much lower cost.

From there, Anne was able to pivot the conversation onto even more intimate ground. Did Miss Walker think they could live a happy life together, and could she now 'give up all thought of ever leaving' her? Miss Walker's response was breathtakingly candid, and not entirely what Anne had been expecting:

> *This led her into explaining that she had said she would never marry – but that, as she had once felt an inclination not to keep to this, she could not yet so positively say she would never feel the same inclination again. She should not like to deceive me and begged not to answer just now.*
>
> 1st October 1832

Anne's reaction, recorded in the long crypt-hand diary entry that now typified her accounts of days spent with Miss Walker, was complex. There was much to digest. On the one hand, it was disappointing that Miss Walker had not yet mentally erased the possibility of a relationship with a man from her future. On the other, the gravity with which she considered

Anne's question was encouraging. Her sincerity was important. It indicated, crucially, that Miss Walker had understood what Anne Lister was offering her: love, loyalty and long-term commitment. Anne had stopped short of proposing her version of marriage, but Miss Walker had received the message loud and clear.

Anne viewed her own relationships firmly within a heterosexual framework. It was, after all, the only one that society had provided. As a Christian, whose own same-sex desires she believed to be the dictate of God, Anne craved the permanency, and, ironically, respectability, of a romantic union solemnised in the same way as a marriage. She saw no reason that she and the woman she loved should not declare their commitment before God. It would have to be more discreet than a traditional wedding, but to Anne, the exchange of rings and taking of the sacrament together in church meant marriage.

Anne was sensitive to Ann Walker's hesitancy. She knew it was early in their courtship for so serious a proposition, and decided to offer Ann until 3rd April the following year to make up her mind:

> *I said she was quite right – praised her judiciousness – that my esteem and admiration were only heightened by it – that no feelings of selfishness should make me even wish my happiness rather than hers, that I should give her six months till my next birthday.*

1st October 1832

If six months felt like a long time, Anne's approach demonstrated the confidence she felt in a positive outcome. Her patience, she hoped, would help to dispel any notion that her interest in Miss Walker was purely mercenary. In the months leading to her forty-second birthday, Anne would have the time to prove to Miss Walker the honourableness of her intentions. She was appropriating a familiar role in traditional (heterosexual) ideals of romance: the ardent lover at the mercy of their coy heroine.

Anne recognised, too, that the time Ann Walker would need to make up her mind could also be of benefit to her. She had suffered over the years at the indecision of women who had ultimately betrayed her. Patience was a virtue. She had waited for sixteen years for Mariana Lawton to commit to her; six months was nothing.

For her part, Ann Walker seemed slightly taken aback by the length of the term offered. She hadn't bargained on Anne's willingness to wait for her answer, but agreed, and told Anne that 'she would give no answer till the time' was up. Anne could not resist the temptation to write in her diary that, 'in spite of her, I should find it out'.

The conversation continued in its romantic timbre. Anne hoped that her 'thorough love speeches of anxiety and impatience' did not seem foolish to Ann Walker. This was false modesty; Anne was blessed with an abundance of self-esteem and privately considered her own behaviour that day 'too agreeable to be found any fault with'.

It seemed that Miss Walker was playing her part to perfection too. Her natural shyness made her appear coy and demure, and it appealed to Anne, who liked 'her all the better for it'. As the life-changing afternoon drew to an end, Anne's conclusion was prophetic: 'She is in for it, if ever a girl was, and so am I too.'

The following day, having stood at her desk 'writing the whole of yesterday' in her journal, Anne returned to domestic and estate matters. She breakfasted with her father, conversed with her aunt, and was out on the land by quarter past ten.

All measure of work was going on across Tilly Holm bridge, Calf Croft and Pit Hill. Anne's workers were carting soil, barrowing loads of stone and breaking ashes to shore up banks and improve the existing roads and walks. Charles Haworth and his son James had begun painting the back of the house. Pickles, sadly, was out of action:

In lifting a heavy stone yesterday strained his back very much. Went home early in the afternoon, and had twelve leeches and a strengthening plaster put on his back.

2nd October 1832

Taking advantage of the tranquillity of the moss hut alone, Anne treated herself to thirty-four pages of French vocabulary exercises. She was drawn back to Shibden in the afternoon by concern for her aunt, who was 'not quite well' again. This time, Dr Sunderland was called, and asked to attend to elderly Jeremy Lister too.

Afterwards, there was a newsy letter to enjoy from Isabella Norcliffe, which included 'Thanks from Burnett for the gown I sent ages ago' and detail of a recent trip to Avranche in France. '1600 English' were living there, Tib had written, and the tour 'cost less than a hundred and sixty pounds'. She had enclosed with her delivery '2 brace of partridges'.

Born in 1785, Tib was six years older than Anne. As young women, they had been lovers, but polar differences in temperament had been among several factors that had prevented their coming together permanently. They had remained close and affectionate friends, and Anne's diaries demonstrate a lifelong loyalty and tenderness towards Tib.

As two distinctive-looking – and by the standards of the day, strikingly 'un-feminine' – women, Anne and Tib had been the subject of occasional rumour. On 12th September 1825, Anne had written of a miniature scandal that took place in York surrounding their sexuality. Mariana's 'tipsy' husband had been gleaning insights from a local Mr Lally. 'You do not know what is said of your friend,' Charles had, somewhat ironically, told Mariana. Mr Lally had commented that, 'He would as soon as turn a man loose in his house as me [Anne]. As for Miss Norcliffe, two Jacks would not suit together.'

Mr Lally's insight that two 'Jacks' (that is, butch women) could not make a romantic match, while not necessarily true, offered a surprisingly nuanced comprehension of lesbian sexuality.

The incident also prompted a noteworthy moment in Mariana's complicated relationship with Anne. It was rare for Mariana to offer any defence of Anne's 'oddity', but now, she supported her: 'the world might say what it pleased'.

By the afternoon, Mr Sunderland had finished examining Jeremy Lister. He did not think, as Anne noted with relief (and some satisfaction) in her diary, that 'he was so fast declining as Marian does'. This was the same Mr Sunderland who Anne had been walking with when she had become aware of Christopher Rawson's game-keeper's trespass on her land in September 1831. She took the opportunity to move the conversation on to blood sport weaponry, quizzing Mr Sunderland on 'the subject of shooting and guns'. 'He promised,' she wrote, 'to lend me Colonel Aker's Sportsman.' The gun was, to her mind, 'the best Sportsman in England' (2nd October 1832).

It was not unusual for Anne to lead her conversation with male visitors into a realm that would have been considered firmly masculine at the time. Her enthusiasm and curiosity for subjects such as business, science and invention made her an engaging conversational partner and, more often than not, she and her opinions seemed to be accepted on a level plane to that of her male peers.

The next day, Anne received a letter from Mariana Lawton. Charles 'had had a severe attack of the cholera' she reported, 'but his health and spirits the better for it'. Moving swiftly on, Mariana told Anne that she had met a Miss Smith on her behalf (Eugenie having not yet been finally settled upon as Anne's maid), but had judged her a 'flippant a sort of girl'. A pity, as 'she spoke really well' (3rd October 1832).

A surprise parcel from Mr and Mrs Edwards of Market Weighton containing '2 brace of pheasants, 2 ditto partridges, and a hare' meant that Anne, suddenly, was awash with spoils of the hunting season. John Booth was dispatched to deliver surplus game to the neighbours. Mrs Rawson of Stoney Royd, the elder Ann Walker of Cliff Hill, Anne's solicitor Mr Parker and Mr and Mrs Sunderland all got partridges. The hare was awarded to Mr and Mrs Priestley at New House. The pheasants Anne kept back for herself.

With typical efficiency, Anne spent the afternoon replying to her friends' letters (from the kitchen, owing to the fact that a plasterer was currently white-washing her bedroom). First was Tib, to whom she appealed 'for a cutting of double yellow rose', and her thoughts on Joseph Booth. The son of her trusted servant John, Joseph was currently working for a family near Langton, and Anne had begun to wonder whether he would be 'at all likely to do for me'. Anne liked to dispense advice as well as receive it, as demonstrated in her response to Isabella's qualms about the recent match of a family member:

> *We ought to congratulate or condole with other people,*
> *according to their failings, not our own – be pleased (as far*
> *as satisfies the demands as kindness and propriety, without*
> *compromising our opinion or sincerity) … Thus I have*
> *congratulated Mrs N on Esther's match 'because I have*
> *reason to believe she is not displeased, and the match will be*
> *a comfort to her' … If Esther is happy, all her friends will*
> *rejoice at her being so. So long as her parents are satisfied,*
> *her not having chosen exactly according to your taste or*
> *mine, is in no respect reprehensible.*

3rd October 1832

Turning next to Mariana's letter, Anne expressed her gratitude for the information about Miss Smith, but agreed that she would not do as a lady's maid. Eugenie was still the front runner. In fact, Anne was still reeling from the departure of her most recent maid, Cameron. Mariana's sister, also named Anne, had been surprised to hear of Cameron's departure from Anne's service. Anne Lister wrote:

Perhaps she [Anne Belcombe] *does not know how unhappy the poor girl was. Surely Eugenie will understand me better. Somehow or other, I never dreamt of anybody being unhappy with me. How little we know ourselves! You did me a lasting service by telling me. Everybody will gain by it. All I dread is changing, and the prospect of this is the worst of Eugenie – but, she may lead me by the nose – she may stay, and save me the trouble of hunting hereafter for the steady woman you talk of.*

3rd October 1832

All of this activity was not to say that Miss Walker had been forgotten. Among the domestic challenges and busy corre-spondence, she had been dominating Anne's thoughts:

I really do get more and more in love with her … Not perhaps a little heightened by the having to wait her answer for the next six months. She has really behaved very judiciously, for I believe she likes me.

3rd October 1832

'She asked me to dine with her at five
and stay all night'

Miss Walker had proven herself remarkably open to Anne Lister's charms. In spite of her nervous disposition and hitherto sheltered existence, she had swiftly become not only comfortable around but enamoured of Anne, and entirely complicit in their intimacy. She had begun to crave Anne's attention almost as much as Anne desired to give it. Now, only three months after their chance re-acquaintance at Shibden Hall, Anne was to find herself on the sofa at Lidgate, with her hand up Miss Walker's petticoat. Over the next few weeks, she would gain intimate knowledge of Miss Walker, and become party to some surprising insights in the process.

On 4th October, Anne arrived at Lidgate a little after ten in the morning, having trusted John Booth to oversee the removal of a window in Shibden's new library passage. After the usual small talk, Miss Walker herself raised the subject of where they should live, should she accept Anne's offer. She was, Anne was pleased to note, finally coming round to the idea of letting out Cliff Hill and moving in to Shibden.

Ann's other preoccupation was less promising. She had started to worry about Anne Lister's 'intimacy' with the Priestleys. She was, correctly, as it would turn out, concerned that the two women's closeness with the inhabitants of nearby New House would lay them open to scrutiny. Anne reassured her that it would be 'easy' for her to distance herself from Mrs Priestley if their liaison were to become official.

Anne, being practised in the art of seduction, preferred to keep the conversation focused more firmly on her intended than her intended's elderly relatives. She dispelled Miss Walker's fears, telling her that it was only the 'pre-engagement of her heart' that mattered to her. The remark was intended to flatter, but it also hinted at an early anxiety of Anne's: that there could be a Charles Lawton or Captain Donald Cameron lurking in the background with designs of his own on Miss Walker's heart.

Anne's account of the day is intriguing. Her full diary entry veers from simple delight at the speed of her progress, to more distanced analysis of Ann Walker's character and behaviour. She appears by turn a calculating seducer and a sympathetic suitor with an increasing emotional stake in the object of her desire.

Any insecurity that existed may have stemmed from Anne's feeling that she was on 'probation' with Miss Walker. In the six-month trial period, she had inadvertently given Ann the power to keep her guessing about her own future. As Anne Lister pushed, Ann Walker's insistence that her mind was 'quite unmade up' stoked Anne's 'fear of disappointment'.

Anne was becoming increasingly cognisant of what she saw as contradictions in Ann Walker's character. Their crux, ironically, was to be Miss Walker's surprising sexual confidence. That afternoon, the relationship had entered a new phase:

I had my arm on the back of the sofa. She leaned on it, looking as if I might be affectionate and it ended in her lying on my arm all the morning and my kissing her and she returning it with such a long, continued, passionate or nervous mumbling kiss ... I thinking to myself, 'Well, this is rather more than I expected'.

4th October 1832

Miss Walker's willingness to respond to her sexual advances thrilled Anne (to whom physical compatibility was imperative in any relationship), but it shocked her too. In many ways, Anne Lister was a conservative woman, and her surprise at Ann's lack of restraint – on 4th October and beyond – reflected the double standards of the society in which she lived. Femininity and modesty were inseparable concepts. She had expected Ann to uphold the decorous image of respectability that her shyness had suggested, for a while longer at least. Instead, Miss Walker 'asked me to dine with her at five and stay all night'.

Anne, of course, accepted. When she returned to Lidgate at 5pm, Ann Walker had changed into an evening gown. The early, formal dinner, waited on by James Mackenzie, was quite different to the more casual suppers Anne usually enjoyed at 6.30 or 7pm at Shibden Hall. After the meal, which had been accompanied by polite conversation about the Highlands, the atmosphere changed considerably. As soon as Ann's manservant left the room, the two women drew nearer:

She sat on my knee, and I did not spare kissing and pressing, she returning it as in the morning. Yet still, I was not to hope too much.

4th October 1832

Amid the kissing and 'pressing' Miss Walker had mumbled something about Anne being infatuated with her, and that when the novelty wore off she would soon forget her. 'Waived all this', wrote Anne, determining to reject any coquettishness on Miss Walker's part. Moving from the stiff surrounds of the dining room to the more comfortable sofa, where they sat 'most lovingly', Anne's ensuing talk of her aunt and Eugenie Pierre had the ring of procrastination. Lidgate was cosy, intimate and far enough from the surrounding Walker properties for the two women to feel safe from interruption. As darkness fell outside, the two women took advantage of the dimming light:

I prest [sic] *her bosom. Then, finding no resistance and the lamp being out, let my hand wander lower down, gently getting to queer* [vagina]. *Still no resistance. So I whispered surely she could care for me a little? 'Yes.' Then gently whispered she would break my heart if she left me.*

4th October 1832

However, their lovemaking was interrupted when Miss Walker began to cry. Breaking away, she told Anne that she was afraid she would think her 'cold' and unfeeling ('How the devil could I?' Anne thought to herself) for the admission she was about to give.

It emerged that until very recently, Miss Walker's 'affections had been engaged' to a man. The suitor, whom Ann described simply as 'one of the best men', had died just three months earlier. Now, she was anxious that Anne should not expect her feelings to be 'transferred so soon'.

Anne appeared to take this on the chin. She found herself able to slip easily into a gentlemanly, gallant role, begging 'a thousand pardons' for her forwardness and describing her own conduct as 'madness' in the hope of allaying Miss Walker's anxieties. She was satisfied with her performance; 'All this was very prettily done ... I shall now turn sentimentally melancholy and put on all the air of romantic hopelessness.'

Privately, Anne was more analytical, and more confused. She was perplexed by the contradictions she had discovered in shy Ann Walker. She even felt that in encouraging her attentions, there had been an element of dissembling in Ann's behaviour: 'She certainly gulled me in that I never dreamt of her being the passionate little person I find her in spite of her calling herself cold,' she wrote.

Her instinct was beginning to pull Anne in different directions. On one hand, it told her to be 'be cautious' and 'mind what I say' to Miss Walker, but on the other, it suggested that 'a little spice of matrimony' might do Miss Walker good.

The business of Miss Walker's former suitor was a further complication. It had been a remarkable and surprising day. 'I scarce know what to make of her,' Anne mused, 'Hang it! This queer girl puzzles me.'

- a lit. cold meat w[...] in for [...] at $6\frac{1}{2}$ - tea at $6\frac{3}{4}$ -

wet [...] very fine day ∓ 5 q$\frac{1}{2}$ at q$\frac{3}{4}$ -

- [...] packd. [...] Trunk bay - [...] & left at [...] -

MISS WALKER'S MUMBLING KISSES AND NERVOUS INCONSISTENCY, JOHN BOOTH'S MISTAKE AND SUSPICIOUS ELIZA PRIESTLEY

'She let out today that there is some who
would now be glad of her, & take her into
a very different rank of life from her present one –
some poor Scotch baronet?'

While she had been at Lidgate on 4th October, Anne
had learned that Miss Walker had been receiving
anonymous letters. Though her diaries do not reveal their
content, Anne noted that they had 'much troubled' Miss
Walker, and the younger woman's appeal for help demonstrates
her growing reliance on Anne as someone to take on the burden
of the issues that caused her anxiety. As Anne wrote, 'she would
get rid of all troubles of cousins, or letters, when with me'.

Over the years, Anne Lister had also received strange
letters in the post. Gleaning that her unusual dress and gentlemanly manner were linked somehow to a deviant sexuality,
men had written with mocking proposals of relationships or
marriage. Anne had grown used to this sort of attention, and
seemed able to dismiss it as nonsense. For Miss Walker, whose
sense of self was more fragile, it was more threatening.

It seems likely that the letters Miss Walker received
concerned her increasingly visible friendship with Anne Lister.
Local eyes were open to the almost daily visits the two women
were paying to each other's homes – and Anne Lister was not
without a reputation.

It is entirely possible that the letters were a warning shot to Anne Lister, sent from inside Ann's family. In contrast to the support Anne had from her loving and remarkably forward-thinking aunt and laid-back father, Ann Walker had no emotional safety net. She was closely guarded by a network of people – the Sutherlands, the Rawsons, the Edwards and the Priestleys – who had their own financial interests at heart. Within her tribe of relations, Mr Priestley and Mr Edwards were particularly mind-ful of Ann Walker's wealth. As joint trustees of the Walker estate, they were duty bound to protect her money. Whether there was a local inkling of the nature of Anne and Ann's relationship by this time or not, the fact was that one woman was spending a dangerous amount of time with their rich relative.

Anne Lister remained troubled by what she had learned about Miss Walker's late former love-interest. From her journal entry of 5th October, it seems as if she had resolved to follow her own advice and 'be cautious' of letting things develop too quickly:

> *I explained how sorry I was. Would have been the last to have intruded on her feelings under the circumstances of such recent grief. But, my being hopeless now, no reason that I shall always be so, and we would leave things as they always were ... wait the six months as agreed.*

5th October 1832

However, pulling back from the relationship was easier said than done. Ann Walker was growing increasingly dependent on Anne's practical advice as well as her emotional support. She looked to Anne for guidance on estate matters, the Walker rent rolls, and how to spend the £1,000 of her £2,500 a year income she had at her immediate disposal. She may not have considered that it was becoming confusing for Anne to be kept at arm's length in some ways, at the same time as being relied upon for affection and so thoroughly implicated in Ann's future plans in others. It is clear from her diary that Anne was beginning to wonder if inconsistent Miss Walker was going to be more trouble than she was worth.

Anne's assessment of this 'queer girl' and her erratic behaviour reflects the disparity in the two women's abilities to process their liaison. It was more than the fact that Anne Lister had experienced lesbian relationships before. It was that she had engaged in years of introspection and analysis to understand her place in the world. Anne's diary, and particularly her crypt hand, had long provided the comfort of a space in which she could explore her deepest emotions and form her complicated identity. She had resolved her Christianity with her sexuality. She had found precedents for her own desires in studies of classical literature. As much as she was led by her heart, the decisions she made were painstakingly weighed up, considered and rationalised. Her journal was a form of daily therapy. It gave her the space to challenge her own behaviour and that of others. It was an important tool that helped to smooth her path to personal happiness.

Ann Walker relied on no such method to untangle her innermost thoughts. The joy of her new experiences competed freely with her anxiety, her desires tussled with her deep religiosity and trust in the Almighty God.

Anne and Ann spent 5th October 1832 together at Lidgate. By just after 10.30am, Miss Walker had given Anne her first 'mumbling kisses' of the day and lay 'languid' on Anne's arm. Anne felt that she 'might have done what she liked' with her, that is, initiated sex. Miss Walker had, after all, been so keen for her to 'stay all night' at Lidgate.

Her restraint on this occasion reflected in part Anne's reluctance to take their affair to the next level with 'no hope' of Miss Walker confirming their long-term commitment. Miss Walker's assurance to her that she 'thought I [Anne] had hope', was not enough.

Miss Walker was suffering with back pain, a frequently recurring affliction, and Anne suggested taking her to see Dr Belcombe in York. Ann's response speaks volumes about the extensive medical attention she had received in the past for her nervousness and depression and their physical effects: 'She said he would only laugh. All doctors would say is "what was the matter with her?" Meaning, that she wanted a good husband.'

Though Anne privately wondered if a diagnosis of hypochondria could be 'near enough the truth', she convinced Miss Walker that a visit to Steph should be arranged for the end of that month.

By now, Anne Lister believed that Ann Walker was 'head and ears' in love with her. However, her own enthusiasm for the relationship was increasingly tempered by the conviction that Miss Walker was less innocent than she had led Anne to believe. She found Ann's anecdote about the poems of George Crabbe particularly off-putting:

> Catherine [Rawson] *maintained they were not fit to be read. Miss Walker was not so particular. Not fit for young girls, but very well for herself and Catherine. 'Oh, oh', thought I, 'this is a new light to me' ... She casually said the other day, she should now know better how to flirt than she used to do. It has struck me more than once she is a deepish hand.*
>
> 5th October 1832

The 'deepish' (i.e. worldly) hand that now led Anne Lister upstairs supported her theory that Miss Walker had been holding back the truth about her level of experience:

> *She took me up to her room. I kissed her and she pushed herself so to me. I rather felt and might have done as much as I pleased. She is man-keen enough. If I stay all night, it will be my own fault if I do not have all of her I can ... she wishes to try the metal I am made of, and I begin to fear not being able to do enough, and to doubt whether even fun will be amusing or safe ... shall I, shall I not give into fun with her, stay all night and do my best for her without caring for the result?*
>
> 5th October 1832

Such a show of insecurity was rare, and Anne Lister's doubts about her ability as a woman to sexually satisfy 'man-keen'

Miss Walker indicate her wider misgivings about her potential partner. On her return to Shibden that evening, she confided her feelings in Aunt Anne: 'Said how I was cooled about the thing – yet still that I would wait the six months for the answer. If it was no, I should not grieve much.' The next day she would add that she 'felt as pleased that it was over as I had done when it began'.

Despite these displays of indifference to her aunt, Anne had by no means completely given up on Miss Walker. Her determination to pursue Ann's hand is reflected in her continued efforts to ingratiate herself with her wider family. It appeared that her endeavours to convince Mrs Priestley of her 'agreeableness' were paying dividends:

> *She had walked with me as far as or beyond the blacksmith's shop, and I returned with her ... She hoped I would breakfast there on Monday, as she was never busy till ten. Very good friends. She said inclination would have led her to turn with me again, had she been able. Either my telling her this day week of her being called fascinating had had a good effect on her, or she made up to me on Miss W's account.*
>
> 6th October 1832

But Mrs Priestley's next comment – that Anne and Miss Walker appeared 'very thick' with each other – worried Anne. Even expressed innocently, Mrs Priestley's observation that the pair had been spending every day together was concerning because it meant that people were becoming aware of their closeness. Anne was keen to play down the relationship: 'Yes, we were very good friends. I had not been every day – not Tuesday or Wednesday ... I should not go there today.'

True to her word, Anne did not go to Lidgate that day. Having left Mrs Priestley, she returned home and filled the day with jobs around Shibden, giving orders to Pickles about the new road through the Trough of Bolland wood, and to Charles Howarth about the library passage outside her bedroom.

On the morning of Sunday 7th October, having taken breakfast at 8.20, Anne walked down the steep Old Bank to Halifax parish church to hear the morning service. She was joined by her father, who had made a good recovery from his recent stomach complaint. The curate, Anne wrote, preached (for '28 mins stupidly') from the second epistle of Corinthians:

> *We have renounced disgraceful, underhanded ways; we refuse to practice cunning or to tamper with God's word, but by the open statement of the truth we would commend ourselves to every man's conscience in the sight of God.*

Anne quite often fell asleep during sermons, finding them either over-long or simply boring. Curates, vicars and priests were a frequent target of her cutting observations, being stupid, 'impedimented' or daring to have dirty nails.

Today, despite her criticism of its delivery, the words of the epistle would have resonance for Anne as someone who lived her life very consciously 'in the sight of God'. Anne had personalised her relationship with God, unafraid to confess her frailties and faults in their daily communication. The confidence with which she was able to view her place in the world was thanks, largely, to Him. She lived her life by the dictates of her nature, a nature ordained and sanctified according to God's holy will.

While Anne observed the rituals of Christian doctrine – prayer and worship – she did not always attend the Sunday service at church or take the sacrament. As she saw it, if she had read the prayers at home she had 'done the business'. Nor did she necessarily devote herself to the bible for hours on end. Holy days could be filled with estate work and business meetings, and sex was not off the cards either. Sundays were not a day of abstinence for Anne Lister.

On that Sunday, while Anne had been occupying the Lister pew in Halifax, Miss Walker had failed to attend Lightcliffe church. As a committed member of the congregation, her unusual absence was noted by Mrs Priestley, who informed Anne. Having observed herself that the blinds had been closed when she had passed Lidgate earlier that day, Anne walked with Mrs Priestley to the house to check up on Ann.

Anne wrote that Miss Walker seemed 'very glad' to see her. Mrs Priestley did not stay long, leaving the two women to take a tea of 'cold tongue, bread and butter, and wine' together.

This was not the first time that a visit to Lidgate had been marked by Anne's concern for Miss Walker's health. On several occasions she had arrived to find Ann still in bed, and would have to rouse her and encourage her to eat or take exercise.

In this instance, the conversation quickly revealed that Ann's suffering was mental rather than physical. Her non-appearance at church reflected her anxiety about what answer she should give to Anne's proposal:

> [She] *began again about wishing me to have no hope, but that she now said enough, and would say no more about it. I had declared I had given up all thought of the thing. Had positively no hope at all. In fact, considered the decisive 'no', as good as said. 'No,' she replied, 'I did not say that. I will think about it, but don't go on hoping.' I declared on my word I* [would] *not do so. Thinking to myself after much pretty talk, I care little about it anyway.*

> 7th October 1832

Though Miss Walker's anxiety and indecision were beginning to take their toll on Anne, her declaration that she had given up hope for the relationship rings hollow. For a start, she remained determined to get inside Miss Walker's 'thick knitted drawers':

> *She kissed me and lay on my arm as before, evidently excited, tho' talking of her coldness, which I never contradicted. Said a little French countess had taught me much of foreign manners, and court scandal. My aunt afraid of her for me …*
>
> *I kissed and pressed very tenderly, and got my right hand up her petticoats to queer, but not to the skin – could*

not get thro' her thick knitted drawers, tho' she never once
attempted to put my hand away. She held her thighs too
tight together for me. I shall manage it the next time.
She said she had now begun with fires in her room. Said
I would sit by it with her. Laughed, and said the dressing
room door should have opened into the bedroom, and
finding my conversation needed not be so strait-laced as for
Catherine Rawson, hinted at the only use of pocket holes
abroad, etc., etc.

7th October 1832

In pocket holes, Anne was alluding to a practice she had observed during her time in Paris. Telling Miss Walker about the public masturbation techniques of French men was a way of pushing their conversation into a different space, creating a very different atmosphere to the polite chit-chat Ann would have known with 'strait-laced' Catherine Rawson.

It was also designed to make her laugh; Anne relied on humour and anecdote to impress women. To Ann Walker, who had spent all of her life in Halifax, outlandish stories like this one came from another world, and the woman who relayed them was equally exotic.

The 'delightful moonlight night' was soon to be spoiled. Having been dispatched to collect his mistress from Lightcliffe after the upset Anne's late-night return had caused on 29th September, John Booth had mistakenly knocked on the Priestleys' door. Quickly realising that he had come to the wrong Lightcliffe property, John left, but not before unwittingly revealing to Mr and Mrs Priestley that Anne had been spending another cosy evening with Miss Walker.

Despite Anne's inner reasoning that Mrs Priestley had no reason to doubt the respectability of her calls on Miss Walker, her instinct told her that this would not end well. The Priestleys' suspicions would be roused. 'They will talk us over and think something in the wind,' she wrote to her diary that night. She was right.

'If you never had any attachment, who taught you to kiss?' I laughed and said how nicely that was said – then answered, that nature taught me'

Anne Lister's conviction that Miss Walker was somehow sexually experienced pervaded the pages of her diary in the early stages of their liaison. Having kept conveniently quiet about her own past encounters ('I had said I was at no time likely to marry. How far she understood me I could not make out'), she was able to laugh off Miss Walker's question about who it was that had taught her to kiss. 'Nature' was her tried and tested reply (8th October 1832).

Despite her own evasive answer, Anne remained preoccupied with the idea that Miss Walker had been practising on someone else. 'And who taught you?' she found herself tempted to respond. Having mentally explored the possibility that Andrew Fraser, Miss Walker's late sweetheart, had had his way with her, Anne's mind wandered to a more fantastic possibility over the next few days: Catherine Rawson. After all, Miss Walker had admitted that 'Catherine Rawson had often said she would like to live with her'. It was enough to make Anne write that she 'fancied that Catherine's classics might have taught her the trick of debauching Miss W' (11th October 1832).

It seemed unlikely that shy Ann Walker and 'strait-laced' Miss Rawson had been lovers, but clearly, lesbian relationships were taking place under the radar of a society that rendered them invisible. Sexual relationships could be hidden behind the veneer of 'romantic friendship', a contemporary conception of platonic same-sex intimacy often used to describe co-habiting, financially independent, female companions.

The two 'Ladies of Llangollen' is one of the best known examples of Georgian 'romantic friendship'. Anne Lister had read about Eleanor Butler and Sarah Ponsonby, who lived together at Plas Newydd in the north-east of Wales, in the society magazine *La Belle Assemblée,* as a young woman. 'I am interested about these ladies very much,' she had noted in her diary when an opportunity arose to meet them several years later. 'There is something in their story, and in all I have heard about them here, added to other circumstances, makes a deep impression' (23rd July 1822).

By the time Anne visited Plas Newydd in 1822, Miss Ponsonby and Miss Butler had lived together for forty-two years. The pastoral utopia that the upper-class women had created in rural Wales, along with their eccentric reputation, had attracted visits from some of the greatest writers of the day, including Shelley, Wordsworth, Lord Byron and Walter Scott.

Whether an endless stream of curious visitors was a lifestyle that appealed to Anne, her visit to 'the Ladies' had a personal resonance. She seemed most struck by the gentlemanly presentation of 'odd' and 'singular' Miss Ponsonby, with her 'shortish waisted cloth habit', 'plain, plaited, frilled habit shirt' and 'thick, white cravat' (23rd July 1822). Her brilliant mind drew praise: 'There was a freshness of intellect, a verdure of amusing talent which, with heart and thorough good breeding, made her conversation more time-beguiling than I could have imagined,' Anne wrote.

Coming immediately after a disastrous visit to Mariana Lawton – who had been married to Charles Lawton for six years at this point and whose behaviour on this occasion left Anne 'convulsed with smothering my sobs' (17th July 1822) – the uncomplicated union she found at Plas Newydd seemed idyllic to Anne.

However, the Ladies' path to personal freedom had not been straightforward. Anne knew that Lady Sarah and Lady Eleanor had fled their native Ireland to escape their respective families' threats of forced heterosexual marriage or convent confinement. Anne recognised how lucky her own circumstances were. Family acceptance, financial privilege, her impressive intellect – all had given her the confidence to live as she wished to; the way she felt nature had intended. 'The utmost I can bear is sometimes to dissemble feelings,' she wrote on 10th July 1824. 'When we leave nature, we leave

our only steady guide, and from that moment become inconsistent with ourselves.'

The uniqueness of Lady Sarah's and Lady Eleanor's situation had a profound effect on Anne's romantic imagination,
and she could not help thinking that their relationship 'was
not platonic' (3rd August 1822). The disparaging assessment
of Emma Saltmarshe, a friend of Anne's, that 'they must
be 2 romantic girls ... it was a pity they were not married'
(10th August 1822) demonstrates perfectly the contemporary
distinction between platonic romantic friendship and marriage,
which involved sex. As they were two women, Emma Saltmarshe assumed that the relationship between the Ladies of
Llangollen must belong in the former category.

It was this thinking that might have worked in Anne Lister
and Ann Walker's favour, allowing them to enjoy the freedom
of an intimate relationship without the risk of public scrutiny.
But, while there were many who would remain ever ignorant
of the true nature of their relationship, Anne's distinctive
image had implications for how their liaison would be viewed
in society.

Physically, Anne Lister stood out. She did not fit into
the image of femininity that romantic friendship had been
constructed around. In fact, she defied categorisation. She
walked like a man, dressed permanently in black, carried a fob
watch and spoke with a deep voice. By virtue of her androg-
yny she unwittingly forced the people around her to consider
their own perception of a 'normal' woman. The unusual figure
she cut attracted attention, and her gender was the subject of

speculation. Though the society she lived in had no language with which to accuse her of pursuing lesbian relationships, it did not mean that some people were not privately speculating about her love life.

Anne was aware that her 'oddity' was not invisible. While she appreciated the protection that the incomprehension of her sexuality provided, she knew that she was courting danger with her transgressive relationships. For their true nature to be revealed would be disastrous; she often talked about disclosure leading to ruination. In public, discretion over her attractions had become second nature.

In private, she had taken risks. At a house party at Langton Hall in 1818 that bore little resemblance to the stiff provincial soirees of Regency literature, Anne and Isabella Norcliffe had entertained a young woman called Mary Vallance into the early hours of the morning. Also the setting of Anne and Tib's affair, the secluded corridors of rural Langton had provided a discreet backdrop for the exploration of a female subculture.

Experimenting at a party at twenty-six was one thing, conducting a lesbian affair on home ground as a middle-aged woman was another. For Anne's relationship with Miss Walker to survive, she knew it must be carried out as carefully as possible.

On the morning of 8th October 1832, Anne shook off the previous night's worry that Mrs Priestley would 'think something in the wind' and decided to pay another visit to Ann Walker at Lidgate. In typical style, she had a long list of social and business matters to attend to first, starting with a call on elderly Mrs Rawson of Stoney Royd.

In spite of their age difference, Anne had been a friend of Christopher and Jeremiah's mother for many years, since around the time she had moved to Halifax as a young woman. On this occasion, she was greeted with a warm welcome and some interesting local intelligence:

Breakfast over but brought in again for me – Mrs R very glad to see me – sat with her till 10.10. Miss Clarke took with her a fortune of five and twenty thousand pounds. Christopher Rawson was told by her, just before the sale of the Walker navigation shares, she would not marry.

Mrs Rawson had a good sense of humour about her sons. She was amused to hear that Jeremiah (who was yet to give Anne an answer about the price of her coal), had offered his services to Anne as land steward:

Jeremiah Rawson commissioned Mrs R to tell me he should be glad to steward for me. Said we should have got on very well together, but he was too late, and laughed and said Miss Walker had provided me so that I had never seemed to be without steward. Joked and told her to take care of Frank Rawson – against Kennys and Clarkes – as I meant to take the best I could of my sister.

After Stoney Royd, Anne judged that there was time for four more visits before heading to Lidgate. After dropping in at the newly established Halifax Philosophical and Natural History Museum on Harrison Street to ask about paying her yearly subscription ('1st time of my ever going there – only one room fitted up but nice enough') there was a quick social call on her friend Mrs Veitch. Anne's third call was to Mrs Briggs, the widow of her recently deceased land steward ('Stayed 1/4 hour and was as kind in my manner as I could') and her last to Throps, the plant merchant ('Two hours there giving him a tolerably large order for evergreens and shrubs and a few trees to be sent to Shibden by noon tomorrow week').

Miss Walker was waiting for Anne at the end of her forty-minute hike up the hill from Halifax. Having only meant to stay at Lidgate for a few minutes, Anne was offered lunch and would be 'kept' by Miss Walker until past six in the evening. Part of the reason for the intended brevity of Anne's visit was the arrival of her period (or 'cousin' as she called it). The preparation, washing and burning of bloodied rags was a time-consuming inconvenience. On this occasion, Anne had also hoped that it might serve as an excuse to put some space between her and Miss Walker over the coming days:

> *On getting up this morning saw that my cousin was come very gently, but put nothing on, and determined to put off breakfasting with my friend for two or three days … She thinks me overhead and ears in love with her, as indeed my manner indicates. She is evidently pleased by my attentions.*
>
> 8th October 1832

In the event, the afternoon was to be a significant one. As the two women settled into 'a good deal of talk', their discussion turned to the nature of happiness. 'Happiness,' Anne told Miss Walker, 'was, in well-bred minds, more mental than in others.' Flattering Miss Walker that she possessed such a mind, Anne asked if she felt she could be truly happy with her, and more specifically, whether she could 'give up the thought of having children'.

Anne Lister was broaching the subject of commitment again. She wanted more than a casual sexual liaison. She needed to be sure that Miss Walker was not the same as the other women who had enjoyed her friendship and sex and then abandoned her for wealthy men. Miss Walker's seeming indifference to her assurance of 'there being no chance of my marrying' frustrated Anne. 'I saw she did not quite enter [understand] this,' she wrote, 'in spite of all the hints it seemed safe to give.' Either Miss Walker was unable to interpret Anne's declaration of her lesbian sexuality, or she was unwilling to engage with the intensity of the conversation.

Abandoning talk, Anne and Miss Walker began 'kissing and pressing' on the sofa. Though Miss Walker had had the foresight to pull the blinds down ('Lucky. James had come in on trivial errands twice') they had not counted upon anyone else materialising at the door of the drawing room. In the midst of their entanglement, just after four o'clock, Mrs Priestley walked in. She had opened the door without knocking.

I had jumped in time and was standing by the fire but
Ann looked red and pale and Mrs P must see we were not

A portrait of Anne Lister as a child.
© Shibden Hall, Calderdale Museum

Anne Lister sitting in a chair –
thought to be the same portrait
mentioned in Anne's diaries in
November 1822 when she 'laughed'
at how good the likeness was of her.
© Shibden Hall, Calderdale Museum

Uncle James (1748–1826), posthumous, by Joshua Horner (1811–1881).

© Shibden Hall, Calderdale Museum

Aunt Anne (1765–1836) by Thomas Binns, commissioned in 1833 – 'Promises to be a very good likeness' Anne Lister said on 8th June, 1833.

© Shibden Hall, Calderdale Museum

Marian Lister c1855 (1797–1882) – Anne's sister and only surviving sibling.

© Shibden Hall, Calderdale Museum

An early mid-19th century engraving printed by Nathaniel Whitley bookseller. His shop, on Crown Street, Halifax, was where Anne ordered ink, blank diaries and books. It is the tall building on the left. Sadly now demolished.

© Calderdale Libraries

Anne's diaries from 1816, 1832 and 1840.

© Shibden Hall, Calderdale Museum

Photograph of Shibden Hall c1930.

© Shibden Hall, Calderdale Museum

Shibden Hall today, now open as a museum to the public.

© Lookout Point

First known page of Anne's diary from 1806 written when she was fifteen years old – 'Eliza left us,' she writes, 'Had a letter from her on Wednesday morning'.

The aborted coal lease in 1833, between Anne and business rival Christopher Rawson Esq. Full of clauses and penalties, Jeremiah Rawson said 'he never saw such a coal lease, would never sign it'.

A travel case belonging to
Anne Lister.

Nous PIERRE BROWNE,

Charge d'Affaires de Sa Majesté Britannique près
Sa Majesté le Roi de Dannemarc,

Prions tous ceux à qui il appartient de laisser

librement passer *Madam Anne Lister, Dame Anglaise,*

nouvellement arrivée de Londres à Copenhague et ayant

l'intention de voyager en très incessament, avec
ses Domestiques et bagage,

sans *lui* donner, ni permettre qu'il *lui* soit donné

Empêchement quelconque, mais, au contraire, toute Aide et Assistance.

En foi de quoi, Nous *lui* avons accordé le

présent Passeport signé de Nous, et muni du Cachet de Nos Armes.

Donné à *Copenhague* ce *7 Octbr.* 18 *33*

N:

Gratis.

Peter Browne

Anne Lister's Danish passport, 1833. Peter
Browne the Charge d'Affaires afforded Anne
entry in to the Danish Royal Court.

Original watercolour drawing by Lady Stuart de Rothesay taken from Anne Lister's album, when Anne was travelling with her in 1830 in the Pyrenees and Spain.

© West Yorkshire Archive Service, Calderdale (SH:7/ML/MISC/8)

A revealing, naive pencil drawing found in Anne Lister's picture album and possibly by her. Is this her 'great dog' Argus who died in 1832? Hanging on the wall is a black cap similar to the one worn by Anne as described in her journals. The desk contains an inkpot, quill, candle and books, perhaps in readiness for the next page of her journal.

© West Yorkshire Archive Service, Calderdale (SH:7/ML/MISC:8)

A portrait of Anne Lister attributed to Halifax artist Joshua Horner (1811–1881). Standing in front is actress Suranne Jones as Anne Lister during the filming of *Gentleman Jack* at Shibden Hall in 2018.

© Lookout Point

particularly expecting or desiring company. She looked
vexed, jealous and annoyed.

8th October 1832

Whether or not Mrs Priestley's timely visit to Lidgate had
been inspired by John Booth's mistaken call at her house the
previous evening, there was no doubt that she now had the
measure of what the two women were up to. She asked, 'in
bitter satire', if Anne had been at Lidgate ever since she had
left her there the day before. The conversation continued
icily:

'No', said I, 'I only ought to have been. My aunt had been
in a host of miseries [about her staying out late]*'. Mrs*
P said, as if turning it all on this, 'Yes, she [aunt Anne
Lister] *was quite vexed with me.' I laughed and said 'I*
really did not intend on doing so [causing aunt Anne
worry] *again. 'Yes,' she replied angrily, 'You will do the*
same the very next time the temptation occurs'.

8th October 1832

Anne's jokey suggestion that the best way to calm Aunt Anne's
fears about her walking home in the dark might be to stay all
night at Lidgate infuriated Mrs Priestley further. She left in
'supressed rage'. 'Plain proof,' thought Anne to herself afterwards, 'of what you think and what you smoke [suspect] a little'.
Mrs Priestley's fears had been confirmed. She had witnessed the
affair between Anne and Miss Walker with her own eyes.

Anne's observation that her friend appeared jealous as well as annoyed is an interesting one. Whether Mrs Priestley feared being locked out of a friendship into which she had poured many hours, was affronted to have appeared naïve about the two women's intimacy, or was simply horrified by it, the friendship would never really recover.

If Anne worried that Mrs Priestley's interruption would put an end to her liaison with Miss Walker, she needn't have. In a surprising show of impetuousness for someone so inclined to anxiety, Miss Walker 'laughed and said we were well matched'. The threat of exposure could be returned to another day. For now, they picked up where they had left off:

> *We soon got to kissing on the sofa ... At last I got my right hand up her petticoats and after much fumbling got thro' the opening of her drawers, and touched (first time) the hair and skin of queer. She never offered the least resistance.*
>
> 8th October 1832

As dusk approached, Ann aired her question about who had taught Anne Lister to kiss. Judging that it was not the right moment to reveal her romantic history, Anne stayed quiet about Mariana Lawton, Vere Hobart, the flirtation with Mariana's sisters Harriet Milne and Anne Belcombe, her affair with single mother Maria Barlow in Paris, experiences with Isabella Norcliffe and Mary Vallance and her passion for Vere's aunt Sibella Maclean. 'Nature,' she maintained, had taught her to kiss.

Anne left Lidgate at 6.25pm. Miss Walker had given her a tartan cloak to wear, owing to the heavy rain, and a 'strong, driving wind' tried at least six times to blow her off the causeway as she walked. So strong was the wind that she struggled to get inside the gate at Shibden Hall. After changing her clothes, she went to her trusted aunt and told her about what had happened with Mrs Priestley:

> *Three or four minutes before dinner and immediately*
> *afterwards with my aunt and father – told them the*
> *adventures and news of the day, and how I had been at*
> *Lidgate yesterday and today. Told my aunt how cross Mrs*
> *William Priestley looked, and that I really thought Miss*
> *Walker was veering about a little and might perhaps give*
> *up Cliff Hill.*

> 8th October 1832

All that remained was to record the events of the day and get ready for the next. 'Sat up preparing for my cousin,' Anne wrote in her diary, 'And washing out stains done since dinner' – an ordinary end to what had been a truly extraordinary day.

CHAPTER 7

A TRIP TO YORK AND BAD NEWS FOR MISS WALKER

'If I can only manage her
tolerably the first night'

The next morning, Ann Walker appeared largely untroubled by the potential ramifications of Mrs Priestley's impromptu visit to Lidgate. She did, however, jump at an opportunity that presented itself to open communication again with Anne. Her tenant, Collins, had removed his cows without permission from her land to a plot in the neighbouring village of Wyke. Her note asking for Anne's advice on the matter began:

> How little did I imagine when we parted last night that I should so soon have had the pleasure of addressing you my dear friend. Under other circumstances I should not have dared to take up my pen, but the plea of soliciting your advice seems at least a tolerably fair excuse.

9th October 1832

Recognising that Ann was seeking assurances following the previous evening's intimacy, Anne Lister knew exactly how to pitch her response. Having thanked Ann for the grapes she had sent to her aunt, and for the loan of the tartan cloak

('Except among Alps and Pyrenees, I know not when I have been out in such a storm of rain and hurricane of wind, which last was so strong against me that I was literally blown off the causeway five or six times'), her language shifted to address the real motive behind Miss Walker's letter:

> *Your note, my love, surprises me, but surprise is not the only or the uppermost feeling which engrosses me. I leave you to imagine what I mean. For surely you already know me too well to wrong in any surmise you may wish to make ... Forgive me if I can hardly regret even your vexation about Collins. Remember that it is to him I owe your note, and to him I owe this present unexpected pleasure of assuring you.*
>
> 9th October 1832

It was amorous and direct. 'I wonder what she will think of this,' Anne mused afterwards. 'In fact,' she continued, 'she will soon I think put me less and less in competition with Cliff Hill – if I can only manage her tolerably the first night.' So far there had been only fondling and kissing. Anne was yet to stay the whole night at Lidgate, and remained somewhat insecure about her ability to sexually satisfy Miss Walker.

By way of a distraction, Anne turned to her books. After ten pages of French vocabulary, she read the first hundred of *Sketches of India* by Captain Skinner. She was 'enthralled' by a passage that described the country's magnificent architecture:

Tomb of Acbar, near Agra, and also near there the Taaja
Mahal, the crown of Edifices, the mausoleum of Shah Jehan
(father of Aurungzebe) … 'they tell you … that it is the
most superb mausoleum in the whole world.'

12th October 1832

Planning her next foreign adventure was a constant preoccupation for Anne. If things with Miss Walker were to stand
any chance of lasting success, Miss Walker must be willing
to accompany her abroad. It was not yet clear whether Ann
had either the inclination or the disposition for travel, but she
certainly had the financial resources. And if she didn't want to
spend her money, it seemed that there were plenty of members
of her family who would be happy enough to spend it for her:

She then showed me the letter from her cousin Mr Edward
Atkinson, thanking her for her offer of lending him five
hundred, but asking the loan of three thousand. Wrote her
a copy of answer which she wrote verbatim, saying she had
meant to give him the five hundred but could do no more,
straitened by her late purchases, etc., for the present. The
magnitude of her expenses uncertain for the future.

11th October 1832

The letter to cousin Atkinson was the first of many that Anne
would dictate for Miss Walker over the coming months. Her
written articulacy and verbal guidance were increasingly relied
upon by Miss Walker, who, Anne noted, consulted her 'about

her concerns' in both estate affairs and personal matters (17th October 1832). Perceiving that Miss Walker had nobody else to defend her corner, Anne was glad, for now, to be depended upon for help.

Her top priority was to arrange the visit to Dr Belcombe in York. Mindful perhaps of a conversation she had once had with Mrs Priestley about Miss Walker's religious melancholy and 'tendency to mental derangement' (30th August 1828), she sensed that Ann's recurring lower back pain was somehow linked to her anxiety and nervousness. She felt that Steph, at the cutting edge of medicine, would be the man to unpick how Miss Walker's precarious psychological state fed into her physiological ill-health.

Anne's determination to take Miss Walker to see Steph Belcombe also reflected the degree to which Miss Walker's illness was starting to have an impact on her too. Her naturally optimistic character was beginning to be tested by the weight of Ann's negativity. She found herself bothered by Miss Walker's lack of self-esteem. Paying Miss Walker a compliment on 'how nice she looked in her evening gown for dinner', she was told that it was nothing but 'proof ... how blind love is' (9th October 1832). She seemed to predict that such a lack of confidence would imperil their future happiness.

Meanwhile, Anne was still considering Eugenie Pierre as a maid. Eventually, after a thorough vetting from her high-class friend, Lady Stuart, the young Frenchwoman was deemed a suitable hire. It had been a long and thorough search. Eugenie accepted the job at 'twenty-four pounds sterling per annum' ('six hundred francs'), but it would be many months until she and her mistress became acquainted.

As she became more deeply involved in Miss Walker's life and affairs, it remained important to Anne to keep on top of her own. The structure of her days was vital to her mental well-being. Ordinary tasks like 'mending pelisse sleeves' or 'planting out the hollies, shrubs, 6 Ragland oaks, and one gigantic weeping elm' were daily personal achievements, recorded diligently in her journal.

Anne's robustly productive days at Shibden were in contrast to Miss Walker's at Lidgate. 'Miss W ... not well and lay on the sofa' is a fairly typical phrase of Anne's diary in this period. On 13th October 1832, the same day that Marian Lister had returned by stagecoach from her extended stay in Market Weighton, Anne's attempts to give physical comfort to Miss Walker were brushed off:

> *She was very tender – I talked soothingly and affectionately, said how gentle I would be, expressed my anxiety for her health, and she said she would go with me to York this month.*
>
> 13th October 1832

Despite this, Anne maintained that Miss Walker 'seemed better tonight of late'. Indeed, 'her affectionate manner did make me feel in love with her'.

There was a change in tone when Anne moved the topic of conversation on to money. Telling Miss Walker that she 'only wished she had but a third of what she had, and no Cliff Hill, and then we might have managed all without difficulty', she was confused by Miss Walker's response. 'Oh no,' Ann said, 'The difficulty would have been far greater.' Unable to fathom Miss Walker's meaning, Anne opened up a little more about her own life, about her inheritance, about her former debts, and about her time in Paris when she got into scrapes with women:

> *I told her my uncle aunt together had given me more than five hundred pounds one year, and my uncle Joseph had had once paid my debts, but if I had not been as I was* [a capable land manager], *perhaps neither I nor Marian would have had the estate. Mentioned having Cordingley with me in Paris, but did not say where we were. Told some of the queer stories, and said I had always been too great a pickle but was quite different now.*
>
> 13th October 1832

Despite Miss Walker's reticence around the subject of their living together as companions, and the resulting uncertainty about the direction of their affair, the two women's physical relationship continued to develop. Anne Lister took this as a sign that Miss Walker was preparing to accept her proposal:

> *I undressed in half-hour, and then went into her room. Had her on my knee a few minutes and then got into bed, she making no objection ... grubbling gently ... She whispered*

> *to me in bed how gentle and kind I was to her, and faintly*
> *said she loved me.*

15th October 1832

However, Anne's accounts of Miss Walker's continued uncertainty proved that it was by no means a done deal:

> *Her cousin came this morning, and I was most tender*
> *over her, till just at ten. I joked about our being just*
> *as good friends if she was settled at Cliff Hill, and I*
> *at Shibden. 'Then,' said she, 'we must give up all this'*
> *(meaning our fondling). 'Could you,' said I, 'Give me*
> *up easily?' This led to, her mind was not made up ... I*
> *had my hand at her queer, spite of her cousin, and we*
> *had gone on just like a married pair, I telling her all*
> *sorts of things.*

19th October 1832

It was 11.20 by the time Anne appeared back at Shibden that night. Cordingley, who had stayed up to await her return, told Anne 'how uneasy' her aunt had been about her staying out so late again. Indeed, when Anne went in to say goodnight, she could see that Aunt Anne was 'vexed'. She decided to put a positive spin on her progress with Miss Walker. 'All had gone on well,' she said, and:

> *Miss W had considered me, and made me stay, and talked*
> *and treated me exactly as if her mind was in reality made*

up to take me, and I felt almost sure, and no two people
could get on more lovingly and well.

19th October 1832

The account she gave her aunt conflicted with feelings Anne
had expressed about Ann Walker elsewhere in that day's
journal entry. Walking home in the dark, she had felt distinctly
'annoyed' at their stalemate, and resolved that she 'had best
care little about her'.

It was a feeling that persisted over the following days. The
more Ann Walker prevaricated, the more Anne Lister faltered
herself, while at the same time maintaining the pressure on
Ann to commit:

Joked, and said I knew Miss Walker meant to say no, that
she would break my heart at last, but she would never
hear of it … Then, said she, 'I must say yes, or give you up
entirely.' Said [I], what else could she expect – people who
feel moderately might act so. How could I do so? I had
nothing for it but one extreme or other … I know she would
like to keep me on so as to have the benefit of my intimacy
without any real joint concern.

20th October 1832

If her feelings about Ann Walker were increasingly conflicted,
it didn't prevent Anne from pressing ahead with the plan to
seek advice from Dr Belcombe. On 14th October she had
written to Mariana, informing her of the upcoming visit to

her brother, and asking for her discretion. 'My taking Steph such a patient,' wrote Anne, 'would not be taken very well hereabouts, if known.' The stigma around Miss Walker's affliction roused a protective instinct in Anne. Of the nature of her 'friendship' with Miss Walker, she revealed nothing to Mariana.

At 11.35am on 22nd October, Anne and Ann set off from Halifax by carriage, and five and a half hours later they arrived in York. For respectability's sake, two rooms had been booked at the Black Swan Inn on Coney Street. Though the circumstances of their first joint trip away from Halifax had little to do with pleasure, Anne would not miss out on the opportunity to catch up with friends. As well as Mr and Mrs Duffin of 58 Micklegate, and Tib's sister Charlotte Norcliffe, she dropped in on Mariana's sister, Harriet Milne.

Anne and Mrs Milne had undertaken a love affair some years previously, and, while Anne was wary of Harriet – who had developed a fixation on her following the end of that relationship – they appeared immediately to resume flirting on this reunion:

> Mrs Milne rallied me about Miss W, but we made 'foot love' under the table. Appeared uncommonly glad to see them, and nothing could get on better – would willingly have spent the evening with them if I could.
>
> 23rd October 1832

But there were other visits to be made in York. Having popped to Barber and Cattle silversmiths for a seal, Anne ran a few errands for Miss Walker, including trips to Myers the coachmaker for carriage repairs and to the Will office to see 'about getting copy of Will of the late Mrs Priestley of Kebroyde for Miss Walker'.

Dr Belcombe began his consultation with Miss Walker soon after their arrival. Rather than at his practice directly behind York Minster, he attended to Miss Walker from the lodging rooms at the Black Swan Inn. The final verdict on her illness was confident and swift. It was delivered to Anne, with the patient herself absent:

> *Nothing the matter with her but nervousness. If all her fortune could fly away, and she had to work for her living she would be well. A case of nervousness and hysteria. No organic disease. Thought I should be sadly bothered with her abroad unless I had the upper hand, and ought not to pet her too much. But going abroad would do her good.*
>
> 23rd October 1832

Dr Belcombe's diagnosis was simple. Miss Walker had too much money and too little to do, and had managed to think herself into being ill. Tincture of henbane was among the treatments he prescribed, along with the advice that Anne should maintain the 'upper hand' by not unduly indulging her patient's nervous complaints. It was a diagnosis typical of its time, reliant on the gendered concept of hysteria to explain away symptoms of mental illness.

There is no record of Miss Walker's response to her diagnosis. It is clear that, in spite of Dr Belcombe's dismissal of the underlying cause of her physical symptoms, her pain persisted. The following day, Anne's crypt hand reveals 'no grubbling last night – she was sore' (24th October 1832).

Though Steph's level of understanding about Anne and Ann's relationship is not clear from Anne's diary, the fact that they were offered to extend their stay in York at the Belcombe residence hints at acceptance. In the event, they declined, leaving York on 25th October. The long journey back to Halifax was punctuated by a stop at Leeds and a little 'grubbling' in the carriage. 'Felt her queer' Anne wrote later, 'it being dark.'

It appears that the two women were becoming carried away in their conversation, too. They would, they decided, buy a bed together out of their joint income, each bring their own crockery to the partnership, and spend only two thousand a year on travelling.

They were talking as if all 'seemed quite agreed', Anne wrote, 'tho' without any decided "yes" on her part. She is evidently much attached to me.'

<hr/>

'We talk and act as if yes was all but said'

Despite the warning signs, Anne Lister was, by now, cautiously optimistic about her future with Miss Walker. There was an attraction and understanding between the two women that overrode her doubts about Miss Walker's inconsistency and nervous disposition. In many ways, she found Miss Walker's dependency on her appealing. As their affair progressed, Anne's emotional stake in Miss Walker was becoming ever greater.

However, on their return from York, Ann Walker was greeted by news which was to trigger a deterioration in her mental health and would prove a significant obstacle to happiness with Anne Lister. Paying a call at Cliff Hill on 26th October, Ann was handed a black-edged envelope by her aunt. It contained the news that her friend, Mrs Ainsworth, had died 'in consequence of being thrown out of an open carriage'. The letter, Anne reported, dropped from Miss Walker's fingers to the ground as soon she had read it.

Her pragmatic response to the death of the friend whose visit she had anticipated in the new year – 'Well now there is no obstacle to our getting off [abroad] in January' – belied Miss Walker's true feelings. Anne Lister was able to perceive that she was in fact 'much affected'. It would, however, be several days before Anne would realise the extent to which the bereavement was affecting Miss Walker, and why.

In the meantime, Anne and Ann settled back into life in Halifax. As October drew to a close, Anne described a healthy sex life ('lay in bed grubbling and love-making till our linen was almost as wet as yesterday morning') and a 'comfortably cosy' routine of overnight stays at Lidgate (27th October 1832). She seemed to be making headway with Miss Walker's family, too. Having taken the opportunity of 'agreeabilizing to the old lady [Ann's aunt]' during another visit to Cliff Hill, a social call of Mrs Priestley's to Lidgate on 28th October served to reassure Anne that the 'supressed rage' in which she had last seen Ann's cousin had subsided.

Mrs Priestley made no comment upon finding Anne Lister in Ann's company again. There was no allusion to her disastrous last visit to Lidgate. It may have been that, without the language with which to accuse the two women of a lesbian relationship, Mrs Priestley felt unable to confront them. Nor would the resulting scandal have reflected well on the family, if she had.

Reporting on their trip to York, Anne told Mrs Priestley about the consultation with Dr Belcombe and his advice that 'Miss Walker ought to get off and leave all pother [sic] behind'. Despite her perceptive reply that 'she would take it with her' wherever she went, Mrs Priestley did seem reassured that in seeking medical advice on her behalf, Anne had Miss Walker's best interests at heart. They parted, Anne wrote, 'very good friends'.

With their own friendship more visible than ever, Anne appreciated the need to maintain her popularity with Miss Walker's family. The charm offensive continued with her attention to the gardens of the Crownest estate. Unfortunately, the gardener at Lidgate proved himself to be somewhat lacking:

Took Sykes the gardener and looked over the Lightcliffe plantation for laurels. Sat about an hour with Miss [Aunt] *Walker of Cliff Hill. Gave Miss W one of the fine large,*

common laurels growing at the Stags Head, and Sykes the
gardener and Eastwood went for it, and just got it planted
here (Lidgate) before dark. Sykes positive and stupid about
it, and I got annoyed and gave him a set down. He had not
got it up well.

30th October 1832

The receipt of another brace of pheasants from Isabella Norcliffe provided an opportunity for Anne to air her positivity about the affair. Without revealing the extent of her feelings to Tib, she mentioned the 'really nice girl' Ann was turning out to be.

Anne demonstrably felt the relationship to be on a good track. She wrote that she was even beginning to consider taking up residence at Lidgate, if and when Ann accepted her proposal. On the last day of the month, she convinced Miss Walker to reduce the term of their arrangement:

At last got her to shorten the time of waiting for her final
answer from 3 April to 1 January. She seemed satisfied this
would be better ... she seems less and less likely to say no. In
fact we talk and act as if yes was all but said.

31st October 1832

If this seemed like good news, Anne's hopes for the relationship were not to last long. On the day Miss Walker had received the news of Mrs Ainsworth's death, Anne Lister had made a passing remark to her diary: 'It instantly struck me. She would in due time succeed her friend and be Mrs Ainsworth' (26th October 1832).

Unfortunately for Anne, her flippant comment was to prove remarkably perceptive. On 1st November, Ann Walker's confidence in their relationship began to unravel, triggered, in part, by the emergence of the widowed Reverend Thomas Ainsworth as a rival for her hand.

CHAPTER 8

THE REVEREND AINSWORTH, MISS WALKER'S INSULTING PURSE OFFER, ATTACKED BY A THUG, AND AN UNCERTAIN END TO THE YEAR

'She must now decide between
Mr Ainsworth and me'

On the first day of November, Anne Lister was shown a letter that convinced her history was set to repeat itself. It seemed to Anne a cruel twist of fate that she should once again be about to lose the object of her affection to a man. A letter from Reverend Ainsworth to Ann Walker had arrived that morning:

> *She begged me to stay till she had read her letter from Mr Ainsworth and this occasioned us such dolefuls* [sadness] *that I offered to stay till tomorrow … Ainsworth hopes Miss W will not forsake him as a friend and begs her to write to him … Oh oh thought I, all this is very clear.*
>
> 1st November 1832

What was clear to Anne was that Ainsworth's letter was more than an informative dispatch on the particulars of his wife's death. From the tone of his appeal for Miss Walker's friend-ship, Anne surmised – very incisively, as it would turn out – that he had romantic intentions. She predicted that this note marked a prelude to a request for Ann's hand:

I candidly told her what I thought. She owned [admitted
that] *she could not misunderstand him ... This led to my
saying that she must now decide between Mr A and me ...
Convinced her of this, and it ended in her resolving to give
me her final answer on Monday.*

1st November 1832

Anne's brisk tone concealed the depth of her feelings.
Behind her call for action was a desperation to know where
she stood with Ann. Despite her frequent claims that she
cared little what Miss Walker should decide, her long crypt-
hand diary entries in the days following Ainsworth's letter
record a period of intense emotional turmoil. For Ann
Walker, bereaved now of a close friend as well as a former
suitor, and grappling with her own sexuality, the letter was
even more affecting:

*Sat by her on the sofa, both of us perpetually with silent
tears trickling down our cheeks. She quite undecided,
fearing she should not be so happy with him as she might
have been. Never knew till now how much she was attached
to me. Should make comparisons to[o] in poor Mr Fraser's
favour ... Torturing herself with all the miseries of not
knowing what to do, she said how beautifully I behaved ...
She said there was as something in me she liked better than
in him. Felt repugnance to forming any connection with
the other sex.*

1st November 1832

The following day, Miss Walker agreed to give Anne a token of her lasting affection: a 'golden lock' of her own pubic hair. Anne, having 'kissed her queer', handed Ann the scissors to cut it herself.

> *She threw herself on the chair by me. We wept and kissed. I thanked her and she left me. She hung upon me and cried and sobbed aloud at parting. A pretty scene we have had, but surely I care not much and shall take my time of suspense very quietly.*
>
> 2nd November 1832

Anne's protestation that she should be 'easily reconciled either way' demonstrated not just bravado but a characteristic desire to retain an outward dignity.

It was a preoccupation that carried into her business concerns, which offered a timely distraction from Ann Walker's impending decision. Thirty minutes after returning to Shibden Hall, Anne found herself hosting Jeremiah Rawson. Mr Rawson, who had finally come to negotiate over the price of her coal beds, found himself at the receiving end of Anne's sharp tongue. She was in no mood to bargain, and swiftly rejected his offer of £160 per acre:

> *I would not abate at all from what I asked when he was here before … that is, the middle price between the two prices at which my uncle had sold the lower bed to Messrs Oates, Green, Hinscliffe & Co.*

Jeremiah was not prepared for such a firm response. He made the mistake of telling Anne he had expected that she 'should have been more reasonable':

If he knew me at all he would know that I should not swerve from what I said, but that in fact I had heard a good deal about the coal since I saw him, and so far from being better, should be worse to bargain with. Said that even if we agreed as to price I would only sell the coal in parts and parcels.

2nd November 1832

Faced with Anne's confident understanding of the small print of a coal lease, Jeremiah continued to falter. Rejecting her request to go down his existing pit until he said they 'had made the bargain' (presumably fearing she would discover their trespass of her land underground), he was met with a firm refusal to cooperate. 'Very well,' Anne told him, 'I will not sell according to the quantity you can get, but according to the quantity I myself choose to dispose of, which I will take care shall be little enough at a time' (2nd November 1832).

Despite knowing that she might eventually have to offer an abatement on her price, Anne remained non-committal. She revealed that she intended to leave for the continent in January, and was reluctant to make a decision until after her return. Her strategy to keep Jeremiah keen appeared to be working. Noting how 'determined' she was, he resolved to go away and 'consider about it again'.

Anne Lister hadn't been bluffing when she had told Jeremiah Rawson that she had learnt a lot about coal since his last visit. Having turned frequently to James Holt for his insights, she had been advised in no uncertain terms that she could expect to make a great deal of money by sinking her own pits and mining the land for herself.

However, it soon became apparent that the Rawsons were prepared to play dirty.

Later that week, Holt returned with some alarming news about their Machiavellian business practices:

James Holt came at 4.5/11 and had him till 6. Something must be wrong that Mr Jeremiah Rawson will not let [me] go into their works – probably they are stealing my coal already – Holt says I should not take less than £200 per acre, but if he was in their place he would not give £250 per acre. Said I had at last asked the price between the two leases (£205 and £230) = £217.10.0, but had said I should be worse to deal with now ... owned afterwards it would be as well not to let him come lower than the Cunnery houses for if he got down to the brook he could throw a quantity of water upon us ...

Holt would meet JR on the ground and see what he wanted ... In making the agreement to have surface measure and the power to send down people into the works whenever I liked, and to have a clause to prevent JR damming or turning on water back into the old

works after he had got the coal. Had I not better have a
bond of indemnity again this? Otherwise he might drown
me in water.

6th November 1832

Anne asked Holt to give her 'an underground plan of a pit in working'. Her intention was to gain a practical knowledge of mining by accompanying her coal steward underground. 'I must understand coal-getting before I have done with it. Holt's pit at Binns Bottom will be ready for working in two months,' she wrote.

With the coal deal progressing, Anne turned to her travel plans. Unwilling to let the cloud of uncertainty around Miss Walker's decision stall her, she forged ahead with her scheme to leave the country in the new year, her aunt's health permitting.

But for this, Anne would need money. The tantalising wealth on offer via Miss Walker relied on her romantic commitment. Without it, Anne would need to explore other avenues.

A trip into Halifax was not wildly encouraging. 'Went to the bank – got £50, and then the balance against me equals £14,' she reported on 3rd November 1832.

However, the visit to town did give Anne the opportunity to undertake some business on Miss Walker's behalf. Still hopeful for their joint future, she remained fiercely protective of Ann's interests and asked her solicitor to draft a request for compensation from Miss Walker's tenant Mr Collins, whose latest misdemeanour was to steal Ann's hay. While she was with Mr Parker, he informed her that:

> *Hinscliffe wants to buy more coal off her* [Miss Walker].
> *He wants a clause inserting to allow him to burn the shale*
> *on the land to enable him to sell it for road making – after*
> *burning it and making a great nuisance in the field.*
>
> 3rd November 1832

Anne made a crypt-hand note to herself to follow up the matter on decision day: 'She [Miss Walker] will wait till she has consulted me on Monday morning.'

Mr Parker had intelligence for Anne, too. Jeremiah Rawson had paid the office a visit directly after his call at Shibden Hall 'to inquire about the particulars of my [Anne's] coal leases'. Anne was gratified to learn that, sharing her suspicion of the Rawsons' methods, her long-standing and trusted solicitor had given away nothing to Jeremiah. Having told Rawson that he had no access to Anne's leases and 'knew not much about them', Parker warned Anne to maintain caution in her negotiations. Her plan to drive the brothers' interest appeared to be working. They 'seemed so anxious to have my coal', she noted (3rd November 1832).

Arriving back at Shibden that afternoon, Anne wrote to Miss Walker a long, advice-filled letter. She appeared to be channelling her nervousness about Ann's final decision into practical management of her estate. It also served as a way to prove her credentials as a partner and protector:

I am not quite certain whether you wished me to keep
Messrs Parker & Adam's letter to Collins, till Monday or
not. You will seal it, fill up the direction, and I hope, send
it by the servant or give it in charge of Washington to be
delivered as soon as possible. You had best explain the thing
to Washington as soon as you can, inquiring if he knows of
anything more taken from the premises than the straw we
saw on Thursday, and adding that, as Collins has so clearly
given you to understand it is his intention to get all he can
out of the land, you have made up your mind too avail
yourself of all the protection the law affords.

3rd November 1832

The only hints at the complicated situation between the women came in Anne's sign-off: 'I am very anxious to hear you are better than when I left you, a verbal answer will be quite enough to tell' – and her affectionate note under the letter's seal. 'Il rest un siècle de trois jours' ('there remains a century of three days') was a romantic framing of the eternity she felt she would have to wait to see Miss Walker again.

But Anne did not have to wait long for a reply. At nine o'clock a note came back to Shibden. 'I feel your kindness,' Miss Walker had written, 'it is consistent with all your actions.' She continued:

I cannot resist the temptation of writing a line or two, for
I so truly feel with you 'il rest un siecle de trois jours' …
Words are powerless to express my thanks [for dealing with

her tenant]. *Suffice that it is your gift ... I have been better today because I have been employing myself for you, but I am still very nervous. I dare not add more. Gratefully and affectionately yours, A.W.*

Anne looked to her diary for answers about Miss Walker's intentions, asking herself:

Now is this or is it not like a person who is going to refuse me? What will be the end of it? Does she or does she not know her own mind already? Or will she really be undecided until the last moment?

Anne resolved to do what she often did in such situations, and put her trust in God to allow her to 'be happy and satisfied and happy either way'.

News soon arrived that Donald Cameron's father had died, delivered in a note from Lady Stuart the following day: 'Donald must return to England – Lady S hopes he will leave Vere where she is, for it will never suit her to winter in the Highlands instead of at Naples' (4th November 1832).

It prompted Anne to reflect on the 'extraordinary fate of things'. It was exactly a year since she had arrived at 15 Pelham Crescent in Hastings, full of hope for a match with Vere Hobart. Now, her mind was full of an entirely new dilemma, 'Wondering, what will be mine tomorrow. Will Miss W take me or not?'

'I have written the words on a slip of paper and put
them in the purse. I have implicit confidence in your
judgement ... the paper you draw out must be the word'

Anne Lister's shock and anger at the method her lover finally
employed to deliver her answer is not hard to fathom. On the
morning of 5th November, after weeks of prevarication, a note
arrived nestled in a basket of fruit which placed the future of their
relationship in the hands of fate. Ann Walker asked Anne, or her
aunt, to choose at random either 'yes' or 'no' from a purse:

I have endeavoured to express myself in the most gentle
and delicate manner possible ... I would rather have
been silent for the present, until grief had become more
subdued ... nevertheless ... I find it impossible to make up
my own mind. For the last 12 months I have lived under
circumstances of no common moment and with my health
impaired, and with vivid regrets of the past, I feel that I
have not the power fairly to exercise my own judgement.
My heart would not allow me to listen to any proposal of
marriage, and this is in effect the same. I would simply go
on and leave the event to God ... I have written the words
on a slip of paper and put them in the purse. I have implicit
confidence in your judgement ... the paper you draw
out must be the word, or if you prefer, let your good aunt
draw ... you may think this an evasive termination of my
promise. Forgive me, for it is really all I can say. Having
heard you say that in one case [if 'no'], *I must give you up*

as a friend, I find myself incapable of consenting to this, as I am under my present feelings what is to be my future course of life. Whatever the event, I shall always remain your faithful and affectionate A. W.

Having opened the note 'in agitation, little expecting to find it a mere evasion', Anne Lister was not impressed. 'All between us as undecided as ever,' she wrote impatiently. Within ten minutes she was on her way to Lidgate, armed with the purse, the insulting slips of paper still inside.

She was to find Ann Walker awaiting her. 'We kissed and she was as affectionate as usual,' Anne wrote, waiting until after the interruptions of visits from Ann's cloth merchant, Mr Outram, and friend, Mrs Dyson, to address the contents of 'the memorable note'.

'I told her I had not been prepared for her note this morning,' wrote Anne, having reminded Miss Walker of the lock of pubic hair she had given her on 2nd November. 'Said she had misled me ... Did not blame her – it was an unlucky inadvertence that had led to all our present difficulties.' Anne was alluding to the death of Mrs Ainsworth. But now, warned Anne, 'There had been too many endearments and too great a tie between us for me to go back to what I had been.' She and Miss Walker had gone beyond the point of friendship and she was losing patience. The time had come, Anne felt, to 'put an end to our travelling together so long as she is undecided'.

Ann Walker did not seem to have considered the prospect of the withdrawal of Anne's affection and support. 'But, said she, she could not now stay at home and be bothered with Mr Ainsworth's letters, and be without protection.' Realising she was at risk of losing Anne Lister altogether, Miss Walker's hesitation all but vanished. As Anne remarked drily, 'She would gladly enough travel with me now.' Walking back to Shibden, guided by the 'fine moonlight', she dwelled on Miss Walker's repeat vacillations:

> On leaving her I repeated myself, 'Come nerve yourself up and never mind', and on getting home, said 'Well, it is an arrow and perhaps a lucky escape. Thank God for all his mercies' ... I have asked myself once or twice – is this a sort of spell breaker? Should she even say yes at last? Should I value it as much as if it had come more freely?
>
> 5th November 1832

Anne remained conflicted herself. She turned to the comfort of her journal to straighten out her thoughts. 'Dined at 6.45 and afterwards till 9.30 wrote all but the first six lines of today,' she wrote, 'much better for it – my mind more composed.' Tomorrow would bring a renewed determination 'to have all ready to be off in January', leaving Miss Walker and her indecision behind.

In an attempt to put the matter out of her mind, Anne attended to business at Shibden. On 6th November, Anne's land steward Samuel Washington was instructed to prepare 'all the bills next week for weaning mystal at Southolme'. A joiner was consulted about the new library passage. Marian was called upon for her opinion on flannel for Anne's new 'waistcoats and drawers', and there were visits to the vicarage and Whitley's bookshop in Halifax.

But Anne found that she couldn't stay away from Lidgate for long. Arriving at the gate, she was met by Samuel Washington, who had called to enquire about Miss Walker's health. She was, Washington told Anne, 'much better and in good spirits' at the prospect of Anne's visit.

Though Ann Walker did seem pleased that Anne Lister had returned to Lidgate a day earlier than she had promised, the resulting meeting did not satisfy Anne:

Talked of the agreeable surprise of seeing but yet seemed more inclined to talk of business than love. I appeared in more than good spirits. She would think them all put on, and perhaps believe me feeling more acutely than I really did. I kissed her but in a common way, and she did not push herself to me as yesterday, and was more guarded.

She will not give me much reason now either to hope or despair. Her self-possession will probably be undisturbed enough. I left her with no pleasant feeling, saying to myself damn her. It is an arrow and perhaps lucky escape. I do not think her answer will be yes, and the more easily reconciled I am the better. Shall I dislike her by and by? At least I shall be more at liberty without her.

6th November 1832

'I reasoned her out of all feeling of duty or obligation towards a man who had taken such base advantage'

The unfavourable terms in which Anne Lister was beginning to write about Ann Walker reflected her growing sense of foreboding for the relationship. Mrs Ainsworth's death and the threat of her widower's interest had cast a dark cloud over Miss Walker's already fragile mental health and impaired her ability to make decisions about her future. Her procrastinations, always an irritant to decisive Anne, had become offensive.

If Anne Lister had begun to suspect that there was more to Ann's refreshed inability to commit than Ann was telling her, she would soon be proven right. On 7th November, Ann received another letter from Reverend Ainsworth. It appeared that Anne Lister's early prediction had been correct. Here, in Ainsworth's floral language and address to 'his affectionate Annie', was unambiguously romantic intent. The letter prompted a confession. Miss Walker revealed that her relationship with Ainsworth had not been platonic:

> Miss W nervous, in tears perpetually ... At last, from little to more, it came out ... I pressed for explanation and discovered that she felt bound to him by some indiscretion. He had taught her to kiss.

> 7th November 1832

It was unclear exactly how intimate Miss Walker had been with Mr Ainsworth. Though she told Anne that 'they had never gone as far as she and I [Anne] had done', Ann was tormented by her implication in what she considered the worst kind of adultery. She had lived the few days since Mrs Ainsworth's death in terror that in consequence of what had gone on, she was morally bound to commit herself in marriage to her friend's widower.

Anne Lister was quick to condemn Ainsworth and defend Ann:

My indignation rose against the parson. I reasoned her out of all feeling of duty or obligation towards a man who had taken such base advantage.

7th November 1832

Anne's confident reassurance that Ann was not bound to marry Mr Ainsworth appeared to lift the enormous weight that had been pressing on Miss Walker. Amazingly, it was at this moment that she finally accepted Anne Lister's proposal:

She said there was now no other obstacle between us and she would be happier with me ... I asked if she was sure of this. 'Yes quite' ... She asked if I would take her and gave me her word ... hoped I should find her faithful and constant to me. Thus in a moment that I thought not of was I accepted and the matter settled.

7th November 1832

It is an extraordinary passage, nestled within a long and ranging crypt-hand diary entry. After months of prevarication, indecision and doubt, Ann Walker was committing to a future with Anne Lister.

The fraught road to their engagement served to subdue the emotion of what might otherwise have been a joyful moment. Privately, Anne Lister was circumspect. She took Miss Walker's admission of her connection with Mr Ainsworth as proof that she had been deceiving her about her level of sexual experience. Her confession, Anne felt, explained the moments of surprising confidence Miss Walker had displayed among her hesitancy. In the weeks leading to Ann's revelation, she had questioned Ann's virginity:

> *I said there was a great deal of relaxation, and at last, said that but for her word to the contrary, I should have believed she could no longer pretend to the title of old maid. She took all very well – denied, but yet in such, sort as left me almost doubtful. She said she did not deny that she had been kissed.*
>
> 19th October 1832

Whatever the truth of Miss Walker's past entanglement with Reverend Ainsworth, the death of his wife had brought to the fore intense feelings of guilt and shame. Ann was deeply God-fearing, and the periods of depression that had marked her life to date had been characterised by bouts of religious mania. Now, her increased anxiety forced her to question how her relationship with Anne Lister would appear in the eyes of the Lord.

Unlike Anne, who had spent years combing the bible for passages that helped her to understand her lesbianism as a

God-given quality, Ann Walker had had almost no time to reconcile the sexual attraction she felt to another woman with her rigid interpretation of the scripture. Now, the memory of the adultery she had committed with Ainsworth forced her to confront the transgression of her relationship with Anne. It would mark the beginning of a rapid descent.

***

'There is some grinding trouble of the heart, some aching voids (if voids can ache), or something other that neither medicine nor I can reach'

The following day, further detail emerged. Miss Walker revealed that Ainsworth had pressed her to have sex with him. 'He had asked her to yield all, assuring her it would not hurt her,' Anne wrote, recording her response ('I held up my hands and exclaimed infamous scoundrel'). Miss Walker went on to tell Anne that the carbuncle ring she wore had been a gift from him. Anne took it from her finger. 'She would see nor hear of it no more.' Miss Walker 'made no reply or resistance' (8th November 1832).

A note from Miss Walker to Anne, sent later that day, demonstrated that Ann was unable to find solace in their relationship. She was depressed and regretful, 'humbled' by her involvement with Ainsworth. Calling at Lidgate the next morning, Anne found her languishing in bed, 'nervous and unwell'. Though she 'talked and reasoned her into being to all appearance better', Anne noted that there was 'no foot or queer washing' in Anne's ablutions, that her personal hygiene was beginning to suffer. It was in contrast to Anne's own fastidious cleanliness (9th November 1832).

A friend of Miss Walker's had also called at Lidgate that day. Miss Parkhill listened with Ann as prayers were 'read aloud' by Anne. But even the bible could bring no comfort. Miss Walker, feeling unable to sit for long, left her friends and retired to the sofa. An attempt was made to rouse her spirits with an outing to Cliff Hill, but there too she lay on the sofa in a hopeless languor. Most strikingly, she began making attempts to rescind her agreement with Anne. 'Thinks she has done wrong to say yes to me,' wrote Anne, 'is remorseful – thinks she was bound to Mr Ainsworth.'

What might under other circumstances have been a happy time for the newly engaged women was anything but. Anne found herself forced into the role of counsellor and care-giver. She inhabited it as best she could, offering words of love and patient encouragement, and gestures from the small – sending a 'stomach tin' (hot water bottle) against Ann's complaints of the cold – to the grand, proposing that she write to her jeweller for a beautiful turquoise ring. Ann was unable to appreciate them. She begged Anne not to send for the ring: 'she could not wear it in mourning'.

In the presence of Miss Parkhill, Anne was careful to moderate her behaviour 'for fear evidently of her gossiping about us' (27th November 1832). Anne knew that to arouse Miss Parkhill's suspicions would be to further increase Miss

Walker's anxieties. 'My conduct altogether bespoke a more than common influence tho' nicely done,' she wrote. 'What will Miss Harriet Parkhill think? But she likes me (Miss W says)' (9th November 1832).

In private, it did not take long for Miss Walker's familiar vacillations to resurface. She now told Anne that she could not possibly think of travelling with her. 'So weak as I am it would be madness in me to leave the kingdom,' she wrote. 'I must talk seriously with you on this subject tomorrow.'

If she was beginning to perceive that it was a hopeless cause, Anne persisted in attempting to allay Miss Walker's anxieties:

> *You know how well I can and do enter into all your feelings ... Excess of sorrow is in the very nature of things its own remedy – our mind and nerves will be stronger by and by. Even conscience is not always strictly just. She may be too lenient or too severe, or lulled to sleep ... We cannot judge ourselves, we are too mistrustful, too confident, too fearful, or too presumptuous. We walk in a vain shadow, but as I cannot believe you to deserve the 'torments of conscience'.*
>
> 9th November 1832

Ann Walker's 'torments of conscience' were not abating. In fact, she appeared inclined to sabotage her chances of happiness with Anne. 'She said ... she should be a deal of trouble to me if I had her' Anne reported on 9th November 1832. In spite of her condemnation of Ainsworth, Anne began to wonder if she was right. 'Shall I let her take the fellow, and myself have done with her? Will she not be more pother than she is worth?'

But Anne would not yet withdraw her support and affection. She promised Ann to 'talk over any plan most likely to re-establish your health' and within two weeks she was back in contact with Dr Belcombe, giving him her own diagnosis:

> *The mind is worse than the body, and in this respect I confess I find a nervous young lady much more difficult to manage than I expected. We have relapses which I can neither understand nor guard against. There is some grinding trouble in the heart, some aching void (if voids can ache), or something or other that neither medicine nor I can reach.*
>
> 26th November 1832

In the face of a problem, Anne Lister's instinct was to seek a practical solution. She was used to managing her tenants, workers, staff and family members on a daily basis. She exercised an uncommon level of control over her life and circumstances. Yet now, she found herself unable to help Miss Walker. 'I see the best way is to speak as one having authority' she maintained, but even having 'parried all her arguments' against Miss Walker's fears of foreign travel, she could not fully convince Ann that leaving the country would not mean imminent death (16th November 1832).

Anne found herself increasingly exhausted by her attempts to cope with Ann's 'moody melancholy pother'. By 23rd November, she had resolved to 'give her back her purse, and "yes" and be off'. More letters from Ainsworth, accompanied by another ring for Ann in remembrance of his dead wife, sent Miss Walker deeper 'into the dolefuls'. Anne started to make plans for 'getting off' in January alone.

The two women were still physically intimate. Suspicions about Miss Walker's level of experience had never left Anne Lister, who now revisited the thought that 'she must have had some man or other' and that consequently, as a woman, she would 'never satisfy her'. Privately interrogating Ann's account of what had gone on with Ainsworth, Anne convinced herself that he had 'deflowered and enjoyed her' (25th November 1832).

That afternoon, Anne was threatened by a stranger as she walked from Lidgate to Shibden. Whether this was a random attack or a premeditated ambush, the man did not appear to have been prepared for Anne's spirited response to his assault:

An impertinent fellow with a great stick in his hand
asked if I was going home and made a catch at my queer.
'Goddamn you' said I, and pushed him off. He said
something which I took as meaning an attack, so said I
'if you dare I'll soon do for you' and he walked one way
and I the other. I did not feel the least frightened. How
involuntarily and bitterly I swear on these occasions!

25th November 1832

The following day, a visit from Jeremiah Rawson reopened the negotiations over Anne's coal. 'He asked if I would take 200 per acre,' reported Anne, who was determined to stay firm on her original quote and replied that she had already 'had £230 bid ... said I was determined not to take less'. Without revealing Hinscliffe's identity as the rival bidder, she sent Jeremiah away to consider her terms. He would have to consult his brother. Christopher, he told Anne, 'would think him mad to talk of that price' (26th November 1832).

Anne had also been trying to purchase a farm and some land on the Godley road, near Shibden. She believed that she had seen right through Mr Carr's inflated price: 'I am of the opinion that he has no customer, and if he has, no-one will give more than the sum [£2,200] I have mentioned,' she wrote. She decided to keep the deal to herself, not saying 'a word of Godley to my father and Marian' lest they should try and dissuade her from taking the financial risk (26th November 1832).

In fact, Anne had already been offered the extra funds as a loan from Miss Walker, but, feeling that it would be wrong to accept it without any formal commitment between them, she had resolved to stick to her original offer. She eventually let Marian in on the deal, but begged her not to tell their father. 'He was so deaf,' she wrote, 'I dread at people overhearing what is said' (30th November 1832).

When a letter arrived from Mariana Lawton, who was full of doom and gloom about 'many vexatious hindrances', it hardly contained the content Anne relished under present circumstances:

What the future brings forward, Fred, we can neither
of us guess at, but I still hold to my not very recently
adopted option that Mr Lawton will outlive me. With

this impression I shall leave all belonging to me here in such
order that there will be little trouble beyond burning one
parcel and sending off another, and something too like a
Will I have made.

27th November 1832

Mariana seems to have known something of Anne's plans to travel. While wishing that Anne 'could learn to have a little more care for old England', there is a hint of relief in her reference to the fact that Anne's next trip should be taken alone: 'Tells me I am far better off without a companion, than if I had one that did not suit me'.

Despite her husband's robust health, Mariana held onto the possibility that she and Anne might someday live together. For Anne, the relationship seemed more firmly at an end:

M's thought of ever being with me is quite gone by. I would
not let her leave Charles and on this account she has made
up her mind to stay with him, and will not be sorry should
her life not last very long. Whatever is, is right. The less I
think of her the better.

27th November 1832

Two days later, Anne heard from Miss Walker. An invitation to visit Lidgate that Saturday would give Anne an opportunity to present the Book of Common Prayer she had ordered for Miss Walker from Whitley's, 'bound in crimson Morocco with purple water silk fly leaves – and richly gilt' (29th November 1832).

In the event, Anne was called upon sooner than expected. On 30th November, James Mackenzie delivered an urgent note. Miss Walker was ill. Dr Sunderland had been sent for but Anne was required too. With pressing business to attend to at Shibden, Anne composed a comforting note for Miss Walker with instructions on how to fill the time until she arrived:

> *Keep yourself as quiet and your mind as tranquil as you can and banish from your thoughts everything that is unpleasing. Remember that the desert has its green spots and that in anger or in mercy, Heaven never afflicts us beyond that we are able to bear. You have at least one comfort if I may hope that it can be a comfort to you to be assured of this affectionate interest and regard of yours, very faithfully Anne Lister.*

30th November 1832

Anne dispatched her business as quickly and efficiently as possible, telling land valuer Mr Mitchell not to 'lose sight' of the Godley deal. A note from Jeremiah, informing Anne that he 'had almost persuaded his brother to let him take the ten acres at £230.10.10' on the condition that they were given the 'whole coal surface measure, and all the coal', was given short shrift. 'They want to smuggle both beds into the agreement which will not do,' wrote Anne, who was only prepared to lease one portion of her land.

By midday Anne had arrived at Lidgate. Though Dr Sunderland was officially attending the patient, it was Anne who made the diagnosis. 'When all trades fail,' she would write drily to Steph Belcombe that evening, 'I will set up for the cure of bodies'. Anne judged Miss Walker's fever to be a result of the medicines that Dr Belcombe had prescribed in York. 'An effect, not a cause, and said I was persuaded she had some mental uneasiness' (30th November 1832).

Ann Walker's 'mental uneasiness' was bound up with her belief that she had lost Anne for good:

> *She had been fretting all yesterday and last night because she thought from my note of yesterday that all was over and I had made up my mind to end the thing between us and she could not bear to part with me. Could not think what she meant. It was that I had concluded with 'affectionately yours' leaving out 'faithfully'. She said if I had gone away, she should never give up the hope of our coming together sometime. She had never felt drawn so close to me since Tuesday and now thought that I could make her happy and had prayed for us to be happy together. I did not say much but asked why, with these feelings, she refused me?*
>
> 30th November 1832

Ann Walker went on to admit that Miss Parkhill, who had left Lidgate 'in a huff' just before Anne arrived, had been bad-mouthing Anne in her absence. 'Miss Harriet Parkhill is all jealous and wrong' Anne wrote, implicating her in a wider network of Halifax gossips with whom she was unpopular, 'and has done all the mischief as Miss Walker owned'. In this instance, her attempt to discredit Anne seems to have back-fired. Praying that she and Anne might 'be happy together', Miss Walker became tentatively protective. Their conversation was testament to how reliant she had become on Anne. When-ever Anne left Lidgate, she told her, she would sink into a depression from which 'nothing could raise her'. 'Said I would do all I could for her as long as I could', wrote Anne. 'She said she should never have much confidence in anybody else.'

If Anne Lister's attitude seems hubristic, nobody else seemed able to give Ann a level of support approaching that which she was offering. Her interest in Miss Walker's welfare remained avid and heartfelt, as did her determination to prevent her from dwelling on her ailments by removing her from the limiting environs of her drawing room. She firmly believed that if Miss Walker could travel abroad, her experi-ence of the wider world would speed her recovery.

In appreciation of Ann Walker's inability to contemplate their agreement in her current condition, Anne Lister reinstated 1st January 1833 as her decision deadline. In a parallel attempt to buy herself more time, Ann Walker told Anne that she would like to write to her sister Elizabeth in Scotland for advice.

Replying to Mariana's letter on her return from Lidgate, Anne was able to be honest about the 'blue devils' she peri-odically experienced, without giving specific mention to her relationship with Miss Walker:

> *Somehow or other, my dearest Mary, your letter is a comfort to me ... you almost persuade me to forget what I have*

*longed for all my life, and to believe that I am better as I
am, than I should be if I had a companion. If I have not the
pleasure, I shall not have the pain, and I shall certainly get
rid of the blue devils which are by no means concomitant of
a temperament like mine ... you will be agreeably surprised
when you see me at Leamington. I am out all day long in
all weathers and it does me good. I am much stronger than
I was a few months ago and my spirit, though bending for
long beneath the tyranny of disappointment* [of Vere], *is
really starting up again with something like its former
elasticity ...*

 *I perpetually talk of getting off in January, but perhaps
I shall not be able, for I have several things in hand not
likely to be settled and done so soon ... what do you advise
me to do about a manservant? Do think about this for
me. I should like to have a good, steady, enterprising
English groom, who would take care of the carriage and
do anything I wanted doing while abroad. If I had such a
man to depend upon I should do well enough for the rest.
And this man of confidence might have the place he liked
at home, and stay with me to my life's end. Do pray give me
your opinion.*

30th November 1832

Though Anne did not name Miss Walker, her 'several things in
hand not likely to be settled and done so soon' may have been
enough of a hint for Mariana, who had heard about the medical
difficulties of Anne's 'friend' as a patient of her brother. In an

otherwise affectionate letter, Anne could not resist signing off with a dig at Mariana. 'I have sometimes been not so good as you thought,' she wrote, 'but very often not so bad. It is probable that you have never appreciated me exactly as I deserved.'

<hr />

'Well! Here is the end of another year!

As the end of 1832 approached, Ann Walker's mental health was deteriorating further. By 6th December, she had abandoned any thought of leaving home, in spite of her sister Elizabeth's advice:

> *Miss Walker read me last night the passage from her sister's letter respecting me. Very sensible. Advised Miss Walker going abroad with me. Thought it would do her good, and be of great advantage to her, all my acquaintances being of a high order. Yet all this did not seem to have much influence. She will not go abroad, and now, will not leave Lidgate on my going away.*

Aunt Anne was there to absorb Anne Lister's frustration. 'Said I had made up my mind, I should not bother myself – but Miss Walker was not fit to be left at Lidgate, and I should contrive some way for her' (7th December 1832).

Lady Vere Cameron, in contrast, seemed deliriously happy. Writing from Rome, she gushed about her husband's 'affectionate nature', which shone forth 'with a degree of unselfishness, and real good feeling, which of many worldlings could not understand'. Following his father's death, Donald Cameron had acceded to the title of twenty-third Chief of Lochiel. 'How can I bear to be left so many weary, long months at such a distance?' wrote Vere, contemplating her husband's premature return to his vast Scottish estate. Her enthusiasm for travel fuelled Anne's own appetite to quit England. She quoted passages of Vere's letter in her journal:

> *Very nice kind letter ... [Vere] recommends Mr Stark's 'Directions to Travellers' as an excellent road book, and very correct as to names and distance with a rarity of names and useful information. I have heard him called vulgar and not remarkably true in his history and chronology, but of that I am no judge. 'Conder's Italy I think a very nice little book, three small volumes ... the Campo Santa will charm you ... do not on any account miss the Cathedral at Siena ... the carved pulpits at Belgium are mere toys compared to the marble one there.'*

7th December 1832

Nine months on from the 'tyranny of disappointment' she had suffered in Hastings, Anne appeared reconciled with Vere's marriage to Donald, wishing the couple happiness in her reply:

> *One of these days I hope to know him much better and to see you both felices ter et amplius. God bless you my dearest Vere*

at this season and at every other. My regard for you is like
the law of the Medes and Persians which changeth not, and
you will find me always and affectionately very faithfully
yours, AL.

7th December 1832

There was more news from Mariana. She had found a potential manservant for Anne:

A man that had lived two years with the Kinnersley's – a
native of Lawton – a remarkably handsome, fine-looking
man ... understands horses and carriages, and as far as
words go, promises very fair and I believe would be most
glad to do anything in the way of making himself useful.

9th December 1832

This was 24-year-old Thomas Beech. Perceiving from this early
account that Beech would suit her well, Anne asked Mariana
to kit him out in the appropriate 'Oxford mixture jacket and
waistcoat and plush breeches and plain yellow buttons'. She
would reimburse her later (26th December 1832).

On 12th December, Anne received some valuable advice
on how to deal with the Rawson brothers. Hinscliffe, who
was competing against them for Anne's land, advised her to
bind the Rawsons in a strict lease, stating 'their heirs, exec-
utors, administrators and assigners under a penalty of £500
not to turn any more water on my [Anne's] coal (both beds)'.
James Holt had offered a similar warning. 'Turning the water'

referred to an underhand tactic by which competitors could flood their rival's mines. Keen to have the clause agreed, Anne resolved to heap pressure on Jeremiah and Christopher to deliver a final answer on the lease:

Dear Sir, if I do not hear from you respecting the coal before the end of this week, I shall feel myself at liberty to dispose of it. The other party have themselves valued at and offered me for the upper or hard bed, the same price at which I said you should have it. I am Sir, etc. etc. etc., Anne Lister.

18th December 1832

In fact, it was this threat of a £500 penalty that would ultimately sound the death knell for the deal. In February 1833, after months of 'blustering', Jeremiah Rawson would tell Mr Parker that 'he never saw such a coal lease, would never sign it'.

Anne found the whole thing 'tiresome'. Though there were moments of triumph – such as Jeremiah's admission on 24th December that 'he was never beaten by ladies' but that 'she had beaten him' on price (to which Anne replied acidly 'It is the intellectual part of us that makes the bargain, and that has no sex, or ought to have none') – she couldn't help feeling that all her 'backwards and forwards work' had been a waste of time. The failed deal left Anne to think more seriously now that she should sink a pit herself and 'set Holt to manage getting coals for me so as to look after Mr Rawson [i.e. teach him a lesson]'. She later said of him, 'He thinks he has me beaten, perhaps he will be disappointed' (25th February 1833).

In the months after the passing of the Reform Act, the spirit of change flourished across the towns and cities of the industrial north. In Halifax, Anne's favoured Tory candidate, James Wortley, lost out in the election to his Whig opponent. Anne vented her frustration to Lady Vere, who was a relation of Wortley's:

So thoroughly unexpected was the disappointment of Mr James Wortley's losing his election, I have not yet got up my political spirits – I hardly thought myself capable of such strong political excitement and mortification. I am completely sick of public events. The unions are still in full force. Many of the delvers [stone quarriers] *have turned into the work again. But they have gained the day, and got the advance of wages.*

31st December 1832

As the last days of December played out, Anne reflected on her year in business in a letter to Mariana, and hinted at her desire to be free to travel again:

Everything seems to go well with me, for though I have no gold mine, I feel I shall work my way through my inconveniences and have little cause to regret what I have done ... In fact, I hope I shall leave all my concerns more satisfactorily than I have ever done before. I have lately been much pleased with some business-like attentions from people upon whom I had no claim. I seem to have established myself

a character at least respectable. I see and feel that I have
nothing to complain of and all I am now anxious about is
to wind up my concerns and be on the wide world again.

26th December 1832

Her love life was judged to have been less of a success. By the
end of 1832 she was resigned to the fact that her situation
with Miss Walker was now one of complete hopelessness. With
Ann's unwillingness to commit to a life permanently with her,
matters had come to a head:

Miss Walker fretted and cried and sighed and said she
should not live long. I proposed her returning her notes,
and having mine. She said she had burned all that were
material, and wished to keep the rest. I begged to see them,
and then had no objection to her keeping them. She begged
me not to send back her history of Paris in three volumes. It
would be of no more use to her, and she wished me to keep it
... Parted in tears, both of us. I saying, I never did or could
understand her.

31st December 1832

After the strain of the last few months, Anne's regret over the
failed relationship was tempered with relief. Taking stock, she
looked to the future:

Well! Here is the end of another year! How different
this new year's eve from the last! Though in each case

unsuccessful love-making ... how different my situation now ... Quite off with Mariana, Vere married and off at Rome ... Miss Walker, as it were, come and gone, known and forgotten ... I have never stood so alone and yet am far happier that I was twelve months ago – in fact, happier than I have been of long. I am used and reconciled to my loneliness.

Believing that all really now *was* at an end with Miss Walker, Anne asked herself: 'What adventure will come next? Who will be the next tenant of my heart?'

CHAPTER 9

MISS WALKER'S DEPARTURE, CATHERINE RAWSON AND PLANS FOR 'GETTING OFF'

❧

> *'Magna est veritas, et praevalebit'*
> *'Truth is great and will prevail'*

T he year 1833 began badly. On New Year's Day, Anne reported that 'poor, old glandered Ball', her beloved shaft horse, was to be shot. Pickles put an end to his suffering as Anne looked on:

> *The poor horse had but a few of those feint convulsive movements and soon died, surely without having been considered in much pain. He was soon covered up where he fell.*
>
> 1st January 1833

Anne remained preoccupied with Miss Walker's declining mental health. Indeed, there had been a hint in her final diary entry of 1832 that Ann would not be as easily 'gone and forgotten' as Anne Lister had claimed: 'This girl, without really having my esteem or affection, somehow or other, unhinges me whenever I see her' (31st December 1832).

Now, in the first weeks of 1833, it was becoming clear to those around Ann Walker that an effective form of special-ised medical treatment needed to be found. Her anxiety was compounded by periods of insomnia and, when she was able to sleep, night terrors. Anne wrote to Steph Belcombe:

> *I never exactly understood before what nervousness meant and God grant that I may know no more of it in any case which concerns me much ... it is dreary to combat sickness without disease, and misery without reason.*
>
> 6th January 1833

Ann was suffering a complete mental breakdown. Symptoms of obsessive compulsion and agoraphobia accompanied her bouts of mania. The successive deaths of her lover and friend, not many years after the loss of her parents and brother, had taken their toll on an already fragile state. Dr Sunderland's precis of her symptoms – 'some little excitement of the mind' – was either euphemistic or a severe understatement (17th January 1833).

Miss Walker pointed to a 'want of confidence in God' at the root of her own illness. A fixation on her sins and the Lord's word characterised her melancholy now as in past patches of ill-health. On 8th January, she pleaded with Anne to pray for her immortal soul. 'It is not only death in this world, but a far worse death that I fear', she wrote. 'If ever the prayers of a so true friend may ever avail for another, may yours be heard for me this night, that the gate of Mercy may not be forever closed upon me, for I am wretchedness itself.'

Anne found herself caught between exhaustion at the 'melodrama' she witnessed at Lidgate and her instinct to protect the woman whose vulnerability continued to 'unhinge' her. Miss Walker talked of 'bitterly' repenting having made the earlier promise to Anne – a promise made from a 'bad motive' and only 'from the fear of being left'. Anne's response to this was sympathetic: 'Be assured of my saying and doing everything in the world I can to cheer and console you.'

Over the next few weeks, Anne turned to pragmatic measures in an attempt to relieve Ann's suffering. She was blunt with her at times, telling her that 'she laboured under mental delusions' (10th January 1833). She instructed Ann to keep a bowl of gruel by her bedside ('kept hot up, to be taken on awakening in the night'), and advised that the 'striking weight' be taken out of the clock to avoid waking her in the early hours of the morning. Ann had told her:

> *It is these hours of the night I so much dread, and they make me feel afraid of going to bed. Oh, my very dear friend, if I could have more faith, it would enable me to support better other afflictions.*

12th January 1833

By this time, Anne was sleeping at Lidgate regularly, to be on hand with advice and reassurance throughout the night. She suggested that repeating the Lord's Prayer might provide an antidote to Ann's insomnia:

> *Talked and reasoned calmly, then turned, and pretended to sleep. She refused all affection, and I did not press it.*

She scarcely, I think, closed her eyes until after 3, when I bade her say the Lord's prayer incessantly until I think she dropped off into a doze for a little while ... She, and the room and bed, smelt of Mr Day's turpentine ointment. I could sleep no better than usual, and longed to be once more creditably free from all this.

11th January 1833

Fearing that she was approaching death, Ann begged Anne to read extracts of the bible aloud. Anne selected and 'paraphrased the 10th of St Matthew', but it seemed that Ann was unable to be reached by its message of resilience and healing. Instead, she preferred to cast herself as the subject of 'Genesis Epistle, St James 1.6', whose lack of absolute faith in the Lord's ability to heal destined them to be cast adrift, 'driven and tossed by the wind, like a wave in the sea'.

'I think her beside herself,' wrote Anne, who understood the depth of Ann's mania (8th January 1833). Though she never doubted her own position as protector – 'It is evident I do her more good and have far more influence than anyone' (14th January 1833) – the emotional strain of caring for Ann was evident. 'Seeing her always unhinges me,' she wrote on 1st January. 'I was low and in tears at dinner and could not get her out of my head and why? For if I had her what could I do with her?' They were questions she could not answer, and on 10th January Anne judged that the time had come to share the burden of Miss Walker's illness with her family. 'I must write to her sister, or get rid of all of this in some way,' she confided to her diary.

Catherine Rawson, who had been drafted in to stay at Lidgate, was alarmed by the deterioration of her cousin's health. 'Miss W frightens her,' commented Anne. She had asked Anne what Miss Walker meant by her reference to 'other afflictions' (25th January 1833).

The Reverend Ainsworth continued to write, but following a thinly veiled threat to expose his adultery if he continued to communicate with Ann, it was Anne Lister to whom his long 'rigmarole' letters were addressed. His feeble promise – 'will not intrude on Miss Walker again . . . he said he hoped she would not, further from vanity, expose him, as her own character might suffer' – confirmed Anne's conviction that he was a spineless scoundrel. 'I assure you of the pardon you desire and that whatever confidence has been placed in me will not be abused,' she replied simply.

A letter she received from Captain George Sutherland on 11th January informed Anne that Miss Walker had written to her brother-in-law in Scotland herself. Sutherland was acutely concerned by the tone of Ann's latest letter. 'I am apprehensive she is in a more delicate state of health than we had any idea of, as it is evidently written under a feeling of gloomy despondency,' he told Anne, asking for more details of Miss Walker's affliction. 'It will confer a great obligation on me if you would kindly give me your candid opinion as to its nature.'

Responding immediately, Anne advised Captain Sutherland not to bring his wife – who was in a delicate state of health herself, having just given birth and nursing another child who had measles – with him on the long journey from Inverness to Yorkshire. She also suggested withholding the purpose of his visit until he had returned with Miss Walker. 'No time should be lost,' she warned, given the degree to which Miss Walker's state had deteriorated since their visit to Dr Belcombe the previous October:

> No occasion for Mrs Sutherland's coming. Your coming on the plea of business will be quite enough, as I dare say you will have no difficulty in persuading Miss Walker to return with you, but would you like Mr Belcombe to be written to and consulted in the meantime? Than whom I know of no-one on every account more likely to be of service. He is certainly a great favourite with Miss Walker, and would probably have more influence than any medical man she at present knows. My own confidence in him is great.
>
> 11th January 1833

With Captain Sutherland's journey south in hand, Anne found time to return to business at Shibden. Commissioning a local cabinet maker to craft her a new writing box, she became keenly interested in timber:

> It is the St. Domingo mahogany, which he calls Spanish, which is most beautiful. And the Honduras looks common but it is this, he says, that pays the best – much less duty paid on it.
>
> 14th January 1833

She was typically exacting about the piece of furniture, giving Greenwood her 'patent, rosewood cased ink bottle as a model for the ink stand place in my new writing box' (31st January 1833).

Work on the estate was progressing steadily. On one occasion, Anne's hands-on approach to the improvements ended with her submerged in the freezing water of the Red Beck:

Cutting and pruning in Lower Brook Ing wood and James Smith's holme. Cut longish Alder there, it fell across the brook, and in trying to walk over it, slipped off into the water and got wet halfway above my knees to my hips or more.

18th January 1833

At the top of the estate, hundreds of tonnes of earth were being moved by hand to accommodate the building of the new road through the Trough of Bolland Wood. As her men continued to dig, excavate and shore up the land, Anne revealed another grand plan to Pickles. She wanted to create a miniature replica of the Simplon Pass, a bridge she had admired during a trip to the Swiss Alps. The bridge that survives today is a testament to Pickles' team and Anne Lister's vision:

With Pickles at the deep cutting, 140 yards done, half way down the wood, 80 to do up to the deep dell. Pickles would fill it up. No! I would have two masonry piers built and throw over a Swiss wooden bridge, such as the one as the bridge over the torrents crossing the Simplon.

2nd February 1833

The 'Scotch Plan' agreed with her family, Anne convinced Ann Walker to consent to her stay in Inverness. She was honest with Ann about what the separation would mean for their relationship. Their contact must be limited, and discreet:

> *Thought she had better not write to me, better not begin a correspondence. I could hear of her from her sister. For being abroad, and uncertain of the fate of letters, must be careful – must begin with My Dear Miss Walker, and end with, Very Truly Yours. She said she would do whatever I liked, but had said before she would rather write to me than anybody.*
>
> 22nd January 1833

Ann Walker gave a hopeless plea to travel with Anne Lister in Europe. Anne replied as sensitively as she could:

> *Told her the time for that was gone by for the moment, but if, in a year's time, she thought she could not live without me, then she must send for me back again. Thus giving her hope that all is not, or needs not be, quite at an end between us.*
>
> 22nd January 1833

In private, Anne's hopes for Miss Walker's recovery were weak. 'Poor soul. Her mental misery must be great, feeling, as she says, it is all over. She has no hope of being saved' (24th January 1833). She was relieved when Ann submitted to the plan which would take her away from the 'evil spirits' she was still encountering at Lidgate. Miss Walker became resigned to her fate, understanding that Scotland, at least for the next few months, was going to be home for her.

A curious by-product of Miss Walker's illness was the friendship that formed between Anne Lister and Catherine Rawson. Catherine's poor opinion of Anne had altered significantly on witnessing her tender care of Ann Walker first-hand at Lidgate:

> *Miss R said she used to think me all that was disagreeable,*
> *and how wrong she was. She said what good I had done her,*
> *and wept over the injustice she felt she had done me.*

2nd February 1833

Catherine had originally perceived Anne to be 'the most dangerous friend and the worst enemy' anyone could have, owing to uncharitable society rumours (4th February 1833).

Anne was intrigued by Catherine's loan to her of Humphry Davy's *Consolations in Travelling, Or the Last Days of a Philosopher,* finding herself perplexed by the scientist's anti-empirical approach to life. Davy had made landmark discoveries in electro-chemistry. His latest work was, interestingly, 'More philosophical than thoughtful, more imaginative than demonstrable ... from the pen of a man who's mind was led by scientific interest' (27th January 1833).

To Catherine, Anne gifted a bespoke seal. Its motto, 'faites-bien laissez dieu', was accompanied with the following words: 'More than human the teacher makes the devil turn preacher, and good stead of evil fulfil, when in scandal's despite he bids

Catherine do right, let serpent-tribe hiss as it will.' The motto encouraged Miss Rawson to do good and put her trust in God.

Trusting in Anne too, Catherine was happy to collude with the Scotch Plan. She was asked not to reveal the nature of her cousin's illness to the wider network of their relatives, should their alarm scupper the effort to remove Ann from Lidgate. A routine of backgammon, garden walks, botany lessons, prayer and night-time vigils continued as the two women prepared for her departure.

In the meantime, Anne had also been consulting with Dr Belcombe. He suggested a complex 'sleeping draft':

> *Take tincture of Henbane – 40 drops, Laudanum – 6 drops, syr. of White Poppies – 1 drachm, Cinnamon or Nutmeg water – 1 ounce. Mix and make a draft to be taken at bedtime. The proportions of these may be increased to 1 drachm of tincture Henbane, and 12 drops of Laudanum.*
>
> 30th January 1833

Miss Walker would have to wait to receive the prescription, for heavy snow had begun to fall at Shibden by the end of January, and when Anne was begged by Ann Walker to go and spend the night with her, Anne was unable to, having been kept indoors by Aunt Anne who had made herself 'wretched' thinking about the prospect of her niece attempting the walk up to Lightcliffe (31st January 1833).

Ann Walker's distress at the prospect of a night without Anne was stifling:

'I will try to get over the night tolerably and pray that the ill I fear may not come upon me but it is very difficult without you. How I long to see you … Yours faithfully and affectionately forever.' Poor soul, she is quite beside herself and I cannot stand all this long.

31st January 1833

With the snow falling from four in the afternoon until eleven in the evening, there was no option for Anne to travel to Lidgate. 'Poor soul,' she remarked, 'she is quite beside herself and I cannot stand all this long.' Recording the temperature in her room as an uninviting 41 degrees Fahrenheit (5 degrees Celsius), she retired to bed.

***

'My conviction is unchanged, that no time ought to be lost in placing your sister under the care of a skilful medical man accustomed to the various shades of mental suffering'

A letter from Elizabeth Sutherland, in which Ann's sister suggested that Anne Lister might accompany Miss Walker to Scotland herself, elicited an indignant response. With a toddler still in recovery from the measles, Mrs Sutherland was worried about her husband's prolonged absence from home:

'As for the reduced state in which our own little boy is (not having yet recovered the use of his limbs) he would feel

reluctant to be absent for the greater length of time than
is absolutely necessary. It would confer a lasting obligation
...' Wishes to consult Dr Abercrombie in Edinburgh. No
mention or allusion to Dr Belcombe.

1st February 1833

Anne Lister's reaction reflected the emotional price she felt she had paid throughout her relationship with Miss Walker, as well as the potential expense of the trip: 'Pretty journey I should have, and must have been paid for into the bargain. No, no, surely I do not deserve to pay so dearly for my folly' (1st February 1833).

Anne made her position clear. She would not be making the arduous 300-mile carriage journey to Edinburgh:

My Dear Mrs Sutherland. I have this moment received your
letter. It would have given me great pleasure to have been
able to be of the smallest service to you in anyway, and in
this particular instance, it would have been the greatest
satisfaction to me to have had it in my power to accompany
Miss Walker to Edinburgh, but I am really sorry that my
leaving home just at present is utterly impossible. Had not
the urgency of my various engagements detained me, I
should have been already on my way back to the continent.

1st February 1833

In truth, foreign travel seemed more distant than ever. With her aunt's health still fragile, Anne could not anticipate leaving

Shibden before the summer. A visit to Mariana Lawton in Leamington seemed more likely. 'I have rather a fancy for going to town with you to have my teeth looked at,' wrote Mariana, in a note expressing her delight at the 'cheerful, satisfied way' Anne had spoken of the future in her latest letter (2nd February 1833). Anne had provided Mariana with a well-curated account of recent events at Shibden ('fuller than ever of things to do' – 18th January 1833).

Mariana still believed that Anne was holding out for her husband's death and the opportunity it would afford for them to live together. Reporting that 'Charles' constitution stronger than ever, tho' not his mind, and he is "more likely to live twenty years than two years ago he was to live as many months",' Mariana warned Anne against 'dwelling too intently upon an event which, to me, every year seems less likely to happen'.

In reality, Anne was dwelling upon nothing of the kind. 'Well, I am reconciled and happy and thankful,' she wrote, 'quite assured that providence orders all things wisely' (2nd February 1833).

A week later, Anne finally received word that Captain Sutherland would arrive at Lidgate with his elderly mother on 16th February. 'What a God-send to have things settled!' she wrote on hearing the news. 'Well, there is at last a prospect of me being free of all this once again' (9th February 1833).

Meanwhile, Ann Walker suggested that they burn the souvenir of their short engagement, the purse with the 'yes' note in it:

Then above half an hour in Miss W's room, hesitating
whether to burn the purse or not – she, not liking to see me do
it. At last, threw it into her fire, purse and 'yes' in it. I, glad
enough to get rid of anything like a tie. She seemed after all
very composed after it, and went quietly back to my room.

9th February 1833

The next morning, Anne, Ann and Catherine conducted their own version of the Sunday service from home. Anne had deliberately kept Miss Walker away from church:

Stayed to keep her from going to church, both morning
and afternoon. She very low all the day … Prayers in the
afternoon as in the morning. Should have returned home to
dine but too rainy and windy and stormy. Dinner before 6
and tea immediately afterwards. All doing a little botany.
Miss W much better this evening. Miss Rawson's and my
philosophical conversations on religion had done her good.
Miss Rawson and I agreed we doubted the doctrine of
everlasting torment in hell-fire.

10th February 1833

The following day, Catherine Rawson left Lidgate. In a mark of their new intimacy, Anne promised to consult Dr Belcombe about Catherine's menstrual 'complaint', the 'three-year stoppage of her cousin' (11th February 1833). The intense environment at Lidgate had acted as a remarkable social lubricant for the two women over the past few weeks.

On 16th February, with the snow having all but disappeared, Captain George Mackay Sutherland and his mother finally arrived at Lidgate. Captain Sutherland ('good looking, very good Scotch countenance') and his mother ('must have been rather handsome – looks perhaps 60, stout and well') were greeted with tea and a thorough appraisal from Anne: 'Good people, but almost vulgar-ish'.

As soon as Mrs Sutherland had retired to her room, Anne cut to the chase about Miss Walker and her illness:

Some talking with Captain Sutherland. Said thought the complaint chiefly on Miss W's mind, but she was perfectly herself on all subjects but that of religious despondency ... She would require very good management. Required a physician accustomed to mental suffering. Mrs Sutherland said Dr MacDonald recommended Dr Hamilton of Edinburgh – at about 70 – but still lecturing there and in great practice. Quite a lady's physician. I agreed to this.

16th February 1833

Anne found Captain Sutherland's other topics of conversation less scintillating. Her commentary of the following day was particularly scathing:

I had been very sorry for myself in such company. Mrs Sutherland vulgar, which would have been sooner and more easily perceived, had she been less quiet. She had dirty nails.

Captain Sutherland good-hearted and well enough, but evidently not a high-bred highlander.

17th February 1833

She felt sorry for Miss Walker. 'Poor girl, what a set she is getting amongst,' she wrote.

⟡

'"Heaven be praised!" said I to myself as I walked homewards, that they are off, and that I have got rid of her, and am once more free'

Anne recorded Ann Walker's last night at Lidgate in detail:

Grubbled her last night, she on the amoroso, and wanted to be near to me – that is, have my drawers off. But I thought it better not. She would sleep in my arms, and snored so shockingly I could scarce bear it. Gooded myself with the thought of its being the last night. She seemed as if she was going to leave all she liked best, and could scarce have enough of me. Poor girl, she could hardly leave me in the morning, and this made us so late. She was a little on the amoroso again; I touched and handled and grubbled a little, but would not do much.

18th February 1833

Without the promise of a future together, Anne was unwilling to give herself fully to Miss Walker.

The day of departure continued with a round of farewells. With Ann Walker and Captain Sutherland at Cliff Hill, Anne Lister was left alone with elderly Mrs Sutherland. Their conversation was illuminating. Mrs Sutherland was very keen to hear if Ann Walker ever mentioned Alexander Mackenzie, Mrs Sutherland's penniless nephew with a benign baronetcy, who had once offered his hand in marriage. 'No,' said Anne, 'I knew she did not like him ... he must have mistaken her civility for something else – she was always civil' (18th February 1833).

Mrs Sutherland brazenly admitted that Alexander Mackenzie had large debts to clear as well as 'his mother and her family to keep'. In fact, Sir Alexander would not have been a good catch at all for Ann Walker. He had a chequered army history. In 1830 he had asked for, and had been granted, special leave from the East India Company to 'settle' his public accounts. In 1832 he had been court martialled on a charge of disgraceful and insulting conduct towards his commanding officer, for the use of gross and indecent language. He had nothing to offer Ann Walker, but the family knew she had everything to offer him. The day before Mrs Sutherland had likened Miss Walker to a kind of valuable commodity, 'Miss Walker had £1500 a year,' she said, 'Now she rated her £2000.'

'I thought Miss Walker would not marry to pay anyone's debts, nor ought she,' Anne replied protectively. 'Surely Captain Sutherland would take care that proper settlements [arrangements] were made?' – meaning for Miss Walker not to be taken advantage of by anyone. It was a response that Mrs Sutherland was not expecting. 'Poor girl,' said Anne, thinking of her friend's vulnerability, 'they want her for some of their kin, if they can get her' (18th February 1833).

Mrs Sutherland's scheme to marry Ann Walker to her penniless nephew was a stark reminder of the way Ann was viewed by her family. Rich and marriageable, she was indeed the valuable commodity who might be used to further the financial interest of her kin. It was a situation that inspired sympathy in Anne Lister, who made no link between Alexander Mackenzie's mercenary motivations and the appraisals she had made of Miss Walker's wealth in the past. For Anne, Ann Walker's money was a useful resource, but one that might only be tapped after a mutual and meaningful romantic pledge. It was also important to her that she was able to bring her own, albeit far smaller, fortune to the partnership.

As the time of her departure drew nearer, Miss Walker was increasingly despondent. 'Very low at going,' wrote Anne. 'Said she would rather go with me.' Countering Ann Walker's anticipation that she would be miserable in Scotland – 'as she was before – felt as if she should never come back' – Anne's attempts to humour her inspired a little hope: 'Smiled and rallied when I joked her about running after me. She seemed quietly bent on being back before June, when she thinks I am to be off.' Ann gave Anne a bronze taper stick she had long coveted as a memento of their relationship.

As the carriage was prepared, Anne had a message for Ann Walker's sister:

Sent my kind regards to Mrs [Elizabeth] Sutherland, and begged her to tell me how Miss Walker was on her arrival at

Inverness, as I thought it better not to write to Miss Walker, as it would only be a harass to her.

18th February 1833

Anne's resolve not to communicate directly with Miss Walker during her recovery in Scotland was a deliberate attempt to open an emotional space between them. The withdrawal of her friendly support may have appeared unusual to someone ignorant of the nature of their relationship. Indeed, as Anne noted, 'the Captain looked, said nothing, but seemed surprised'.

Just after one o'clock in the afternoon, the carriage left Lidgate. For Anne, sadness at Ann Walker's departure was diluted by a huge deal of relief. The last few months had been draining. She had supported Ann through illness and personal trauma, balancing the duty she felt towards her with her own desire for freedom. She had courted dangerous attention, all the while questioning Ann's experience and motives, and attempting to reconcile her own conflicted feelings for the woman whose vacillations frustrated and 'unhinged' her in equal measure. All told, she felt she had made a narrow escape.

'For he shall give his angels charge over thee, to keep them in all thy ways'

That afternoon, Anne set about tying up a number of loose ends on Miss Walker's behalf. There was a sovereign to be given to

Mrs Armitage of the missionary society, and a message for Samuel Washington 'to pay for two children at a little school'. For Mrs Sutherland, she posted two letters, bound to make their way from Halifax to the West Indies. She enjoyed the opportunity to re-establish her routine of home improvements and reading:

> *From 2.35 all the afternoon with Charles and James Howarth in the library fitting the wainscot doors to the two larger book cupboards taken down, till dinner at 6 1/4. Afterwards, read the first 62 pages of Latrobe's 'Alpenstock or Travels on Foot in Switzerland'.*

> 18th February 1833

Before the day was out there came a hint that Ann Walker would not be so easily erased from Anne's life. Leafing through the bible Ann had gifted her for the promotion of her 'Christian knowledge', Anne noticed an inscription on the flyleaf: '18th February 1833, psalm 91.11', and, at the back, 'AW to AL'. Anne turned to the reference and was touched by the words she found: 'For he shall give his angels charge over thee, to keep them in all thy ways'.

With sadness, Anne reflected on how different things could have been if Miss Walker had only had the courage to love and be loved. 'Poor girl, what a pity,' she wrote. 'What a pity she has not more mind to be happy herself, and make others so.'

It would be ten months before the women would see each other again.

'Miss Hobart, nor Miss Walker, nor M, were for me. I must wait and see what heaven vouchsafes'

Over the years, Anne frequently commented that her embroilment in estate affairs stunted her travel ambitions. 'I should have been half the world over by this time, but for the foolish potherations I have let myself be drawn in to,' she would write later. Now, in addition to her concern for her aunt, a series of domestic issues conspired to keep her at Shibden throughout the spring of 1833.

The 'potherations' of March included interactions with Halifax's over-inquisitive postmistress Tabitha Bagnold, the close supervision of Charles Howarth as he carried out her commission of a bespoke walking-stick barometer, and pressing John Oates to complete the blow-pipe she had ordered from him six months ago. At Shibden, she placed Rachel Hemingway under surveillance when a book went missing. 'Does our reading housemaid Rachel ever meddle with my book?' she wondered. 'I have caught her going out quickly in the evening, not seeing her so as to be quite certain' (28th March 1833).

At the same time, travel arrangements must be made. Sending five pounds to Eugenie Pierre in Brighton for temporary board and lodgings, Anne enclosed a warning to her new lady's maid 'to be in readiness to be off in a few hours' notice'. In an attempt to save money, Anne wrote to the French customs office at Calais informing them she would be using the same carriage as she had on a previous trip, and therefore 'wished to avoid paying duty for a second time' (4th March 1833). Expenses were adding up in a worrying way:

> *Making a calculation of what I have to pay and what to*
> *receive from this to next rent day ... To pay everything, I*
> *shall want eleven hundred pounds and cannot make up*
> *more than seven.*
>
> 5th March 1833

Before she was to leave England, Anne also needed to finance her business concerns. Her request for a £2,000 letter of credit from Rawson's Bank resulted in a rare instance of bonding with Marian, who was misinformed by Christopher Rawson – presumably with malign intentions – that her sister had taken out the loan against the deeds to Shibden. Marian was upset. Anne was furious:

> *I said I had never offered any such thing. Explained, then*
> *got my business letter book, and read her the copies of the*
> *two letters, one to Mr Briggs* [her late land steward] *and*
> *one to Mr Rawson I had written on the subject. Marian*
> *struck at the unfairness of Mr R's conduct – thought it*
> *was a fetch to get to know how Shibden was left ... She*
> *owned, she thought, that if anything happened to his wife,*
> *he would be very glad to take her, if by so doing he could*
> *get Shibden.*
>
> 5th March 1833

On 22nd April, Anne invited Christopher Rawson to Shibden to confront him over his 'unhandsome' behaviour towards Marian:

At 11½ Mr Rawson – stayed an hour. Began with the
letter of credit, mentioned his mention of the thing to my
sister, how much she had been uneasy and alarmed about
it, wondering about the Shibden papers being offered on
security, and how much I had been annoyed on hearing of
this. He said, he had only joked about whether I was going
to be married – all joke and, 'she was a great thickhead – he
did not think she could have been such a thickhead', and he
would tell her about it.

I quietly said it was not always easy to calculate people's
wit or the contrary, but it was always better not to joke on
such subjects. I mentioned what I thought proper, and no
one liked to hear of their affairs mentioned by their banker.
Settled that he would give me another letter of credit
(£2000 as before) – whenever I wanted it.

22nd April 1833

Anne's defence of her sister was spirited but short lived. On
2nd June, they fell back into their usual arguments. This
time, Marian had angered Anne, understandably, by imply-
ing (somewhat ludicrously) that she shouldn't necessarily be
allowed to attend their father's funeral, when the time came:

She [Marian] *has changed her mind it seems, and now says*
not only that I may come, if I like, to my father's funeral,
should anything happen to him, but she would even rather
I was here on that occasion. For all her fear was of my
interfering in her affairs, and now she knows I should not

do that (which, by the way, she owns I always promised her).
She was satisfied.

Anne's commission of a painting of the Shibden Dale for
Marian suggests that the women were on better terms by
the advent of summer. The pedigree of the local artist John
Horner appealed to her aristocratic sensibilities:

> *Horner came at 4. Paid him for the pictures. Agrees that*
> *the painted rounding off of the pictures of my 3rd great*
> *uncle does not look well, but it was the fashion of the day.*
> *Thinks they were probably painted by* [Thomas] *Hudson*
> [1709–1779], *the master of Sir Godfrey Kneller – Sir*
> *Godfrey Kneller who found fault with Joshua Reynolds*
> *when he first returned from Italy … Saw his, and praised*
> *his sketch of Shibden Dale for Marian – to be, or rather not*
> *to, exceed 20 guineas. Subscribed (desired my name to be*
> *put down), to his views* [of Halifax] *about to be published.*
> *Asked to send Binns up tomorrow to paint my aunt's*
> *likeness in oils.*

6th June 1833

The paintings commissioned by Anne in the summer of 1833
still hang at Shibden Hall. 'Marian's View' of the Dale can be
seen over the oak stairwell, and Aunt Anne's portrait ('promises to be a very good likeness' she had said on 8th June), is a
feature of the central housebody, next to Anne's own portrait
and that of her uncle, James.

The first news of Miss Walker had arrived from Scotland on 2nd March. Captain Sutherland cheerily detailed that she had 'declined having medical advice ... wanted nothing but air and exercise – travelled from Dunkeld to Inverness on the 26th and she suffered no inconvenience.' Anne, who may have been expecting to hear about an arduous journey, dismissed it sarcastically, privately exclaiming 'So much for nervousness!' Her journal entry continued acerbically:

Will she continue better? Or will she tire of Scotland and want to be back again? I shall be off as soon as I can. I do not want to be in her way soon again. I have had enough of it, and tis likely enough she means me not to escape without her. Though who knows, an amoroso fit may come on and she may marry and very luckily think no more of me.

2nd March 1833

Ann Walker appeared keener to bridge the geographical and emotional distance between them. On 13th March, a conspicuously large box arrived at Shibden Hall. At first, Anne assumed it to be the willow cuttings she was expecting from her memorably named Scottish friend Breadalbane McLean.

A conversation with Samuel Washington exposed the true identity of the sender:

Washington asked if I had heard from Miss Walker as the box was from her. Said no! I expected nothing from her, had heard nothing of it. Expected a box from another friend in

the Highlands. Washington surprised but persisted in it. It
was the box sent to him with orders for him to send here in
his cart.

Anne instructed Charles Howarth, who was working in the
library passage, to open the box. It contained a round rosewood table. Inside, there was a note addressed to Aunt Anne
and dated Edinburgh, 25th February 1833:

Miss Walker hopes Miss Lister will do her the favour to
accept the small table which she trusts may prove a useful
appendage to her work. Miss Walker begs to present her very
kind regards to all the family at Shibden Hall.

Aunt Anne understood well enough that the piece of furniture
was meant not for the family, but for a specific Lister. As she
speculated on Miss Walker's motive, Anne commented:

My aunt thinks Miss Walker means not to let me escape her.
This, I owned, would be the natural interpretation of the
table, if sent by a person knowing the world, but for Miss
Walker, I know not what to make of it. She may mean it as
a sort of acknowledgement of all my attention and kindness.

The following afternoon, Anne trudged through the snow
that had returned to pay a polite call on Ann Walker's aunt.
Their conversation was marked by the sad news that one of
Miss Walker's tenants, William Hutchinson, had hanged

himself following the breakdown of his second marriage. A lighter dispatch arrived from Mrs Norcliffe, who parted with gossip and an invitation to Langton Hall: – 'Mr Duffin an invalid – Mrs Belcombe senior better – Burnett does not know of a place likely to suit Martha but will think of her ...' She bade Anne 'write to me soon, but come where you will be welcome' (14th March 1833).

That evening, Anne prepared to break her self-imposed ban and drafted a letter to Ann Walker. Her language was high-flown. 'Feeling may be quick without being transient,' she wrote, 'and that which has lasted a dozen years, is neither the empty bubble of a moment, nor the vain imagining of an idle dream.'

The next day, Anne had second thoughts. Loath to give Ann Walker false hope via what she now conceded to be her romantic tone, she was also aware that Ann's sister and her brother-in-law might have access to her correspondence. 'Corrected my letter to Miss Walker leaving out the sentence vid. last 3 or 4 lines of yesterday,' she wrote. The resulting letter was 'kind, but perfectly judicious and proper'. Miss Walker, said Anne, 'May do what she likes with it' (15th March 1833).

Miss Walker appeared to have been thrilled by the edited letter, which 'seemed like a sunbeam and raised a hope of her getting better' on its arrival. However, a week later, her reply indicated that 'this hope seemed to have subsided'. Miss Walker – true to form – was doleful, sad and repentant, determined to remember what Anne Lister had said to her before she had left, that she must think of her in her hour of need:

*Any progress that I make one day I lose the next, and my
fears accumulate upon me. I fervently trust change of scene
will be more beneficial to you, and that all the unhappiness
I have caused you will eventually be productive of good
instead of evil ... whatever I do it brings me no peace. I feel
inexpressibly your desire to remember you in case of need. I
cannot forget you, nor can a few weeks or months obliterate
remembrance of the past. With every feeling that friendship
can offer to yourself, believe me, yours faithfully and
affectionately Anne Walker.*

30th March 1833

'Whatever you ask me to do, I consider as an especial favour
conferred on myself,' Ann had written, promising to knit
Anne a pair of woollen kneecaps, and Anne was pleased to hear
that she had resumed her 'botanical drawings in pencil'. On
balance, however, the letter was not encouraging. 'Miserable',
Anne judged it. 'She is as bad as ever. What shall I do? Write
again or let it drop and leave her to her fate? I must think of
it. I really feel for and pity her. But what could I do with her?'
(30th March 1833).

Anne's tendency towards introspection had also been
triggered by a dispatch from Vere. Lady Cameron had been
effusive on the subject of her recent Italian tour, and of
reminder a day in the past significant to both Anne and Vere:

*Left Naples at 3pm on Wednesday the 6th and anchored
off the harbour at Leghorn at 6am Friday the 8th inst*

by the Francesco Primo – very good vessel ... Did not
attempt Vesuvius – Donald been up before! Saw Pompeii
... We are going off to Pisa where the Ussero is said to be
the best hotel in Italy, kept by two cidevant courtiers ...
Think of leaving Florence the 18th, which will bring us to
Nice by Lucca and Genoa 30th, and I suppose at Paris by
the 15th April. Do you recollect anything of consequence
on that day?'

26th March 1833

The date alluded to was the day when Captain Cameron had
offered Vere his hand in marriage. Having been drawn back
to her own diaries to recall the event, Anne was cast back to a
time of heartbreak that she had taken pains to bury:

Casually recollecting Vere's inquiry if I recollected anything
particular on the 15th April. Turned to my travelling
journal of 1829. Left London Saturday 18th April that
year with V. Then, turned to the 15th April last year. The
day Captain Cameron made his offer. I had quite forgotten
it was that day. A tear started as I read of my then misery,
but it was soon dried. I am more than reconciled, and have
been for long. Some difference between her and Miss Walker.
I hope to be off both?

30th March 1833

It was a month before Anne replied. She was careful not to
reveal the full impact of Vere's remembrance:

My dearest V, I see, to my great surprise, it is near a month since I received your most astonishingly agreeable letter ... Yes! I do recollect something of consequence that happened on the 15th of this month last year, and thought of it on the morning and the evening of that day. Perhaps it is one of those circumstances I am least likely to forget. It can never be indifferent to me, unless (which seems to me as impossible as at this moment as it did 12 months ago), your happiness can cease to be one of the most earnest desires and interests of which I am capable ... The name of Cameron has lost all disagreeable association ... God bless you my dearest Vere, my love to yourself and Donald and believe me always affectionately yours, Anne Lister.

21st April 1833

'Providence orders all things rightly,' she had reminded herself. She cemented the feelings of acceptance and resolution about other former flames too: 'Miss Hobart, nor Miss Walker, nor M, were for me. I must wait and see what heaven vouchsafes' (30th March 1833).

As her forty-second birthday arrived, Anne remained sanguine. 'I am more single than ever, un-companioned and alone,' she admitted, 'Yet still, I feel happier than this time last year.' She spent the next twelve hours dusting her books and placing them onto the shelves of her newly constructed library passage.

'I have more enjoyment, am in stronger health and vigour of mind,' she wrote, and 'Again and again, God be thanked' (3rd April 1833).

"I try not to disquiet myself in vain, tho' my mind is so tim'ly rebell'd" — but a lit. energy & determinat. to set yr mind to rights — go straight forw. to start — said Champ. Consc'e, & happ's. is wch in reach of us all — the exercise — ride — amuse yrn. — do as mch good as you ha. been accust'd to — like yr Norcliffes, bt. do not minish & bring yours. low by dwell'g. up. much — yr. let. fr. wch. you gi. me a lit. quotat., is clear as yr day — yr. ghd. is mth. bet. &c. &c. — she wd. gain right toga to chch. at Lawton — "there will be mo. tranq'l. on yr. melanch'y. subj't. by bly" — conclude they at — mington — "do tell me if miss Cholm'bley wr" — & if she be — will beg. & — ask aft. mr. Bestle. Congrat's. town'd miller on being a fav'r — & tho: yr paragraph concern'd her — I do not fancy he partic'y likes, but — tell me what you & Grantham told her his wages were to be. I ga. poor — offer'd on sist. Ho. no. — I consid'd. yr. und. stood, bt. he says you & Grantham told him 20£ — per ann'm, yt. it may catch yr. eye, &yt. you may be sure not to forget — yr in yr. next — I really go on very well, & I am very comfble" — Sing — which. set'n. for yr Queens 6th. day ball on Wed. — impoff. to go & abirth — &. throw it off for yr. night — two. present's. last word. — I am ind. for — social." — few peop. in town, yet Kno. &c. so not like yr. to be dull — &y — as mch. spoilt here as elsewhere — hind., indeed, many, ev. bod. is so — so very. Kind & attentive, yt. I am ahead. as mch. at ho. here as — domiciliat'd for years — I shall not. ever. ha. yr. potter'd of yr g8. in yr line of — s., especially aftord's; as they. in offers fr. frd's who ha. yr entire, yr — la ligue" — yr. gay gaieties do not begin. tile Jan'y. bt. yr. will be pleas'd — & amus'd present with; know yr. in a not. agreeable socials. Kind of socie. — very mch. — In fact, I am seldom. an wd. at ho." ——————— I put. 2 do. — on night with. a charm'd frd. of Ld. Harrot' — I shall be quiet tile a — an — find no fault with. yr climate. yet — uncert'n. like Eng'd. — East & — togi. rheumatism — not felt incommod'd as at Hearth'. — East wind & scarbro' — agues in yr spring. — shall be off bef. yr. tho' may delay a — well rec'd. & comfter — bott. of p.3. "But I reserve yr. remark — to say yt. I shall hear hittd. fr. Hammersley, tell yr and ofr yr. course, acknowl. yr. recpt. off yr £200 to yr. immed'd. yr. and £100 — ha. £500 in my hd. at 4pc. dating for. yr 1st. of Jan'y. next — w. not. payment. yr lot. when lve you agn — yr. prest. memorandum wil. — you a mo. regul'r. acct. & acknowledgmt., wch. will do. bef. leav't. here — v. good health so far — I am in very good health so far — thro. amtht. happ, & with. out yr. leav't. any directs. or cont's., I shall consid'r. yr. as hr — ream officer's hund'd. fund's. & all accumulat'd of simple int't. yr. up. dr —

CHAPTER 10

HALIFAX, LONDON, PARIS AND BEYOND

'Soon I took my leave, merely saying good morning,
not contradicting the thought of my being back
for a little while before winter'

Anne Lister had left her home county for the first
time at the age of fifteen. On 25th August 1806 she
recorded the excursion with excitement in her diary: 'Rode
with Mr Mitchell to Bacup – the first time I was out of Yorkshire'. Though the journey she made into Lancashire that day
was of only a few miles, the thrill of experiencing somewhere
new had made its impression.

As Anne grew, so did her ambition to travel. Her dream
destinations became further flung and more exotic. It did not
satisfy her to leave England for a week or two; throughout her
adult life she spent months at a time away from home, including periods of residence in Paris.

Having also explored Italy, Belgium, Holland and Switzerland, in the summer of 1833 Scandinavia and the Baltics were
in Anne's sights. After months of indecision, she finally 'determined to go north' on 17th July that year, resolving to end
her journey in Denmark. The protracted episode with Miss
Walker had of course delayed Anne from travelling earlier, and
Aunt Anne's prolonged bout of ill-health had also kept her
longer at Shibden than she had intended.

In an age of carriages and steamers, foreign travel was no small undertaking. Routes had to be painstakingly planned. Anne had mapped out a constellation of stops even before she had settled upon Copenhagen as her final destination. After York, she decided, would come Leamington, and then London. From the south coast she would cross the water and begin her travels through the continent.

On 16th June 1833, Anne left Shibden. Her farewell to Aunt Anne and Marian was brisk: 'soon I took my leave, merely saying good morning, not contradicting the thought of my being back for a little while before winter'. Arriving in York after a journey of nearly five hours, she was irritated to find that neither Thomas Beech and Eugenie Pierre, the servants who were to make up her much-anticipated travelling entourage, were at the Black Swan as arranged:

Reached the Black Swan, York at 5 3/4. Thomas not there, potheration. Met him in Blake Street coming for me. Annoyed, but he excused himself so tolerably about the mistake of his that I hoped it would be the last time and said no more.

No Eugenie at home. Had to send for and wait for her 1/2 an hour. Annoyed again, begged it might happen no more and she looked pale and was so sorry. I said I hoped it would be for the last time.

16th June 1833

It was a poor first impression, and indeed there were bumps in the road ahead for Anne's relationship with her lady's maid in particular.

The diary accounts of the two trips Anne had made to York the previous month displayed a growing dissatisfaction with what she judged to be a distinctly provincial place and people. She craved the society of her upper-class London set. Her restlessness was manifest in a snobbish evaluation of the East Yorkshire side of her family, the Inmans, about whom she had spoken to Mrs Henry Belcombe:

> *Mercy, thought I to myself, all this would never suit me, the place of one's youth may not be that of one's age and York will never do for me. I had spoken to Mrs HSB yesterday about the Inmans, of the relationship, but that I really did not mean to begin the acquaintance. My uncle had not wished it, and my sister went to them and I should keep aloof. She thought me right. All this and scandal and vulgar finery of some and misconduct of others would soon disgust me. The fine ones are the best, but I should soon be sick of them all.*

> 30th May 1833

In spite of this, Anne seemed keen enough to pay calls on her York friends on 17th and 18th June. After visits to the Cromptons and Duffins, she met Harriet Milne, the sister of Mariana, with whom she enjoyed a long-standing flirtation. While she couldn't resist paying court to Harriet, it seemed that, by forty-two, Anne was wary of taking things too far:

> *Latterly rather flirting but not much … Gave her the carbuncle ring while in the fly, obscurely or round aboutly*

explained that that stone was the emblem of long and deep feeling, alias passion. She said she was glad of it. Kissed her rather lovingly but not much. Might go as far as I liked but too cautious nowadays.

17th June 1833

The same day, Anne and Harriet visited another of Anne's former lovers. In fact, Eliza Raine had been Anne's first. The two had formed an intense bond as teenagers when they studied together and shared an attic bedroom at the Manor School in York, where Anne had been sent as a fourteen-year-old in 1805. Though the romantic relationship had broken down by adulthood, and Eliza's mental health had suffered a sharp decline, Anne maintained contact with her for the rest of her life. By 1833, Eliza had been living in a mental institution for almost twenty years.

Went for Mrs Milne, who accompanied me to Mrs Barker's to see poor Eliza Raine. Mrs M sat in another room while I was 10 minutes with Eliza. Her gown made straint, waistcoat-wise. Kept her eyes shut and would not speak, becoming cross so I came away. Thought her thinner in the face than when I saw her last. She is often cross and riotous – curses and swears and makes herself ill ... and keeps the people awake all night.

17th June 1833

'I can amuse without entangling myself'

On 19th June, Anne travelled on to Leamington to collect Mariana, who was to be her companion on the trip at least as far as London. In spite of Anne's frequent claims that Mariana meant very little to her, her recounting of the recent flirtation with Harriet Milne was transparently intended to make Mariana jealous. Mariana's lack-lustre reaction to the news shocked and upset Anne: 'From the manner in which M took it, could not think she cared much. I was really affected. In tears' (20th June 1833). She had not got the desired reaction she was expecting.

On the other hand, with her full inheritance of Shibden being within tantalising reach (given the advancing years of her ailing aunt and father), she found herself able to see through Mariana's renewed desire to one day move in with her. 'She owned the other day that if William had not died she would not have tried to get me back,' Anne wrote on 28th June. William Lawton, Mariana's nephew-in-law, had recently died in a tragic accident, having had his arm ripped off by a piece of machinery when visiting a fulling mill. The death had major implications for Mariana's future financial stability, seeing as William had stood to inherit her home, Lawton Hall, from husband Charles. Mariana had hoped to benefit from his kindness in the event of her being left a widow, with her husband having as yet made absolutely no provision in his will for *her*. Anne Lister was shocked to find herself playing second fiddle to poor William. She remarked:

I said not much, but how astounded I had been to find myself second to William Lawton. 'Tis now quite evident how much she wants to bring all on again but, though I am very kind, I always avoid this.

By the time Anne and Mariana had reached London on 3rd July, the cracks in their relationship had opened into a chasm. En route Anne had engaged in reluctant sex with her, which was only marginally satisfying for Anne having only received 'a tolerable kiss [orgasm]' (23rd June 1833).

Now, busily reacquainting herself with high society in visits to her titled friends, including Vere – who had just given birth to a baby girl named Anne – Anne Lister effectively ignored Mariana. Mariana, now finding herself waiting at the hotel or in the back of the carriage during Anne's calls, 'felt alone and bitterly repented having come' (5th July 1833). On one occasion, she secretly trailed Anne to see where she was going.

By the time Charles Lawton arrived on 10th July, the situation had deteriorated further. It seemed as if Charles and Mariana were having relationship problems of their own. While Anne had been courting Ann Walker, Mariana had been playing up to the pointed charms of Cheshire man, a Mr Willoughby Crewe. Anne heard Mariana and Charles arguing. They were 'shouting and bawling. I was ashamed of them and thought myself lucky to be engaged and out of the way,' she wrote. She had resolved to leave Mariana in England and travel on to the continent alone.

Anne remained keen to impress her high-ton friends. Trawling the streets of London for a late wedding present for Vere, she made three stops over two days, and agonized over the expense of the resulting coffee pot:

> *For £33, handsome, second-hand plain coffee pot and tea pot (with lamp, I think, included), and for £39 choice of 2 very handsome modern chased coffee pots and tea pots, but no lamp. A new one would be £8 or £9 more.*
>
> 9th July 1833

> *Choosing also the lamp, which makes this second hand concern come to about £40. I could have done better at Rundle Bridges. Vexed at heart but said nothing even to M. May I manage better another time. Mind how I make promises of coffee pots. They have managed well to get* [a] *teapot into the bargain. Vere told me at Hastings she had no remorse for me. I had money enough, but she will not get much more.*
>
> 10th July 1833

She displayed more confidence in a visit to a mathematical instrument-maker in Cheapside, buying herself a 'small compass and a pair of blue spectacles' as part of a mineralogical tool set she intended to use abroad. There, she also learned that the walking stick barometer she had taken with her and had agreed to get valued on behalf of tenant Charles Howarth's elderly father, was 'not worth a farthing' (9th July 1833).

The round of social engagements continued. A Miss Tate said Anne 'reminded her of her father, who used to say the world was like a stagecoach, if one was not ready to go with it, one must be left behind.' She had told Anne, flattering her, 'How many would be glad of me [Anne] for a companion.'

Anne, still undecided about the final destination of her travels, had been toying with the idea of going as far as Russia: 'Lady S[tuart] and Miss Tate against my doing more than St. Petersburg and Moscow – (I had talked of an excursion to the Ural mountains) – it would be odd and talked of' (12th July 1833).

Her plan to travel just to the continent, let alone Russia, was raising eyebrows among Anne's society acquaintances. She was humbled by Lady Stuart's honesty and concern:

Said I, 'I am sure you were right about my oddity of my going alone. Nobody would tell me the truth, not even Vere and I shall never forget my obligation to you.' She seemed affected and said she had done it because she had a real regard for me. All this was done so kindly, I myself was affected and thought to myself, she is the only friend I have amongst them … said I should write all my adventures to Lady S. She should have them all and should tell just what she liked.

17th July 1833

Visiting Vere at Wimpole Street during her packed itinerary of farewells, there was no hint of the tense, anxious Anne of Hastings. 'Laughed and told V, if she liked the coffee pot and

I would have the credit of the choice, if not, all the blame should be on Lady S', Anne wrote in good humour on 16th July.

Elderly Lady Stuart seemed particularly saddened at Anne's departure. 'It was a small thing at her time of life to take leave of anyone.' She kissed Anne, who was once again touched by her kindness. 'Not everyone has much heart as she. I felt moved and full of gratitude. Thought I would send her thread stockings from Paris and leave her £300 [in her will] and V[ere] at most 1.'

Having now settled upon Copenhagen over Russia, Anne had made arrangements to meet a young woman called Sophie Ferrall in Paris. Sophie, who was the niece of her friend Madame de Bourke, would travel with Anne all the way and be delivered to her sister, Countess Emily Blucher, who lived in the Danish capital.

Boarding the Ferret Steamer, a 140-tonne 'fine, fast vessel' bound for Calais, Anne looked back on her time in London and made grand plans for the future. 'Reflected, did not read, but very fairly happy today,' she wrote. 'Castle building about writing, publishing and making my book pay my expenses' (18th July 1833).

<hr />

'This solitary journey may do me good. It will show me how far I may really trust to the resources of my own mind. From the moment they fail me, or threaten to do so, I shall date my return'

Anne was thrilled to be on the road again. Her natural optimism was suited to the pursuit of new adventures:

I always feel a certain indescribable something within that always helps me from without, and if believing all things not unreasonable and hoping all things not impossible be the character of the philosopher, I have some small pretention that way.

29th July 1833

Anne conceded that the addition of Sophie Ferrall to her traveling entourage was a sensible one. Together with her servants, their group would 'do very well, and very respectably too, into the bargain' (29th July 1833). That said, she had not actually met Miss Ferrall yet, and her unfavourable first impression of Eugenie had not been helped by what she considered some seriously inappropriate behaviour for a maid as their travels together began:

She certainly does not know how to behave en femme de chambre ... *Walks before me, begins the conversations, and tonight took her place almost in front of me from a gent who offered it, and kept it to the exclusion of a young lady, a friend of the gent's!!! This was just going too far and so I have just told her. Said I could not do with this sort of thing. If she could not conform to the place she had taken, she had better give it up.*

28th July 1833

Eugenie did have her good points. On 1st August, she made a conciliatory rice pudding for Anne, who commented sweetly

262

that if 'we can possibly keep up going on as well as we do now, I shall think of my servants as treasures'.

By this time, the party had arrived in Paris. Anne took advantage of the superior French fashion scene to purchase stockings, sleeves and black satin shoes, and for both her and for Mariana, a pair of stays (corsets). Anne's bespoke corset was more expensive, the maker Madame Calis having to pad out the breast area in order to give a more feminine shape – Anne referred to them as 'stuffed concerns' (6th August 1833). A letter to her friend Mrs Dalton gave a brilliant critique of the latest styles:

> *Though London imitates as well as she can, 'tis merely that a substitute shines brightly as a King, until a King be by. Bonnets not much larger than a good sized breakfast cup, skirts of an ampleur, reminding one of the pea-filled rotundity of a Dutch doll,* cheveux en hatte. *The hair plaited very broad and set upon so as to form something very like a medimmus on the head of Isis. Large rooms and folding doors are nowadays quite necessary, for sleeves are so enormous that each lady's breadth across the shoulders is doubled. Pelerines very large, much worn with longer or shorter ends confined by the ceinture* [belt] *in front ... black lace very much worn. But dress not for nothing – things cheaper in London.*

11th August 1833

'My greatest pother is dress, but I find I must have it. My days of one small portmanteau and merely the hat on my head are gone by,' wrote Anne to Tib the same day. She was aware that in Copenhagen, where she would be mixing with the cream of Danish society, she would need to dress immaculately.

Anne laid out more funds on gifts to the academic friends she had made during her scientific studies in the 1820s. There were medical implements for Etienne Geoffroy St-Hilaire, a 'four-blade mother-of pearl pen-knife' to Monsieur Desfontaine – a bold choice for someone now 'blind from cataract and looking very old and infirm' (11th August 1833) – and '5 bistouries and one scalpel' for Monsieur Julliart, who had instructed her in dissection. Of those, she kept 'one of each' back for herself, having 'hoped to do something again in the study' on her return from Denmark (12th August 1833).

Though Anne was never to formally resume her studies, she retained a lifelong interest in human anatomy and physiology. Having long 'wished to be, in some sort, a naturalist', she was also aware that the restrictions of her sex meant this would never be a profession. Dissecting bodies in a secret attic room was one thing, but in the male-only field of early nineteenth-century medicine, she was destined to remain an interested amateur.

On 2nd August, Anne was introduced to Sophie Ferrall for the first time. Her friend, Madame de Bourke, had given Anne the background on her niece a few days previously:

Heard all the story of her refusing a Russian with 2000 sterling a year but 20 years older than herself. The young lady 24. Madame de Bourke determined to get rid of her. I promised never to tell all she had told me and she not to say to the girl herself she had told me. When at last I rather fought off she said it would be a kindness, a charity and I agreed. How extraordinary, thought I. Well, I am at any rate companioned.

30th July 1833

Anne's first impressions of Sophie were favourable. She judged her to be a 'pretty looking', 'nice, sensible girl' on the first two occasions of their meeting. On 3rd August at the fashionable Rue de Fauberg, the home of Madame de Bourke, Anne was treated to a fine selection of 'madeira, champagne, Bordeaux, sherry, Burgundy, and an old Sicilian wine, a liqueur (blue)'. She concluded that she 'liked Mademoiselle Ferrall very well'.

Before setting off on their journey, Anne pointedly told Sophie that she would not be going direct to Copenhagen, meaning that Sophie would have to fit in with Anne's protracted journey and resultant adventures through her decidedly more scenic route through Luxembourg, Treves, Koblentz, Kassel, Hanover and Lubeck. Sophie made no comment, most likely not quite understanding just exactly what was meant by Anne deciding she was 'not going direct'.

'How extraordinarily things happen'

On the 8th August a three-page letter arrived from Elizabeth Sutherland from Udale in Scotland, about Miss Walker:

*Mrs S perplexed about her sister. Better in bodily health,
at least fatter, but still it seems no better in spirits. 'I am
aware, from what my sister has repeatedly stated, that
there is no individual living by whom she would be so much
influenced, and my only consolation is that through your
kind interference and influence, she may be directed to do
that which will promote her happiness.'*

8th August 1833

Ann Walker had, she said, been waiting anxiously to hear from
her. 'How extraordinarily things happen,' wrote Anne to herself,
considering her elevation from a figure of suspicion to one of
trust in the eyes of Ann's family. Despite the ocean's distance
between them, she maintained a feeling of moral duty towards
Miss Walker's wellbeing. The next day, from her lodgings at the
Rue Neuve de Luxembourg, Anne Lister penned her considered
reply to Mrs Sutherland, sounding like a physician-in-waiting:

My dear Mrs. Sutherland,

*I received your letter yesterday and lose no time in
answering it and in expressing my very sincere regret that
your sister's health is not more entirely re-established. I hope
your not having written more explicitly is unimportant,
as I have so long contemplated the possibility and probable
circumstances of the case, that I am perhaps already nearly
as well acquainted with it as you can desire.*

*I was aware, when your sister left home, that something
more than a mere visit to you was necessary, and that you*

must discover this sooner or later. I was aware also that Lidgate was not the place where she ought to be left alone, and she will remember with what earnestness I represented this to her, again and again. I entreat you to show her this letter and say, if my influence is still unshaken, I am sure that, with your approbation and under your direction, she will follow my advice, I shall give it without reserve, as the best means in my power of proving how much I am really interested for her.

It is, in the first place, necessary to ascertain the real state of morbid disturbance under which the mind is labouring. I have not mentioned my own opinion on the subject to anyone but your aunt, Miss Walker, just before my leaving home, and Dr. Belcombe, in whose security and honour I have as much confidence as in his experience and skill in this particular branch of medical practice. I strongly recommend your writing to him to take your sister under his care, to provide a proper person to be with her, and a lodging and every comfort and everything cheerful.

You need be under no apprehension, you may safely leave all to him. He is too well accustomed to this sort of thing and will do his upmost for his own sake as well as for mine, as he knows how much I feel interested. You will mention your wish that that thing should not be known. Your sister can take any name she likes for the time, and you can so manage both friends and business for her in the interview, that no one needs know she is not still with you. I have always told her everything plainly, and without the least concealment. I have even, in some sort, suggested this plan to her before. Do give my love and tell her that if she will only consent to do what I so earnestly advise, I am persuaded she will be better and happier by and by.

I leave here on Monday for Copenhagen. Any letter directed there to Madame Lister, aux soins de *Messrs Kortwright, Banquiers will be quite safe and will meet me on my arrival, about 3 weeks hence. With kind regards to Captain Sutherland and for your sister's recovery.*

Believe me, my dear Mrs. Sutherland, very truly yours, Anne Lister.

An addendum to the letter demonstrates an impulse to include something more heart-felt:

I can't close my letter without again begging you to give my love to your sister, with a repetition of the assurance that she may count upon my doing all I can for her, and that, her having too often prevented my doing the best I could, will never deter me from doing whatever may remain in my power. Tell her to consider what I have urged and not reject it too hastily. Removal and skilful medical treatment are, in the first instance absolutely and immediately necessary. Half measures never answer and feeble ones but seldom.

9th August 1833

Ann Walker was to stay in Anne's thoughts throughout her journey. She remained a sexual preoccupation too, the coded words 'incurred a cross thinking of Miss Walker' appearing at regular intervals in her diary over the coming months.

⁂

'Eugenie heated and very much tired and Thomas tired too. I, not at all'

Anne, Sophie Ferrall, Thomas Beech and Eugenie left Paris on 18th August 1833. The journey, which was not without its mishaps and adventures, saw Anne determined to eke out as much as she could from the sights, sounds and spectacles of the foreign landscapes. She often dished out orders to her two weary and possibly shell-shocked new servants, and occasionally pandered to the needs of an impatient and flirty Sophie Ferrall. Anne's carriage veered up hills, down tracks, over narrow bridges into the cobbled streets of the villages of rural France and Germany.

The 'boulder stone pavement, all in holes' was a contrast to the smart neighbourhoods she had occupied in the French capital. Occasionally, so soft was the ground that the carriage wheel sunk into the 'deep rutted sand', as on 13th September.

At the end of each day, the weary group would settle at whatever *auberge* or inn they could find, regularly judged by Anne to be over-priced and under-par. As protection against the filthy sheets, she often found herself sleeping in her great coat. Sophie, she noted, was sometimes so exhausted that she slept 'without nightcap and in her day shift' (25th August 1833).

But Anne's descriptions of the flora and fauna in the passing villages spoke of a beautiful landscape. The wooded hills and dales of oak, beech and birch trees reminded her of the Shibden valley. Rivers were compared with those in Yorkshire too, though not always favourably. The River Lahn in the Moselle region was 'not so good at the moment as the Calder at Salterhebble' (26th August 1833).

Each location was appraised in precise detail. In the central German town of Kassel, the street she stayed on 'seemed the essence of dullness' (28th August 1833). In Luxembourg, there was 'nothing to be seen in the town' but 'several curiosities in the neighbourhood' (22nd August 1833). Treves (now Trier, in south-west Germany), was a 'nice, clean, good town', with an attractive church and Roman amphitheatre.

Local people were observed from the windows of the carriage. In Germany, the men wore 'singular cocked hats and white smock frocks to their knees', and the women wore caps 'with their hair plaited from before and secured behind with a large silver pin, like a blunt, long knife blade' (26th August 1833). The women of Holstein got a special mention for wearing 'men's black beaver hats' (13th September 1833).

There were additional detours to be made to visit interesting people and attractions. At Épernay, Anne, Eugenie and Sophie explored Moët's Champagne caves. 'Each of us a candle in our hand,' Anne wrote, describing their descent into the eerie blackness where the bottles were stored:

Inscription in memory of Napoleon La Grande, having honoured with a visit in 1807 ... [The wine left] in the wood two years and in the bottle four, before ever sold – there was a great deal of wine of 1828 but the oldest was 1825 – will be very much and very good this year – 40 to 50 workmen employed.

Mr Möet himself was out:

While at dinner, came a very civil message from him, begging my acceptance of a bottle of Sillery, and one of pink champagne. The latter was most excellent, tasted so good we drank the whole bottle, and were admirably unfitted for doing anything but go to bed and sleep.

19th August 1833

By 29th August, they had reached Kassel. The famous statue to Hercules was described as a 'large, rough building surmounted by a gigantic bronze statue that one sees from all directions approaching Kassel'. On closer inspection, Anne was unimpressed:

The famous waterworks commence from the foot of the building but all has been long out of order and the great building itself is propped from behind. The present Elector will do nothing, nor will the town of Kassel and the people are dissatisfied to pay 300,000 thalers of revenue to Prince, who leaves his wife ... and spent his money anywhere but at home.

29th August 1833

Anne did concede that climbing '3 or 4 ladders into the very body of the Hercule' resulted in a magnificent view, 'the palace almost as it were at our feet'.

At Göttingen, Anne engineered a meeting with Professor Johann Friedrich Blumenbach, the scientist, physician and teacher famous for his studies in comparative anatomy:

> *At 4.05 called and sat 1/4 of an hour with Mr Blumenbach*
> *... Mr Blumenbach is about 80 to 84 but received me with*
> *as much vivacity and pleasure and civility as if he had been*
> *30 or 40 years younger. But it was easy to see nature could*
> *not support this exertion for very long. His countenance*
> *still fine with an agreeable expression of goodness, his voice*
> *thick. I, with difficulty, understood his French. Said I was*
> *English and found he spoke English much more intelligently*
> *than French, and apparently with much more ease ... I*
> *complimented him on his looking so well. He said he minded*
> *not long life – but, to be useful – that was another thing.*
> *His wife older than himself and much more infirm, but he*
> *stoops a good deal, has a little rheumatism.*

Anne returned the next day to see Blumenbach's famous cabinet of skulls. His theory of classification relied on the idea that human crania could be classified by race:

> *There at 4.20. Delighted to see me. Showed me the presents*
> *he had had from different people. Our late Queen Charlotte*
> *had given him part of an elephant's tooth, which grown over*

a lead bullet – the bullet (now cut through), remaining quite round, as if it was at the time of lodging in the poor animal's tusk, which must have been young. Spoke of the large caves and Meiningen.

... Blumenbach showed me into his cabinet of skulls, observed the same sort of model as the one at the museum. The original, he said, is at Darmstadt, (Hesse-Darmstadt). It was picked up in some church yard and bought by the Duke at a great price. Monsieur Jussieu of Paris has one, and there is a 3rd at Prague. The complaint had no name till Blumenbach himself gave it that of Osteonecrosis.

He has a specimen of a dried man taken from a church in Magdeburg, much finer specimen than the one at the museum. No accounting for this kind of drying, can't tell why it should be, especially why one should be so dried among so many which perish like the rest.

Blumenbach never could make out the great distinguishing mark of a Jew till breakfasting one morning with Sir Benjamin West. He, West, told him, it was the ridge formed by the suture of the two bones just under the nose, into which the upper teeth are set. On returning home, he found the remark verified, and pointed out to me a Jew's skull that was a remarkable illustration of the observation.

1st September 1833

'Nothing very particular, several foetus in spirits, snakes etc, etc, some skulls and a few stuffed birds and animals, sea clothes, spears etc, and a dried man (with his feet gone),' Anne wrote of a visit to Göttingen's University museum on the same day. In the crypt of the gothic church in Bremen the following week there were,

> *8 dried bodies, dried up like leather ... a large, old Swedish General, and his young aide de camp, a man who fell from his work on the top of the cathedral and broke open his neck, and a man who died from a large cut in the arm, both these wounds very evident ... all lying in large, clumsy black coffins, the lids of which are all lifted up to show the cadavers within.*
>
> 8th September 1833

Other coffins held 'an English major with half the hair on his head', and a 'large, old, English countess' with 'cottage-knitted gloves and stockings and cap, said to be those she was buried in'.

Anne's journal gives little indication of what her servants made of their unusual journey. Generally, she seemed to take only Thomas Beech with her into museums, leaving Eugenie and Sophie Ferrall behind at their current lodgings. It is clear that Sophie, who did not share Anne's fascination with dead bodies, had begun to grow impatient to reach Copenhagen. Sensing resistance to her plans, Anne started to feel hard done by herself:

> *Miss F so little thinking of my pleasure. I had said this morning, sorry for the delay but really I might have been a month longer but for her anxiety to get to Hamburg ...*

If she was to be long delayed, she thinks she may be mad.
Perhaps she is half so already ... shall be heartily glad to be
rid of her. Her German has served me little.

7th September 1833

There had been moments of flirtation between Anne and her twenty-four-year-old travel companion. 'Playing with Miss Ferrall. Very good friends now', she had written just the evening before. 'She sits on my knee tonight and has kissed me these three nights but I do it all very properly' (6th September 1833). But this diversion seemed no more than a game to Anne. 'I behave very kindly to her,' she said, following it with a less than complimentary, 'Glad enough to see her but should do very well without her, and shall be glad enough in reality without her' (11th September 1833). It seemed that Sophie Ferrall had a touch of the Miss Walker about her – suffering from low self-esteem, hinted at when Anne wrote, 'She sat on my knee this evening. I tell her she is not ugly and she is well enough inclined to flirt with me but I am very prudent' (11th September 1833).

Over their many hours in the carriage together, Anne had learned more about the Russian count Sophie's aunt had been keen for her to marry. Feigning ignorance on the topic, Anne listened with interest to Sophie's conflicting account of the man who had, according to her 'first said he had 60, then 40 thousand francs a year. A club foot and 47 years older than herself. I gave no hint of knowing anything about it before' (25th August 1833).

In an interesting coda to this story, Sophie Ferrall went on to marry Federico Confalonieri, the Italian revolutionary who had led the insurrection against allied forces in favour of an independent Italy in 1814. Much to the delight of Madame de Bourke, their marriage in July 1841 drew attention from all areas of Parisian society. In February 1840, Sophie wrote to her sister: 'One knows how nobly he behaved during all his sufferings one cannot help loving him. He is about fifty, but looks more in his face ... We are the greatest of friends in the world.' Though the marriage would last only five years, Sophie's match had given her access to a new realm of society. In the years after Confalonieri's premature death, she was able to count Rossini, Verdi, Liszt, Victor Hugo, Balzac and Alexis de Tocquville among her acquaintances.

Back in the summer and autumn of 1833, Sophie Ferrall was caught between her attraction to Anne Lister's charismatic personality and her growing impatience at her uncompromising and eccentric itinerary. By the time they boarded the steamer in Travemunde on 17th September, it was a relief for both of them to be in sight of their final destination.

'Should have been comfortable enough without Miss Ferrall and her snoring, disagreeable little dog', Anne had written on 13th September. She looked forward to the luxury of being on her own again, of being left to her own devices – 'I shall not wish for a companion again,' she said. To this she now added that Sophie was 'the most disagreeable girl I ever saw' (17th September 1833).

Now, at last, they were bound for Copenhagen. The carriage, which had been loaded onto the deck of an eighty horse-power steamer, would provide a makeshift cabin for Anne during the eighteen-hour journey ahead. 'Lay across it with my feet upon my travelling bag pretty comfortably', she wrote, 'dozing or slumbering, then sick about every 1/4 of an hour till 8 or 9 in the morning.' She wrote three pages to Vere's sister Lady Harriet de Hageman to say that their arrival would be imminent, asking her to reserve two rooms ('comfortable, but not splendid'), at the Hotel Royal. Miss Ferrall would go direct to her sister, Countess Emily Blucher.

Almost twelve weeks to the day after leaving Shibden Hall, Copenhagen was finally in sight.

... acorns in Wallrope upper brow where John ... sow!
... gates & turnstile are put up post ab.t John Mallins ... pigsties ...
... w.th a turnstile, acr. y.e r.d just on y.e Wallrope side off ent.ce to low.r
... so y.t ... stray cattle c.d n.t even get down fr. Geo. Robinson ... by gap fr.
... thro' Daisy bank corner int. Low.r bra wood o be well made up — speak.s
... been present.d at court, to y.e King & Queen, ... rest, h.d sept.e audiences
... & w.s at y.e Queen's ball on her birthnight, & at y.e ball y.e other night —
... is heir presumptive to y.e throne; this princess is one of y.e handsom.st ...
... w.m seen — she is clever, too, & m.st grac.y & genteel. — y.e Queen is a v.ry
... of g.t tact & talent, v.ry handso. in earl.r life, still goodlook.g, & tells
big, & good style & dress — you w.d be pleas.d to see how well I am rec.d here — I am
... at ... not doing for y.e post & bag fr. y.t w.ch goes off y.e office at 7) my lett.r to
Skircoat Hall, Halifax, Yorkshire, England" — y.e last d.nr any wine to-d.
... 47 to-day — How time slips away! — out at 5 ... to L.d Hawt. and sat w.
till 8 ... by.d h.e & tête kiss During h.r! tête kiss Galli apart.t at 50 l/s
carpet all complete — L.d Hawt. r.d y.e cook the sp.a of w.ch he gl.d to co. on...

$5762 = 1 - 3 = 240\,4 \sqrt{5} \neq 32\,2 : \sqrt{5}\sqrt{2}13\,3213 \quad 2\phi32 \quad 73 = 83 : \sqrt{3}\leftarrow240\,486. \; 13$
$358\sqrt{2}\wedge\,4\rho l - 4\cap\odot\wedge - 213\,64\wedge5 - 34\wedge3\frac{1}{4}30 \quad C6\wedge4 + 272 : 2\phi3\wedge45\wedge5$
$2\wedge3\rho2 \cdot = 3 - = \sqrt{5}\wedge04 \neq 32 = 30 - = +321\,4\wedge\wedge\neq =\wedge62\rho\wedge\sqrt{5}6\rho\wedge3\langle27 \quad \sqrt{3}\sqrt{5}6$
$4\wedge82 = 204 = 20 \,\supset2\wedge\wedge\supset3\sqrt{2}\wedge\#4 = \wedge3\rho040\sqrt{5}\wedge1\sqrt{5}8\odot3\rho \quad 4\wedge!\sqrt{5}\wedge4\supset3\,C6\wedge$
$3\phi304 - 4\wedge\odot\wedge\sqrt{5}\wedge\langle32 = 130\wedge5 - ;\wedge \quad 1\sqrt{3}8\sqrt{5}\sqrt{5}\wedge2\wedge2\langle4\wedge = \wedge C6\wedge\odot2\odot\sqrt{5}\wedge - 57$
$\wedge4\wedge2\langle7\,2\supset\wedge6\,24 = \wedge2\wedge3\wedge$ ... $\wedge2\wedge\supset3 = - $ ho. al
... ey — F 53° in y.e salon n.w at 12 tonight —

... frosty morn.g. F 46° on my writ.g desk in my bedr.m, at 9 a.m. w.
... on Bluch.r. Will y.e fine morn.t tempt you to tt. n.drive? if it will, fix ...
... call for you in my own car.t fr. out of w.ch one can see (conseq.y) I shall
... eyes like y.rs useless) h.nce will go where you please — v.ry truly y.rs &
...ever. 1833" — 1.st off st.r ... y.e ab.t to the countess de Blucher" at 10 — dressi...
... v.d (N. p.64 to go lamps lit. hit. of Denmark — y.e Eugenie ha. left ...
... y.e house up to pick y.e lock on find a key to y.t ... — v.d st.t pray.d to
... it. & g.d ph. to st.t till 12 & out in my own car.ge at t.t Blucher's at 12...
... Cottenham — 40 mins. walk y.e — & th.r dr.m at home & ... call.d
... Eckhart — fnd M.r Hockschieser y.re — M.r E. ca. in than.g me d.n by ca...
$354 + 13 \quad 484 : \odot2\supset3\wedge5 - 573\wedge\sqrt{3} -,$ left my card for in.r Wheaton y.e americ...
... at 3 ... Eugenie annoy.d by his expenses — dress.d — M.r & de Hagema...

CHAPTER 11

COPENHAGEN

❦

*'I have been presented at court to the King and
Queen and the rest. Had separate audiences of
the Queen and the 5 princesses and was at the
Queen's ball on her birth night'*

Anne was delighted by Copenhagen. From the
window of her stylish room at the Hotel Royal,
she could see the sparkling new Christiansborg, built on the
site of the former palace which had been destroyed by fire.
She felt welcome in Denmark, noting none of the stares that
followed her masculine apparel and gait in the English prov-
inces. In a letter to her aunt, Anne described a routine of
walking '7 English miles on the Roskilde road about 3 days a
week' and of being 'out almost every evening' (9th November 1833). The small city lent itself perfectly to a busy social
life. Vere's half-sister, Lady Harriet de Hageman, lived a short
distance away on a street called Amaliagade. Countess Emily
Blucher lived close by at Blancogade, all of which made for
an instant and ready-made community for Anne to call upon.

A letter from Mariana Lawton attempted to pour cold water
on Anne's new adventure. Mariana wrote that she had heard
that Copenhagen was 'the court of dullness' and that people
had told her that Anne would 'not like it here'. Anne replied
that she had not had any 'time to find it so'. She told Mariana
that she had dined with the de Hagemans 'yesterday and

Thursday', had 'refused today', but 'should go tomorrow and should go, if I could, to Countess Blucher this evening' (21st September 1833). The de Hagemans were indeed turning out to be genial hosts, almost fawning and wishing to do as much as they could to make Anne feel welcome and comfortable.

Anne took pleasure in filling in Mariana on her schedule of social engagements, and her 'very pretty', 'very agreeable and useful' travelling companion. The uncharacteristically complimentary account of Sophie Ferrall was an attempt to provoke Mariana. 'Let Mariana take Willoughby Crewe,' she wrote a week later. 'She will not get hold of me again in a hurry' (8th October 1833).

Amongst the first packet of letters she had received Anne was struck that there had been no word from Scotland about Miss Walker. Anne was puzzled, wondering if Elizabeth Sutherland had taken offence at her detailed advice for Ann's recovery. 'Perhaps she did not quite like my last,' she mused on 19th September. 'Well, I am easy about it. If I can only make my income do, it is all I want.'

Anne found her new surroundings intellectually stimulating. She took daily German lessons from a Mr Christiani and practised her newly acquired skills by reading the memoirs of German dramatist August Kotzebue and the *Hamburg Reporter*. She devoured travel volumes, memoirs and books on astronomy. During her ten weeks in Denmark, she wrote nearly 40,000 words in her journal, observing the people and places around her.

Her own 'gaucheries' were unflinchingly recorded. The aristocratic circles in which she found herself moving were thrilling, but they provided frequent opportunities for embarrassment. Introduced to Madame Rosencrantz, a Russian royal and widow of the late Danish Prime Minister, Anne misread her social cue:

> *She shook hands with difficulty last night. Like a goose I offered my hand this morning, which she positively declined, and on my hoping to see her often this winter she said as little as possible.*
>
> 11th October 1833

During a night at the theatre, she made another faux pas:

> *Made a grand mistake in supposing the music of* Robert le Diable *by Rossini! By Meyerbeer ... Got over my blunder as well as perhaps such a blunder could be got over. What in the world do I know of operas?*
>
> 3rd November 1833

She was now mingling with people who had more knowledge than her 'about the theatres of Paris', who talked 'excessively' about them, leaving her to conclude that she must learn more about these things in order to contribute effectively in 'company conversation'.

She remained a confident theatre critic in the privacy of her journal. Of Goethe's *Faust* she wrote that 'the dancing was very fair, but the women had such bad legs' (21st October 1833).

Anne's social slips did not impede her entry into the highest level of Danish society. Invitations to be presented at court and, subsequently, to attend the Queen's birthday ball came astonishingly quickly. They were facilitated by the connections she had begun to cultivate through the de Hagemans with important high society people like the Swedish minister Mr Hockschild, the Russian Ambassador Baron Nikolai and Mr Sarmento, the Portuguese chargé d'affaires,

Peter Brown, a British chargé d'affaires, proved a particularly useful figure. Overcoming her initial judgement that he was a 'common Methodist' with 'dirty nails' (7th October 1833), Anne accepted his offer of royal introduction in appropriately courtly language:

> *Miss Lister regrets very much being in the country when he was so good to call on Friday. Finding that being presented at Court might make her winter here more agreeable, Miss Lister would be glad to have her audiences before the Queen's birthday.*

15th October 1833

The evening of 23rd October did not begin well. Dressed to impress in black satin with her 'thinnest black silk stockings and silk shoes', Anne made a royal blunder:

> *Unluckily took the chief maid for the Queen because of her broad red ribbon and star. Got over it well enough and did not care so much as I might have done.*

Having eventually identified the right woman to curtsey to, Anne seemed to recover well:

About 10 minutes audience of the Queen. At about 65, a nice neat little figure, looking very well but sadly too much rouged. Very gracious. Then to Princess Caroline, the King's daughter, that was burnt. Her throat and lower part of her face still bearing strong traces of the fire. About 5 minutes with her. Not au fait *at audiences like the Queen, not much to say for herself but very civil.*

23rd October 1833

Princess Christian, the wife of the heir to the throne, was Anne's favourite. She was deemed 'very handsome, very dignified but pleasing and agreeable', and their lively conversation, which ranged from the Notre Dame cathedral to beech trees, prompted Anne to feel, by the end of the night, quite 'in love with Princess Christian'.

Returning to her 'great gaucherie' as she completed the day's diary entry, Anne was matter-of-fact. 'I wonder what they all thought of me,' she wrote. 'I joked about it to the Bluchers this morning gently. I shall learn in time.'

As her stay in Copenhagen progressed, Anne perceived that her new friends were competing to impress her with their royal connections:

I shall tread my ground cautiously with the Browns. Neither they, nor others, like the de Hs. I see they [the de

Hagemans] *are vexed at my have gone to court and would gladly have kept me away. What could be their reason? She* [Harriet] *thought I had been very often at the Bluchers ... There is jealousy at the bottom. Well, she may make herself unhappy but not me.*

26th October 1833

Harriet de Hageman had also refused to introduce Anne to the Spanish minister's wife over dinner and, though she subsequently apologised, Anne was beginning to tire of the intricacies of etiquette. As someone who exercised a great deal of control over her life at home, she disliked feeling like a pawn in a game of society rivalry. 'I always think I can do without the world if I can't have it to my mind,' she wrote on 27th October 1833.

Having acquired a 'good travelling carriage' which gained her 'several smart unknown bows' from Copenhagen locals on 28th October – as well as a pleasing degree of personal independence – Anne's pressing task was to find a suitable outfit for the Queen's birthday ball.

It was not an easy one. Anne had always found dressing for society a 'potheration', and on this occasion her dress must be not only appropriately feminine, but white. The last time she had visited the palace, the court had been in mourning for the King of Spain. Now, as well as shedding the armour of her usual masculine great coat, pelisse and gaitered boots, she acknowledged that it would be 'impossible to go to a birthday wearing black'. Gamely, she resolved to abandon her uniform ('throw it off for the night') and enlisted Eugenie to make her a white satin gown.

The evening before the royal birthday party, Lady Harriet de Hageman, Sophie Ferrall and her sister the Countess Blucher assembled and approved Eugenie's efforts. Silk stockings and two birds of paradise feathers, to be affixed to Anne's hair by a French coiffeur, would complete the look.

Amidst the excitement of preparing for the party, Anne's thoughts turned to Ann Walker. Though she had received intelligence from her aunt that Ann was intending to return to Halifax – 'though she had not mentioned it to Mrs Sutherland, on account of her (Mrs Sutherland's) not being well' (15th October 1833) – Anne had still not heard back directly from Ann's sister in reply to her own letter from Paris. She was torn about whether to try again. 'I have thought much about Miss Walker lately,' she wrote on the afternoon of the ball, 'In doubt whether to write again to Mrs Sutherland or not. What could I do with the poor girl?' (30th October 1833).

That evening, Mr Brown called for Anne in the stylish carriage that would take them to the palace. Luckily, his wife was able to deal with a wardrobe malfunction en route. 'One of my birds of paradise came down in the carriage,' wrote Anne. 'Mrs B arranged it on arriving.' As they entered, the outfit was praised:

> *Princess Christian admired my headdress. I said I had had* grand peur [great fear] *about it. It had come down and Mrs. Brown had arranged it. One of the Queen's Maids of*

Honour observed my magnificent blonde [cape] *and said*
it was not from Paris. Yes, but I had bought it here. Was in
black and had nothing white with me. Could get everything
good but stockings.

Though Anne began to worry that her address to the royal had
been over-familiar – 'I generally, on coming away, remember
some gaucherie' – she judged the rest of the evening a success.
The palace and people were sharply observed in her diary:

Might be about 50 ladies in front and as many behind
and perhaps half as many more. The Queen, the Princesses
Christian (Caroline Amalia), and Caroline Princess
Royal, and then her young sister Wilhelmina followed
round the circle. Mrs Brown stood between Mrs Stuart
Courtenay and myself, to present us to the King. As the
Queen began with the Lady's half circle, the King began
with the gent's half. Each went the whole round, and then
to the ballroom, all following the Royal family. Dancing till
12, then 30 ladies and 30 gents drew lots for each other and
all the rest of us went to the Grand Marshall's table (in the
King's palace), up and down dirty narrow stairs and along
long, low passages, at which his deputy, Mr. Crow presided.
The ex-Dresden Minister's wife on his right and I on his left
... handed round supper, but nothing looking particularly
good to eat but took some quince and some blancmange
and a glass of goodish red wine and a glass of tolerable
champagne, to drink the Queen's and Princess Charlotte's

birthdays. The president gave their health. Drank in silence. A third birthday today but not mentioned.

We then went back to the salon, only 5 ladies besides Mrs Brown and myself, all the rest had gone home. Saw the Royal party again (except the King and Queen), and then got to our carriages as soon as we could. Set down Mr and Mrs Brown and home at 3.35. Everybody very civil to me, very well amused but now that I have seen the thing once, will not trouble the Marshall's table again. Not fond of second tables, even in the houses of Kings. The party said to be unusually small. No diamonds but those worn by the Royal family. Princess Christian the finest woman in the room and Miss Ferrall the prettiest, best dressed girl. No magnificence of dress but everything assez bien. The palace moderately handsome. All the Princesses spoke to me conversationally. Particularly Princess Christian and the Princess Wilhelmina.

30th October 1833

Minor criticisms aside, which included having to sit at the 'second table' next to the King and Queen rather than the top table, Anne was relishing her stay in the Danish capital. Her intellect, energy and charisma were quickly recognised, and her company sought after. 'I am invited everywhere,' she wrote happily to her aunt on 9th November 1833.

Madame Hage, another of the de Hagemans' set, took a particular shine to Anne. She asked Anne if she 'knew Latin and Greek' and if she 'had read Virgil, Horace, Homer in their originals', to which Anne replied, 'guilty'. Anne told

Madame Hage that poetry was not her strength, leaving the latter feeling somewhat deflated. Madame Hage seems to have imagined herself as a possible travelling companion for Anne, saying how she 'envied' Anne's talk of journeying to Russia. 'In fact,' said Anne, 'she would gladly go with me if I gave this the least encouragement' (11th November 1833).

If her friendships were going from strength to strength, Anne's relationship with her servants was not so harmonious. Neither Thomas Beech nor Eugenie had reached the level of skill or devotion that Anne had been expecting. At times they were incompetent, losing her clothes and misplacing their keys. Eugenie, Anne noted, 'seemed to think it hard to hem a towel and duster' (24th November 1833). She had also taken to going out at night without Anne's permission:

> *Eugenie came back at 9 ½. I see there is no trusting her. Her excuses are ready enough, but that she only went out when I went out to dinner was an untruth. She did not seem to care a great deal (though very civil as to servant like propriety in saying not much). I told her I should try to take better care of her in future, and if I could not manage her, should send her back to her parents. Said I had a right mind to write to her mother, but this seemed to make no great impression.*

11th November 1833

Her manservant unwillingly corroborated the facts – 'Thomas did not like to say much but owned to her being out ½ a dozen times or more.'

On 19th November, news from home signalled a premature end to Anne's stay in Copenhagen. A worrying letter arrived from Marian about Aunt Anne's 'exceedingly precarious state of health'. The first two pages had been written by Dr Kenny:

Both legs have been more or less oedematous for some time past but one in particular became very much so within the last few weeks, and a small ulcer which latterly formed upon it has assumed a most unhealthy aspect. Indeed, within the last few days it has increased rapidly in extent by a gangrenous state of the surrounding skin and cellular membrane. At present, it has a defined margin, but the slough has not yet wholly separated.

In this enfeebled state in which your aunt's general health is found at the present day, it is impossible to say whether the gangrene may at any time extend rapidly beyond the present limits and lead to a fatal termination. With so much constitutional disturbance, the pulse is, as might be expected, constantly above 100.

If I were to hazard an opinion, which might tend to influence your plans, it is whether you should or should not return to the country at present, it would be this. Gangrene possibly, may upon any day, extend rapidly and destroy life long before you could possibly arrive in this country. On the other hand, the gangrene, having at present set limits to itself the sphacelated part may slough away, leaving an ulcer which need not of necessity destroy life, though I do

not anticipate under any circumstances its evidencing a
disposition to heal soon, if ever.

19th November 1832

Anne found herself conflicted. Though she suspected that Dr Kenny – who, along with Marian, she had long branded as an 'alarmist' – was being melodramatic, her aunt's health was too dear to her to run the risk.

A week later her decision had been made. The newly rented flat at 158 Amaliagade, where she had intended to live until the following spring, was let go, and plans were made for her immediate return journey to England. Despite the 'real and flattering kindness' that she would leave behind, and the inhospitable winter weather that she knew she would encounter, there was only one thing on Anne's mind. 'Deeply anxious to be home,' she wrote, 'in time to see my poor aunt alive' (28th November 1833).

***

'Terrible night, tremendous wind and rain, could not
sleep for the noise of this and the water dashing against
my head and the vessel striking every now and then
against the wooden break water'

The journey was as treacherous as Anne had feared. On board the *Columbine*, the ship that was to bring her party home following several days on the road through Germany, Anne did not need to be warned that there was 'a tremendous sea outside' by Captain John Corbin. 'Our vessel heaved about so much before the tide raised her quite off the ground' she wrote. 'I was really sick and got rid of all my tea and bread and butter ... I can't stand all this motion.' (11th December 1833). On 8th December the wind had severed the bowsprit from their ship, leaving them stranded at the port of Cuxhaven. Other vessels had fared even worse:

> *The water muddy looking, great deal of muck, seaweed*
> *floating about and several floating logs and boards of*
> *vessels. Passed the wrecks of two brigs, the last with half of*
> *her mast standing up out of the water was the Hamburg*
> *brig lost on Sunday morning in the gale that broke our*
> *bowsprit at 12 on Saturday night.*

12th December 1833

Anne's sea-sickness continued as the journey progressed:

> *The rough water made me sick immediately. Threw myself*
> *on the hard covered bench at the foot of the cot and sick and*
> *retching almost incessantly for the next 11 hours ... Tho'*
> *somehow about ten at night crawled in the dark into the*
> *water closet and had a tolerable motion. So far a good effect*
> *of my sickness. The wind was soon getting out of the river in*
> *our favour towards evening the vessel rolled so tremendously,*
> *nothing not very fast could keep its place. My table and stool*
> *were turned upside down to slide about that way. My candle*
> *would sit in a basin jammed in the table bottom that the*

candlelight danced about so in the basin I could scarce help
laughing. Cooler on the bench than in the cot and more
convenient for being sick so there I lay in my cloak and my
travelling cap with my travelling bag for a pillow.

12th December 1833

Between the bouts of sickness that punctuated the two-week voyage, Anne attempted to spend as much time as possible alone. She found the company of her fellow passengers tedious – particularly the American merchant who said 'nothing worth hearing' – and the conversation of the ship's captain lacking – 'after one or two insufficient answers to my observations [he] said no more' (10th December 1833).

She preferred to read. Having made her way through the 'first large edition of all Lord Byron's works', she moved on to a pamphlet on handy household hints. To cure a corn, she noted, one must 'roast a clove of garlic on a live coal in hot ashes and bind it on the corn on going to bed. This should be repeated 2 or 3 times in the 24 hours' (8th December 1833).

Thomas and Eugenie were not good travellers. They were wet, tired and struggled to withstand the rigours and hardships of the inclement weather. Anne branded her manservant 'sadly soft and cowardly about himself, and a great lout'. He was worse even than George Playforth. 'It seems to be my fate to have louts about me,' she lamented on 4th December. Eugenie, told that she was 'headless and useless' by a mistress who had been considering giving her the sack throughout the journey, promised to try harder. Anne agreed keep her on.

On 15th December 1833, fifteen days after leaving Copenhagen, a weary and dishevelled Anne, Thomas and Eugenie disembarked the *Columbine* at Gravesend docks. Their return to dry land was welcome. Apart from having splashed her face with cold water, Anne had not washed, or removed her clothes, for the last fifteen days.

The Ship Tavern at Gravesend was a 'sad, dirty place' with rumpled bedsheets, but there was at least 'good, thickish broth (mutton) and toast' and soap for a 'thorough scrub'. Relieved to be back on terra firma, Anne slept for five hours, with a towel for a pillow case, dressing gown as a top sheet, and her damp, filthy great coat for a nightshift.

Of the five days following her return to England, Anne wrote nothing. The blank pages of her diary, presumably left so for her to return to, stand out in a volume in which every other inch of space is tightly and meticulously filled with letters and symbols. The missing days encompassed a visit to Mariana at Lawton Hall, and a letter that Anne received two days after her return to Shibden hints at what may have passed between them over the 16th–20th December. 'I think she begins to be sorry for herself. Likes me better than Willoughby Crewe, and thanks me for my uniform kindness and generous conduct' (23rd December 1833). It sounded as if Anne and Mariana had been going over the old, painful ground of their past relationship.

On her return to Shibden, Anne discovered that she had been right about Dr Kenny and Marian's alarmist impulses. Aunt Anne's demise did not, thankfully, appear to be as imminent as she had been led to believe. Writing to Lady Stuart, Anne recounted:

> *Found my aunt a great deal better than it was possible to expect from the very alarming accounts I had received. She is certainly in a precarious state and suffers a great deal, but, if I might venture to depend at all upon my own judgment, I would say the danger was less imminent than it had been represented and that life might be prolonged for a considerable time, at least for many months. I have no fear of her not getting over the winter unless there should be some sudden change, which I do not at present see any reason to apprehend.*

21st December 1833

Anne found the time to admonish Dr Kenny for summoning her back in the mid-winter. 'Told him it was unfair and absurd to send for me under such circumstances. I had come at this risk of my own life and that of my servants,' she wrote. Dr Kenny masterfully passed the buck. 'He said it was not his doing, he wished Marian not to send for me but she did it in her fright' (23rd December 1833).

But Anne could not stay angry for long. Nor could she truly regret coming home. Her aunt's health, and her delight at their reunion, meant everything to Anne. 'I shall never repent not having hesitated about it,' she wrote on 21st December 1833, and reflecting to Lady Harriet de Hageman a few months later:

My poor aunt suffers a martyrdom and may well survive
some months. It was her arms that first held me – hers was
like a mother's care, and to her liberal kindness, were owing
half the comforts of my early life. I see her sinking slowly,
painfully into the grave, and at such a time the heart even
of a casual bystander would not be hardest, nor his spirits
lightest. I shall feel lonely when she is gone.

9th March 1834

She acknowledged that she had done right to leave her life in
Copenhagen behind. 'My coming made her happy, and I am
satisfied.'

frosty morn. F 43° at 10½ — brkft. at 10¾ — wait ½ hr. w. ...

N. ca. sw. — sup. st. read & talk & tea 3 — out fr. 3¼ to 4⁴⁰ walkd. ...

din. at 5¾ — coff. tea — ca. upst. at 11½ p. N. in bed — morn. out & ...

bed r. fr. p. 360 to p. 384 end of vol. 1. "Transatlantic Sketches, comp...

visits to ye m.t. interest & scenes in N.th & S.th Amca., the West Ind. w.

notes on negro slav. & Canadian emigrat. By Capt. J. E. Alexandr.,

Royl. Highlanders. F.R.G. S. M.R.A.S. etc. auth. of Travls. in Ava, Persia,

in 2 vols. vol. 1. Lond.: Rich.d Bentley, New Burlington St. Publishr.

ord. to his majesty. 1833." 2 vols. 8vo pp. 384 and 320.

"Print. by Saml. Bentley, Dorset St."

... made sent. Sat. fr. ... abt. 2 vols. — R. als. ... 1st. 72 pm. vol. 1. McGregor's

tide 12¾ tonight — y. ... ... abt. of today — ver. fine day F 43° now at 12²⁵ tonight

morn. F 42° at 10½ a. m. — ... st. at 11 — ho. N. wife Belco. today diffi...

who left us ...

— wr. a few lines by Norcliffe, enclos. in C N's let. ... milne, & Jo...

d. bien york ys. tomor. — wr. als. to m. milne sent. ... seal of C N's let.

... man. hap. ... opp. ... & to assure h. opp. remembce. ... ... opp. imp...

— out let 3. walkd. on ye wood, and ho. at 4³⁵ — drop. din. at 5 — c...

Causes célèbres ye trial opp. marquise de ~~Bren~~ Brinvilliers to head

ye burnt & thrown to ye winds, in Paris, in ye time of Louis 14 a. d. by

... by broth. ... attempt. to pois. her sist. & broth. ...

head draw at Bremen hav? — R. als. in ye course opp. day fr. p. 7...

macgregor's Brit. Amca. — ca. upst. at 11½ — ver. fine frosty day F ...

tonight —

morn. F 41½ at 10¾ a. m., — M. N. lent me ye 2 vols. 8vo opp. ...

w. D lost away w. me — talk to 1 or oth. — off br. laugh. at 3²⁰...

& stopt slept to at M. Belcombe's in ye minster court at 5¹¹ — y. ...

at M. Belco's — ca. off Black swan at 7 — drop. — at M. B's at 8...

... lodg. for miss W — supp. & if Phillips ... twd. exam. ... for travl. — th...

... W. to Copenhagen w. ... — M. H. Belco. w. to ... ... at 9¼ —

... tea ... B's — tea ag. — ment. ye Washington Capt. Jefferson ...

sail fr. Liverpool to Canton 1st. next ... — Hamlin mild. w. be lucky if ...

keep ... as a com. sailor — all ye support. by M. Bulcock & ...

at M. Belco. Louisa & W. ... / M. ... miss Belco. at ... ... p. ... — ...

din. in chain at 11 — fine, soft, muggy warm day — F 45° in ye bedr. at ...

GENTLEMAN JACK

FINALE – STANDING BEFORE GOD

'Miss Walker returned to Lidgate!!! Fred, is this to be your fate?'

On 27 December, Anne Lister received a letter from Ann Walker. It conveyed a remarkable coincidence. Ann was not in Scotland, but at Lidgate. She had arrived on Christmas Eve, just a few days after Anne's own return to Shibden. She had known nothing of Anne's serendipitous homecoming until she had called at the hall, to see Anne's aunt and uncle.

Anne was fifty miles away, at the Norcliffe's estate near York, when she received the news. She and Miss Walker fell into a correspondence immediately, making plans for a reunion in the first days of January. Anne was hopeful that she would find Ann much recovered after her period of recuperation in Scotland:

> *My letter altogether a kind one, she should cheer up now as she had so much reason to hope all she could desire. Will do all I can for her, never to think of repaying me. Once well again, her health and happiness would be enough and all that I desired.*

30th December 1833

Ann Walker was as eager as ever to see Anne Lister. She promised to 'count each day and hour' until her arrival.

'How extraordinarily my return and hers too so close and unexpected on each other!' wrote Anne in her diary (27th December 1833), and it was not long before she relayed the news to Mariana. Her former lover suggested that Anne's destiny was preordained:

> *Miss Walker returned to Lidgate!!! Fred, is this to be your fate? How strange her return this time. It puts me in mind of the gypsy's prophecy to me, and the thought would almost persuade me that we are not free agents.*
>
> 4th January 1834

Anne was more circumspect. 'Miss W's return is indeed odd,' she replied. 'Your surprise could not exceed my own, but do not let your conclusion run on too rapidly' (7th January 1834).

On 4th January, Anne made the familiar brisk journey on foot from Shibden to Lidgate:

> *Miss Walker delighted to see me, looking certainly better in spirits than when I saw her last, but probably this improvement is merely the result of the present pleasure and excitement on seeing me.*

After ten months apart, the two women had a lot to discuss:

> *Much talk last night till 4 this morning and then not asleep for a long while. She repented having left me. Longed*

to go after me to Copenhagen. Had had Mr Ainsworth
writing and offering again. Once thought she ought to
marry, lastly refused him. Her sister told him she was
not able to judge for herself, but he did not mind that, so
both Captain and Mrs Sutherland got annoyed at him. I
suppose saw through him.

5th January 1834

It seemed that Miss Walker now spoke of wanting to commit to Anne, to try again, as if there was a degree of certainty in her thinking that they could now be together. Anne Lister was less sure, and commented how, 'Miss W talked as if she would be glad to take me, then, if I say anything decisive, she hesitates.'

Anne was on her guard, and she wondered whether the real reason Miss Walker had arrived back in Halifax so suddenly was purely based on her need 'to get away from the Sutherlands'. Was Anne only the second reason for her return? This was why Anne saw Miss Walker now feeling 'the want' of her.

Anne had neither the energy nor the inclination to fall back into the circuitous pattern of their old relationship. If there was to be hope of a romantic future, she needed Ann Walker to finally commit to her. To exchange rings and take the sacrament with her before God. To become her wife. 'I am older in these matters than I was twenty years ago,' wrote Anne. ''Tis well my care for her will not kill me, whether she says eventually, yes or no' (6th January 1834).

There remained a question mark over Ann Walker's ability to undertake a life-changing decision. She had not received medical attention in Scotland, and Anne Lister was keen that she should be reassessed by Dr Belcombe in York. 'She seemed lowish,' Anne wrote on 8th January. 'Getting a little into the old way, despairing of being quite well ... felt so oddly afraid of not caring for anybody.'

Soon, the arrangements had been made. On 23rd January, Anne settled Ann Walker into a discreet facility at Heworth Grange on the outskirts of York, where she could recover under the care of Dr Belcombe, within visiting distance of Shibden.

It was during a return to Lidgate in the middle of February – which Ann Walker made ostensibly for the reason of visiting an ailing aunt, Mrs Atkinson – that their union was finally agreed. Calling there on 9th February, Anne Lister noted that Ann was 'looking and being considerably better than when I saw her last'. There was talk of a trip to Paris, which could be carried off in tantalising style thanks to Miss Walker's wealth. 'She will pay all and I will make all answer as well as I can, however things may be' Anne wrote, ever-honest about the draw of Miss Walker's financial circumstances.

Though Anne remained determined to resist Ann's desire for her to be fully naked during their lovemaking without her commitment – 'She has often said she wished to be near myself' (12th February 1834) – their physical connection appeared stronger than ever:

She was, at first, tired and sleepy but by and by roused up
and during a long grubbling, said often we had never done

*it so well before. I was hot to washing tub wetness and tired
before it was half over. We talked and never slept till 5.*

10th February 1834

The same day, Anne Lister stated her case for their union a final time:

*Better make up her mind at once or what could I do? She
agreed and it was understood she was to consider herself as
nobody to please and being under no authority but mine. To
make her will right directly and on returning from France
and on my aunt's death, then to add a codicil leaving me
a life estate in all she could and I would do the same to her.
Well then, is it really settled or not?*

10th February 1834

Two days later, the decision appeared final. She and Ann Walker
were to pledge themselves to each other in a lifetime of commitment. The coded line in her diary on 12th February 1834 is
small, understated and momentous: 'She is to give me a ring
and I her one in token of our union, as confirmed on Monday.'

<hr>

'You have made up your mind – you therefore have, or ought to have, courage to avow it'

Anne Lister was wary of counting her blessings too soon. Her
diary entries display a level of caution as she began to prepare

the ground for the life she hoped to live with Miss Walker. She confided the plan to her aunt:

> *Talked to my aunt tonight as if the thing was nearly done but I should know better in York, tacitly meaning that I should then make her give me a ring and bind herself by a decided promise.*

17th February 1834

Her reflections on a letter to Ann Walker demonstrated a similar instinct for self-preservation until the union had taken place:

> *She seems to have been pleased with my affectionate letter, 'do come quickly for I am getting dull and I want you in a thousand ways.' I see she will be fond of me by and by. If she will bind herself so that I can have confidence, I hope and think we shall get on together happily.*

21st February 1834

On 27th February 1834, Anne and Ann exchanged rings. As they travelled together towards a call at the Norcliffes' estate, the pact was quietly made:

> *I asked her to cut the gold wedding ring I wore and leant her sixpence to pay me for it. She would not give it me immediately but wore it till we entered the village of Langton and then put it on my left 3rd finger in token of*

our union, which is now understood to be confirmed forever
though little or nothing was said.

27th February 1834

Ann was to wear the onyx ring that Anne had purchased for
her in York. Though it would be another month before the
two women took the sacrament together at Goodramgate
church, the symbolic exchange of rings appeared to be enough
for Anne Lister to have complete confidence in their bond.
That day, she allowed herself to be 'near' to Ann:

No drawers on last night. First time and first attempt to
get really near her. Did not succeed very well but she seemed
tolerably satisfied.

27th February 1834

Though Ann had agreed to move into Shibden Hall in princi-
ple, she remained reticent about going public with (a sanitised
version of) her decision to live as Anne Lister's companion.
She was wary that she and Anne should not be too explicit in
their letters to one another, for fear of attracting the attention
of the notoriously nosy local postmistress and, by extension,
the interest of the community:

Said that as I wrote for the eye of Mrs Bagnold more than
ordinary caution was required. Miss W had begged me not
to write anything particular – not to get ourselves laughed
at. I believe she is fond of me and however unreserved and

on the amoroso at night in bed no allusion to these matters
ever escapes her in the day. In fact she is then r[e]ally modest
and nicely particular enough.

4th March 1834

Anne responded sensitively but firmly to Ann's reluctance to brave the judgement of her extended family. As Anne had always been true to her nature, she now wanted Ann Walker to find the same kind of inner strength to respect her own desires. Guilt and grief had dogged Ann's adult life; here she had a chance to live it as she wanted to. It would be a difficult task, but Anne hoped to convince Ann that together, they could be happy:

A proper respect for public opinion is due from all, but it
is best shown by paying a proper respect to ourselves, and
that is always difficult under circumstances which seem
equivocal. You have made up your mind – you therefore
have, or ought to have, courage to avow it.

12th March 1834

Anne was able to be so confident about their shared future partly because she had the full support of her family. Her relationship with her sister seemed to have taken a positive turn since 11th January, when she had had a 'long talk with Marian about her always crying when I say anything to her'. In fact, Marian now revealed her delight with Miss Walker as a match for Anne:

Stood talking to Marian near an hour till after 7 in the hall.
Laughed and asked which would suit me best – M, or Miss W – ?
She thought the latter would be more convenient, and then
agreed with me that she would suit me in every respect the best –
I said I would rather take her connections than Mariana's –
'Yes,' said Marian, 'And so would I. They say in York Mrs
Henry Belcombe's father was a tea dealer and her first husband
a spirit merchant'. (Said I did not know.) Both my father and
Marian seem pleased about Miss W. Said I thought I should
be happier with her than I should now be with Mrs Lawton, to
which Marian seemed to agree without the least surprise.

7th March 1834

Four days later, Anne was able to offer Marian support in her
own love life, rebutting the unwanted attentions of a local
George Brearley on her little sister's behalf:

'Sir, my sister has just received your letter, which she has
very properly put into my hands, as also a copy of her
answer of the third January to your previous letter, which
answer ought to have prevented your giving her any further
trouble. I hope you will deem this communication from me
sufficiently explicit, and that you will see the necessity of
forbearing either to write again, or to call at Shibden Hall
on any plea whatsoever. I am, Sir, etc. etc. AL.' Marian
much pleased and obliged and being just going to Halifax
put it into the post herself.

11th March 1834

As the spring progressed, Anne Lister shared her confidence in the future with those outside her family circle. To Mrs Norcliffe, to whom she had introduced Ann Walker directly after their exchange of rings, Anne wrote a letter full of heartfelt thanks:

Come what may I never do and never shall forget all your kindness. I always think with gratitude and pleasure that you at least have done me the justice to believe I had some sincerity, some steadiness of heart, some deeper and better feeling than many have given me credit for. I have been annoyed and hurt by those from whom I least deserve and least expected it. But you have never changed in kindness, nor I in gratitude in 4 and 20 years. Believe me Mrs Norcliffe, always very affectionately yours, AL.

16th March 1834

Mariana Lawton had been made aware of the events that had followed Miss Walker's return from Scotland. Her emotionally charged letters to Anne spoke of her regret that things must now be at a firm end between them:

Freddy, since you have been in York, my thoughts have been perpetually full of you. I do love you dearly and fondly. Come what may, my heart is not unfaithful, and still as formerly and for ever my joys by yours are known.

11th March 1834

On 30th March 1834, Anne Lister and Ann Walker performed the second act of their symbolic union. At 10.35am, the two women, in the escort of servant Thomas Beech, stepped into the tiny church of the Holy Trinity just off Goodramgate in York, and took communion together:

> *Miss W and I and Thomas stayed the sacrament. Almost all the congregation stayed, and though the church too small to hold many, the service took 40 minutes. The first time I ever joined Miss W in my prayers. I had prayed that our union might be happy.*
>
> 30th March 1834

To Anne Lister, their commitment had been solemnised. They had been joined together in the eyes of God. The afternoon of an historic day passed quietly and mundanely, with a routine of social calls. The next day, the couple made a trip to town to pay for a number of silver forks at Barber and Cattle's and to enquire about a new manservant. Thomas Beech, fittingly, was leaving Shibden to marry his sweetheart.

It was September 1834 before Ann Walker moved into Shibden Hall. While the Listers welcomed her, her own extended family were less enthusiastic. Interpreting the move as an abandonment of her elderly aunt at Cliff Hill, they cast Anne Lister as a coercive force who had stolen away their relative for her own mercenary purposes. Making their feelings clear over the coming years, Miss Walker's family were known to call unannounced at Shibden to see Ann, pointedly refusing to acknowledge or shake hands with Anne Lister.

The two women stood firm and, as Shibden was reno-
vated around them, remained companions until the end of
Anne's life. Though their relationship was never free of the
strain of Ann Walker's anxiety, and was frequently the site of
financial disagreement, they honoured their early promise that
it should be as lasting and 'as good as a marriage'. Anne Lister
had found the domestic security she had craved all her life. In
celebration of their first anniversary, on 10th February 1835,
she wrote, 'Ann and I had excellent plumb pudding today in
commemoration of the first anniversary of being together so
comfortably and so happily – may we live to enjoy many more.'

Jeremy Lister and the elder Anne died within a few months
of each other in 1836. Anne was heartbroken to lose her aunt,
saying, 'She was always good and kind to me – none will ever
think so highly of me – none was more interested in my interest
– none' (10th October 1836). She lamented the passing of a
generation that had given her much, emotionally and financially, but Shibden was now under her sole ownership.

Marian Lister moved to Market Weighton the same year.
Their parting was surprisingly tender, with Anne comment-
ing how Marian 'Stood talking as if she had not resolution to
leave me – poor Marian! My heart aches for her and for myself
too' (1st May 1836). Anne commissioned a bespoke writing
box for her as a leaving present.

Mariana Lawton eventually became reconciled to Anne's
new life with Ann Walker. Agreeing to spend a week together
at Shibden in the November of 1836, the three women seemed
to find a respectful and contented way of being in each other's

company. Anne remarked how, 'M really likes Ann – and the liking is mutual' (7th November 1836). At first Mariana was shocked at just how settled Anne and Ann were as a couple. Occasionally she tried to tempt Anne with an 'open-lipped' kiss but Anne resisted, refusing all intimacy. 'The fact is,' said Anne, when Mariana left to return to Lawton Hall, 'I am not sorry she is gone' (12th November 1836).

By the end of the 1830s, Anne and Ann's travels were taking them away from Shibden for long stretches at a time. Their tour of Russia was to be Anne's final adventure. In the September of 1840, she died of a fever while travelling through what is now Georgia. She was just 49. Ann Walker returned her body to Shibden in a process that would take six months, the last act of devotion to a woman who had altered the course of her life.

Ann Walker continued to live at Shibden. Sadly, her mental health deteriorated in the period following Anne's death, and following concerns for her safety she was removed from the hall a few years later. Staying for a time in an institution in York, she eventually returned to live at Cliff Hill in Lightcliffe. She died in 1854.

If Anne Lister was a figure of interest in her own lifetime, she leaves an extraordinarily rich legacy today. In 2018, a plaque was erected by the York Civic Trust to commemorate her marriage to Ann Walker, nearly two centuries after their private union at the church of the Holy Trinity in York. The wording on the plaque courted controversy as it referred to Anne as 'gender non-conformer' as opposed to lesbian. It has since been changed to the latter, and is indicative of the importance Anne occupies in lesbian history and consciousness today.

Anne Lister led her life fearlessly. Let's leave the last words to her:

> *With all my faults, Heaven grant me still the virtue of sincerity; and though I walk through many a darksome shade of folly and remorse, still let there be one light, the light of truth to guide me right at last.*

ACKNOWLEDGEMENTS

This book has been a joy and an honour to write. I am indebted to the following people who have helped me bring it to publication.

To my friend and collaborator Sally Wainwright, for her loyalty and encouragement during our wonderful Anne Lister journey together. For the unique opportunity of being able to work with her as creative partner on this project, as well as her adviser on the TV drama, I will be forever grateful.

To Yvonne Jacob of Penguin Random House and Commissioning Editor for BBC Books, for her embracing of my ideas for the book from the outset, and for being a wonderful source of encouragement to me throughout the writing process. To Liz Marvin and Nell Warner at Penguin for their brilliant editing and proof-reading of the manuscript – and for enlightening me about dangling modifiers! A special thank you to my editor Stella Merz, for her expertise in shaping the manuscript, and her support as a member of the Lookout Point team.

To my agent Hilary Delamere for her legal expertise and patient handling of all things business-related during the contract phase – and particularly for putting up with my emails asking, 'Is there any news yet?' Grateful thanks also to Bethan

Evans, whose initial input during the pitching of the book to BBC Books proved invaluable.

To all of my friends at Lookout Point (Team Gentleman Jack!) – Faith Penhale, Will Johnston, Yasmina Hadded and Laura Lankester – for their support and appreciation of my work over the last two years.

To actresses Suranne Jones and Sophie Rundle for so brilliantly bringing the characters of Anne Lister and Ann Walker to life, which helped me to visualise new aspects of their complex relationship as the book progressed. For use of the iconic Anne Lister image on the front cover, I would like to extend further thanks to Suranne.

Love and thanks to Belinda O'Hooley and Heidi Tidow (O'Hooley & Tidow) for sharing fun discussions and for travelling the Gentleman Jack journey with Sally and myself over the last two years.

I am grateful to the staff at West Yorkshire Archive Service in Halifax and to Angela Clare, Collections Manager at Shibden Hall, for assisting myself and the team at Penguin Random House with requests for archival material.

To my wonderful family and friends for realising how important the writing of this book has been to me personally, I send heaps of love and gratitude.

Lastly to Sarah – for her love, for being a patient listener, and for giving me the freedom to read, to think and to write.

INDEX

AL indicates Anne Lister.

Ainsworth, Mrs 116, 174, 176–7, 191, 194, 195, 196, 201, 220
Ainsworth, Reverend Thomas 116, 177, 179, 181–2, 192, 194–5, 196, 197, 198, 199–200, 201, 220, 223, 303

Bagnold, Tabitha 239, 307
Bagot, Sir Charles 11
Barlow, Jane xxxi
Barlow, Maria xxix, xxxi, 158
Beech, Thomas 210, 254, 269, 274, 290, 294, 295, 311
Belcombe, Anne xxx, 130, 158
Belcombe, Dr Stephen (Steph) xxx, 86–7, 99, 142, 166, 170–1, 172–3, 175, 200, 205, 207, 220, 224, 228, 230, 232, 267, 304
Blucher, Countess Emily 261, 277, 281, 282, 285, 286, 287
Blumenbach, Johann Friedrich 272–4
Booth, Charlotte 82
Booth, John xxxiv, 82, 128, 130, 131, 148–9, 157
Booth, Joseph 73, 129

Booth, Martha 82–3
Bottomley, Benjamin 47–8
de Bourke, Madame 261, 264–5, 276
Brearley, George 309
Bremen, Germany 274
Briggs, James 55, 56, 155, 240
Briggs, Rawdon 94
Brontë, Charlotte 83
Brown, Peter 284, 285, 287–8, 289
Bulwer-Lytton, Edward: *Eugene Aram* 17
Burrell, Arthur xxvii
Butler, Lady Eleanor 150–2
Byron, Lord xxiv, 151, 294

Cameron (AL's servant) 3, 17–18, 130
Cameron, Captain Donald 13, 14, 15, 22, 28, 29 30, 77–8, 98, 132, 189, 208–10, 247, 248
Cameron, Lady *see* Hobart (later, Lady Cameron), Vere
Canning, George 10
Caroline of Denmark, Princess 285, 288
Charlotte of Denmark, Princess 288–9
cholera 4–5, 13, 128

Christian of Denmark, Princess 285, 287, 288, 289

Christiansborg, Copenhagen 281

Church of the Holy Trinity, Goodramgate, York 307, 311, 313–14

Cliff Hill, Lightcliffe estate 61, 123, 131, 159, 164, 174–5, 198, 235, 311, 313

Cobb, Dr Charles 50, 51–2

Collins (Ann Walker's tenant) 163, 164, 186–7, 188

Collins, William: 'The Passions. An Ode' 18

Columbine (ship) 292–5

Confalonieri, Federico 276

Conservatoire des Artes, Paris 6

Copenhagen, Denmark 18, 98, 254, 261, 264, 265, 268, 274, 277, 281–97, 303

Corbin, Captain John 293

Cordingley, Elizabeth xxxiv, 29, 77, 83, 118, 168, 169

Cornewall, Sir George xxxii

Crabbe, George 143

Crewe, Willoughby 258, 282, 295

Crownest estate, Lightcliffe 61, 175–6

Cuvier, Georges xxv, 19–20

Davy, Humphry: *Consolations in Travelling, Or the Last Days of a Philosopher* 227–8

Denmark xxiii, 18, 98, 100, 253, 254, 261, 264, 265, 268, 274, 277, 281–97, 303

Denmark, Frederick VI, King of xxiii, 279, 285, 289

Denmark, Marie Sophie Frederikke, Queen of xxiii, 279, 284–5, 287–9

Desfontaine, Monsieur 264

Dodgson, Mr (AL's tenant) 100–1

Duff-Gordon, Lady Caroline xxxii, 4, 7, 13, 14, 22, 29, 33, 34, 57, 58

East India Company 235

Eastbourne, East Sussex 21–2

Edwards, Mr and Mrs (friends of Ann Walker) 63, 70, 80–1, 94, 128, 140

Épernay, France 270–1

Fawthorpe, Jabus xxiii

Ferrall, Sophie 261, 262, 264–5, 269–70, 274–6, 277, 282, 287, 289

Fraser, Andrew 134–5, 140, 149–50, 182

Germany 265, 269, 270, 271–2, 292

Gibbon, Edward: *The Decline and Fall of the Roman Empire* 3, 19, 25

Godley Road 104–5, 202, 204

Goethe, Johann Wolfgang von: *Faust* 283

Gordon, Lord Cosmo 11

Gottingen, Germany 271–4

Greenwood, James 73–4, 80, 225

Grenadier Guards 13

Hage, Madame 289–90

Hageman, Lady Harriet de 18, 89, 98, 277, 281–2, 284, 285–6, 287, 289, 296–7

Halifax, West Yorkshire ix, xi, xii–xiii, xiv, xviii, xx, xxii, xxiii, xxxiv, 35, 41, 42, 46, 47, 53, 56, 59, 64, 65, 76, 82, 88, 93, 94, 99, 105,

107, 114, 118, 145, 146, 148, 154, 155, 171, 173, 174, 186, 193, 205, 212, 238, 239, 242, 287, 303, 309, 316

Halifax Philosophical and Natural History Museum 155

Hamburg, Germany 274–5, 293

Hamburg Reporter 282

Hanover, Germany 265

Hare, Augustus: *The Story of Two Noble Lives* 10–11

Hastings, East Sussex xxxiii, 3–5, 13–32, 41, 44, 47, 49, 55, 58, 59, 61, 73, 74, 75, 84, 98, 189, 209, 259, 260

Hemingway, Rachel xxxiv, 72, 100, 118, 239

Highcliffe Castle, Dorset 5

Hinscliffe, James 64, 87–8, 187, 202, 210

Hobart, Earl of Buckinghamshire, George 5

Hobart, Vere (later, Lady Cameron) xxxii, xxxiii, 3–35, 89, 158, 189, 212

Donald Cameron becomes suitor to 13–15, 22, 28

engagement and break from AL 29–35, 41, 42, 47, 58, 71, 75, 84, 93, 96, 109, 209–10, 214, 246–8

family 5

first meets AL 4, 6

friendship with AL after marriage 98, 258, 259–60

Hastings with AL xxxiii, 3–5, 13–32, 41, 44, 47, 49, 55, 58, 59, 61, 73, 74, 75, 84, 98, 189, 209, 259, 260

Lady Cameron, becomes 97–8

marriage 208–10, 246–8

Paris with AL 6–13, 18

provides pointers to AL on behaviour in society 11–12

relationship with AL deteriorates 21–8

wedding 77–8

Holdsworth, Mr 103–4

Holstein, Germany 270

Holt, James 53, 64, 185–6, 210–11

Hope Hall 45, 47

Horace xxiv, 41, 289

Horner, John 242

Howarth, Charles 81, 88, 126, 145, 238, 239, 244, 259

Howarth, James 81, 126, 238, 259

Hudson, Thomas 242

Hutchinson, William 244–5

James Church, Hebden Bridge 83

Julliart, Monsieur xxv, 264

Kant, Emmanuel xxi

Kassel, Germany 265, 270, 271–2

Kenny, Dr Mason Stanhope xxiii, 69, 119, 120, 291–2, 295, 296

Kirton, Mr (AL's tenant) 100–1

Kneller, Sir Godfrey 242

Koblentz, Germany 265

Kotzebue, August 282

La Belle Assemble 150

Ladies of Llangollen 150–2

Langton Hall, North Yorkshire xxix, 50–1, 73, 104, 153, 245

Lawton, Charles xxxi, 28, 34, 71, 77, 85, 100, 128, 132, 151, 203, 231, 257, 258

Lawton Hall, Cheshire xxxi, 34, 71, 78, 257, 295, 313

Lawton (née Belcombe), Mariana
    19, 77–9, 82–3, 86, 158,
    212–13, 214, 295, 309
  AL's Copenhagen trip and
    281–2
  AL's depression and 39–40,
    206–7
  AL's flirtation with Harriet
    Milne and 255, 257
  AL's relationship with Ann
    Walker and 113, 114, 125,
    127, 170–1, 206–8, 302,
    310, 313–14
  AL's relationship with Vere
    Hobart and 6, 22, 27–8,
    32–3, 58
  AL's restlessness, questions
    73
  AL's search for new servants
    and 99–100, 102, 128,
    129–30, 210
  breaks AL's heart, marries
    Charles Lawton xxx–xxi,
    27–8, 71, 79, 93, 109
  first meets AL xxx–xxi
  marriage xxx–xxi, 27–8, 71,
    79, 85, 151, 202–3, 231,
    257–8
  pivotal role in AL's life after
    marriage xxxi–xxxii, 27–8,
    59–60, 82–3
  resumption of romantic relation-
    ship with AL, holds onto
    hope of 203, 231, 310
  sexual relationship with AL
    xxix, 34, 258
  Shibden Hall renovations and
    80
  travels to London with AL
    257–8
  William Lawton death and
    257–8
Lawton, William 257–8

Leamington, Warwickshire 207,
    231, 254, 257
Lidgate, Lightcliffe estate 61,
    62, 69, 70, 72, 83, 94,
    96, 106, 107–8, 114,
    116, 131, 133, 134, 139,
    142, 145, 146, 153, 154,
    155, 157, 159, 163, 164,
    167, 174, 175–6, 191,
    193, 197, 198, 201, 203,
    204–6, 208, 220, 221,
    223, 226, 227, 228, 229,
    231, 232, 233, 234, 237,
    267, 299, 301, 302, 304
Lightcliffe estate 56, 60, 61, 64,
    69–70, 118, 119, 146,
    148, 175, 228, 313
Lister, Anne:
  ambitions viii, xvi, xvii, xx,
    xxxiii, 5, 16–17
  appearance xi–xiv, 93–4, 113,
    152–3, 263–4, 286–8
  author, ambition to be an xvii,
    16–17, 261
  authoritarian landowner viii,
    xviii–xiv, 43–8, 80, 88–9,
    128
  birth xiv
  childhood xi–xv, xvii, xx, 75–7
  death xi, 313
  depression/'blue devils' 39–40,
    206–7
  diet 87
  diaries vii, xxi
    coded words, use of 95, 106,
      119, 173, 174, 234, 258,
      268–9, 304–5
    decoded xxvi–xxvii
    importance of xx–xxi
    importance to AL's mental
      equilibrium of 33–4, 58,
      141
    literary influences upon xxi

John Lister hides xxvii
physical nature of xx–xxi
secret code/crypt hand
vii, xxii, xxvi–xxvii, 7–8,
13, 27, 58, 71, 95, 109,
123, 141, 173, 182, 187,
195–6, 305
size/length of x, xx–xxi
travel journals xxiii–xxv, 7, 8,
11, 12
UK Memory Bank of the
World Register, added to
the xxi
writing style vii, xxi–xxii
finances xv–xvii, xx, xxix, xxxiii,
4, 12, 16, 17, 33, 59, 60,
63, 70, 71, 72, 79, 84,
103–4, 151, 165, 167–8,
186, 202, 236, 239–40,
259, 312
fitness vii, viii, xv, 56
gender as subject of speculation
xiii, 152–3
'Gentleman Jack' nickname xiii
health 86–7, 99
human anatomy, interest in
xxiv, xxv, 19, 56–7, 264,
272–4
inheritance xv–xix, xxxiii, 4, 39,
63, 72, 77, 257, 312
intelligence vii, viii, xiv–xv, xvii,
xxiv–xxvi, 9, 19–20,
56–7, 114, 151, 282,
289
introspection and self-analysis,
periods of 11
legacy 313–14
Lister lineage and 40–1, 123
markswoman 43–4, 128
mathematical skills xiv, 64
'oddity' xiv, xxviii, 59, 97, 127,
153
optimism 57–8, 166, 261–2

politics xviii–xix, 56, 84, 88,
89, 97, 98–9, 212
polymath vii
portraits xi–xii, 242
reading/love of books vii, xxv–
xxvi, 3, 16–17, 29, 41, 61,
83–4, 87, 106–7, 164–5,
227–8, 238, 239, 248,
282, 294
religious faith xxv, xxvii–xxviii,
9, 124, 141, 145–6,
196–7, 311
school xiv–xv
servants/workers and xxiii,
xxxiv, 3, 13, 17–18, 29,
43, 48, 49–53, 55–6, 57,
72, 73–5, 77, 80, 81–3,
99–100, 102–3, 105, 118,
120–1, 126, 128–30, 131,
133, 134, 148–9, 154, 155,
157, 166–7, 168, 169, 188,
192–3, 200, 207, 210, 225,
238, 239–40, 243–4, 254,
262–3, 269, 274, 290, 294,
296, 311
sexuality vii, viii, xv, xvii–xviii,
xxiii, xxvi–xxxiv
attraction to wealth and
pedigree xxxix xxx, xxxii,
xxxiii, 5, 29–30, 60–1, 63,
71, 89, 186, 304
butch lesbian xxviii, 96
confident and experienced
lover of women 95–6
first sexual relationship xv
gender as subject of speculation xiii, 152–3, 313–14
'going to Italy' (making love
or having full sex) 95, 106
'grubbling' (using her hands
to bring another woman
to orgasm) 95, 173, 174,
234, 304–5

'incurred a cross' (orgasm achieved through masturbation) 95, 119, 269
'kiss' (word for orgasm) 95, 258

relationships xxix–xxiv *see also individual partner name*
sexual curiosity xxviii–xxvix, 95–6

Shibden Hall and *see* Shibden Hall
snobbishness xix, 40, 88, 255
society and/societal ambitions xx, xxii, xxxiii, 5, 6, 8–9, 11–13, 27, 32–4, 59, 71, 98, 255, 258–61, 281–90
style/dress xii–xiv, xxvii, 3–4, 12, 32, 113, 139, 152, 263–4, 286–8
tenants and xvii, xviii, xix, xx, 47–8, 53, 54–5, 56, 73, 81–2, 83, 89, 100–2, 200, 259
theatre and 283
translations xvii, 56–7
travel xxiii, 4, 6–13, 73–5, 81, 100, 102, 103, 106, 109, 114, 115, 116, 164–5, 174, 186, 199, 200, 203, 206, 209, 213–14, 230–1, 238, 239, 253, 253–97
Ann Walker and 100, 102, 103, 106, 109, 114, 115, 116, 118, 165, 173, 174, 186, 191, 192, 199, 200, 206, 226, 313
Copenhagen, Denmark xxiv, 98, 254, 261, 264, 265, 268, 274, 277, 281–97, 303
dream travel plans 100, 253

France xiii, xxiii, xxiv, xxv, xxxii, xxxiii, 5, 6–13, 18, 32, 51, 53, 70, 76, 89, 100, 148, 158, 168, 213, 247, 253, 261, 263–71, 273, 276, 283, 287, 288, 304
Hanover, Germany 265
Hastings, East Sussex xxxiii, 3–5, 13–32, 41, 44, 47, 49, 55, 58, 59, 61, 73, 74, 75, 84, 98, 189, 209, 259, 260
human anatomy studies and xxiv–xxv, 264, 272–4
journals xxiii–xxv, 7, 8, 11, 12
Kassel, Germany 265, 270, 271–2
Koblentz, Germany 265
London 5, 13, 14, 29, 32–3, 74, 78, 247, 254, 255, 257–61, 263
Lubeck, Germany 265
Luxembourg 265, 266–7, 270
Mount Vignemale, Spanish Alps, climbs xxiv
Paris, France xxv, xxxii, xxxiii, 5, 6–13, 18, 51, 70, 76, 89, 148, 158, 168, 213, 247, 253, 261, 263–9, 273, 276, 283, 287, 288, 304
Spain, plan to travel to with Lady Caroline Duff Gordon 4, 29
Russia 260, 261, 290, 313
Switzerland xxiv, 100, 225, 253
Strasbourg, France xiii
Treves, Germany 265, 270
voice xiii, 152
walk xii–xiii, 113, 139, 152

walking, love of xiii, 56, 61, 78, 108, 115, 145, 146, 159, 201

women in politics, opinion on 89

working-class, thoughts on xviii–xix, 42–4, 81–3, 88–9, 98–9

Lister, Anne (AL's aunt) xv, 109, 134

AL's childhood and xv, 76, 77

AL's confidant 77, 159

AL's inheritance and xvi

AL's management of Shibden Hall and 47–8, 54, 55

AL's relationship with Ann Walker and 72, 75, 94, 114, 117–19, 144, 147, 157, 159, 163, 169–70, 190, 208, 228, 244, 287, 301, 306

AL's relationship with Vere Hobart and 15–16, 28, 35

AL's return to Shibden Hall and xxxiii, 31, 35, 41

AL's sexuality and 77, 140, 159

AL's travels and 281, 289, 291–2, 295–7

death of xvi, 312

health xxii–xxiii, xxxiii, 100, 116, 119, 120, 126, 186, 230–1, 239, 253, 257, 291–2, 295–7

portrait 242

Lister, James (AL's uncle) xv, xvi, xvii, xviii, 242

Lister, Jeremy (AL's father) xiv, xvi, xxxiii, 12, 40, 41, 48, 53–4, 75, 79, 80, 105, 126, 127–8, 140, 145, 159, 202, 241–2, 257, 312

Lister, John (AL's descendant) ix, xxvi–xxvii

Lister, Marian (AL's sister):

AL's Copenhagen trip and 254, 291, 292, 296

AL's relationship with Ann Walker and 117–18, 119, 167, 308–9

AL's search for new servants and 74–5

Christopher Rawson and 240–1

Dr Kenny and 119

health of father and 128

health of aunt and 100, 291, 292, 296

hysteric 117–18, 119, 291, 292

Market Weighton, moves to 312

relationship with AL xvii, xxxiii–xxxiv, 4, 28, 41, 47–8, 74–5, 117–18, 119, 122, 168, 192–3, 202, 240–2, 308–9, 312

return of AL to Shibden and xxxiii–xxxiv, 4, 41

Shibden renovations and 80, 81

Shibden tenants and 47–8

Shibden trespassers and 80

Lister, Rebecca (AL's mother) xiv, 75–6

Lister, Sam (AL's brother) xvii

Locke, John xxi

London 5, 13, 14, 29, 32–3, 74, 78, 247, 254, 255, 257–61, 263

Lubeck, Germany 265

Luxembourg 265, 266–7, 270

Mackenzie, James 106, 107, 133, 204

Mackenzie, Sir Alexander 63, 235, 236

Maclean, Sibbella xxx, xxxii–xxxii–xxxiii, 5, 158

Mallinson, Jonathan 54–5, 83, 88–9
Manor House boarding school, York xv
Married Women's Property Act (1870) xvii–xviii
McLean, Breadalbane 243
McRea, Arthur ix
Merat's Botany 79
Milne, Harriet xxx, 158, 171, 255–6, 257
Moët 270–1

Napoleonic Wars 13
New House, Lightcliffe estate 69–70, 114, 129, 131
Nicholls, Arthur Bell 83
Norcliffe, Charlotte 171
Norcliffe, Isabella ('Tib') xxix, xxx, 50, 81, 96, 104, 126–7, 129, 153, 158, 171, 176
Norcliffe, Mrs xx, 43, 104, 120, 245, 310
Northowram Road 80–1

Oates, John 101–2, 239

Paris, France xxv, xxxii, xxxiii, 5, 6–13, 18, 51, 70, 76, 89, 148, 158, 168, 213, 247, 253, 261, 263–9, 273, 276, 283, 287, 288, 304
Parkhill, Harriet 62, 198–9, 205–6
Paxton and Harrison's gardening magazine 79
Pelham Crescent, Hastings xxxiii, 3–32, 44, 58, 59, 98, 189
Penny Magazine 70–1
Pett Levels 25

Pickles, George 80, 81–2, 85, 101, 105, 122, 126, 145, 219, 225
Pickles, Joseph 106
Pickles, Robert 80, 85
Pierre, Eugenie 99–100, 102–3, 120–1, 128, 130, 134, 166–7, 239–40, 254, 262–3, 269, 270, 274, 287, 290, 294, 295
Plas Newyd, Wales 150–1
Playforth, George 3, 13, 49–53, 73, 120, 294
Pollard, Matty 73
Ponsonby, Lady Sarah 150–2
Pre-Raphaelite painters 10–11
Priestley, Eliza viii–ix, 61, 62, 63–4, 69–70, 114, 122, 129, 131, 140, 144–5, 146, 148–9, 153, 156–9, 163, 166, 172, 175
Priestley, Mary 63
Priestley, William 61–2, 63–4, 69–70, 114, 129, 131, 140, 148–9, 159
Pye Nest 80
Pyrenees 4, 16–17, 164

Raine, Eliza xv, 256
Rawson, Catherine 62, 70, 93, 143, 148, 150, 223, 227–8, 232
Rawson, Christopher xviii, 44–7, 63, 65, 87, 103–4, 128, 154, 202, 210–11, 240–1
Rawson, Delia 107–8
Rawson, Jeremiah xviii, 64–5, 87–8, 103–4, 154, 183–4, 185–6, 187, 201–2, 204, 210–11
Rawson, Mrs 128, 140, 153–4
Rawson, Stansfield 107–8

Rawson's Bank, Halifax 46, 47, 240

Reform Bill (1832) xviii–xiv, 56, 97, 99, 212

Reynolds, Joshua 242

Rosencrantz, Madame 283

Rossetti, Dante Gabriel 10

de Rothesay, Lady Stuart xxxii, xxxiii, 4, 5, 8–9, 10, 12, 13, 14, 17, 78, 89

Rousseau, Jean Jacques: *Confessions* xxi

Russia 260, 261, 290, 313

Saltmarshe, Emma 94, 152

Shakespeare, William 16, 17, 29

Shelley, Mary: *Frankenstein* 3, 17

Shibden Hall, Halifax ix, xi, xii, xiii–xiv, xv, xviii–xix, xxxiv, 11, 12, 15, 28, 64, 79–84, 85–6, 100–1, 106, 126, 183–7, 192–3, 201–2, 204, 210–11, 212–13, 224–5, 239

AL as authoritarian landowner viii, xviii–xiv, 42–8, 81–3, 88–9

AL inherits xv–xix, xxxiii, 4, 39, 63, 72, 77, 257, 312

AL's childhood and xv–xvi, 76–7

AL's complex relationship with xix–xx, 39–40, 60

AL's return to xv, xxxii–xxxiv, 4, 35, 39–40, 41, 53–9

Ann Walker moves to 116, 119, 123, 307, 311

Ann Walker's life with AL at 312–13

Blue Room xv, 29, 77

Calf Croft 81, 85, 102, 121, 126

chaumière 53, 80, 85–6, 102, 108–9, 121, 122

coal reserves xviii, xx, 47, 53, 64–5, 87–8, 103–4, 126, 183–6, 187, 201–2, 210–11

cultivation of land 79–80

eviction of tenants 47–8

gothic library tower 83–4

Hall Croft 101

library passage 79, 102, 131, 145, 192–3, 244, 248

Listerwick pit xx, 53

'long chair', (rustic red seat) 81, 102

Lower Brook Ing Wood 80, 85, 125

Lower Place, Kirton 100–1

Pit Hill 85, 103, 126

portraits in xi–xii, 242

profitability xx, 48, 53–6, 103

public footpaths 43–7

Red Beck 125

renovation of xix–xx, 53–6, 80–1, 84, 85–6, 102, 104–5, 108–9, 121–2, 225, 312

rent collection day 48, 54–5

servants/workers and xxxiv, 3, 13, 17–18, 29, 43, 49–53, 55–6, 57, 72, 73–5, 77, 80, 81–2, 83, 99–100, 102–3, 105, 118, 120–1, 128–30, 131, 134, 148–9, 157, 166–7, 168, 169, 188, 192–3, 210, 225, 238, 239–40, 243–4, 254, 262–3, 269, 274, 290, 294, 311

size of estate 63

tenants xvii, xviii, xix, xx, 47–8, 53, 54–5, 56, 73, 81–2, 83, 89, 100–2, 200, 259

trespassers 43–7, 80, 128

Shibden Hall(*Continued*)
  Trough of Bolland 65, 104–5,
    145, 225
  Willy Hill pit 65
Ship Tavern, Gravesend 295
Skinner, Captain: *Sketches of India*
  164–5
Sowden, Samuel 83
Stag's Head Inn 48, 54–5, 83, 88–9
St-Hilaire, Etienne Geoffroy xxv,
  9–10, 264
Stuart, Charles xxxii, 5
Stuart, Charlotte (later, Viscount-
  ess Canning) xxxii, 10
Stuart, Lady xxxii, 5, 8–9, 10, 76,
    78, 97–8, 99, 102, 166,
    189, 260, 261, 296
Stuart, Louisa (later, Marchioness
  of Watford) xxxii, 10–11
Stump Cross Inn, Godley Lane
  78
Sunderland, Dr 44, 126, 127–8,
    129, 204–5, 220
Sutcliffe Wood Farm 83
Sutherland, Captain George
    Mackay 62, 63, 140, 223–4,
    229–30, 231, 233–4,
    235–6, 243, 268, 303
Sutherland, Elizabeth 62, 140,
    223–4, 229–30, 236–7,
    265–7, 282, 287, 303
Sutherland, Mrs 63, 231, 233,
    235–6, 238, 287

Treves, Germany 265, 270

Vallance, Mary xxx, 153, 158
Veitch, Mrs 155
Victoria, Queen 10
Vignemale, Mount, Alps xxiii
Voltaire 61

Walker, Ann ix, xxxiv

Ainsworth death and 174,
  176–7, 191, 194, 195,
  201, 220
AL death and 313
Andrew Fraser death and
  134–5, 140, 149–50
anonymous letters, receives
  139–40
childhood 60–1
clandestine nature of relationship with AL 131, 139–40,
  144–5, 146, 148–9, 153,
  156–8, 163–4, 175
contradictions in character of
  132–5, 141–3
death 313
dependency on AL 140–1,
  165–6, 173–4, 186–9,
  206
Eliza Priestley discovers in
  embrace with AL 156–8,
  163–4, 175
family/extended family 61,
  63, 64, 70, 94, 114, 118,
  119, 140, 144, 156–8,
  163–4, 174–5, 22–3, 226,
  235, 236, 308, 311
finances 63, 141, 167–8, 202,
  235–6, 304, 312
first meetings with AL 60–1
first public outing with AL
  93–5
'golden lock' of pubic hair,
  gives to AL 183, 191
inheritance 63
lesbian identity of AL and
  96–7
mental health 62, 122, 146–7,
  166, 167, 170–1, 172–3,
  174, 175, 190, 196–201,
  204– 8, 213, 219–24,
  226–38, 243–6, 265–9,
  303–4, 312, 313

plaque erected by the York Civic Trust to commemorate marriage to AL 313–14
proposal of living together as companions, AL's 123–6, 147–8, 168–70, 176, 187, 189–94, 195–6, 206, 213, 221, 231–2, 303–4
relationship with AL unravels 176–7, 181–208, 213–14, 219–38
religion and 196–7, 198, 203, 220, 221–2, 232, 311
reunion with AL after Copenhagen trip 301–4
Reverend Thomas Ainsworth and 177, 179, 181–2, 192, 194–5, 196, 197, 198, 199–200, 201, 220, 223, 303
rings, exchanges with AL 306–7, 310
romantic relationship with AL begins 69–72, 73, 75, 79, 84, 106–9
Scotland, recovery from mental health problems in 226–30, 243–6, 265–9, 301, 304
sexual relationship with AL 86, 95, 116–17, 119, 131, 132–4, 142–4, 147–8, 149–50, 156–8, 168–9, 174, 234, 268–9, 304–5

Shibden Hall, life with AL at 312–13
Shibden Hall, move to 116, 119, 123, 307, 311
shyness ix, 64, 113, 125–6, 133, 135, 150
similarities with AL 63
Sir Alexander Mackenzie and 235–6
travelling companion for AL, as 100, 109, 114, 115, 116, 165, 174, 186, 199, 200, 206, 313
union with AL 304–14
Walker, Elizabeth 60, 62, 63, 206, 208
Washington, Hannah 57
Washington, Samuel 43, 55–6, 57, 105, 188, 192–3, 238, 243–4
West, Sir Benjamin 273
Wilcock, Mark 44, 45–7
Wilhelmina of Denmark, Princess 288, 289
Wortley, James 99, 212

York, North Yorkshire xv, xxiii, xxix, 54, 127, 142, 166, 167, 171–5, 205, 254–5, 256, 301, 304, 306, 307, 309, 310, 311, 313
York Civic Trust 313–14